BOARDS

THAT

WORK

David Fishel

DIRECTORY OF SOCIAL CHANGE

Published by
Directory of Social Change
24 Stephenson Way
London NW1 2DP
Tel. 020 7209 5151; Fax 020 7391 4804
e-mail books@dsc.org.uk
www.dsc.org.uk
from whom further copies and a full publications list are available.

Directory of Social Change is a Registered Charity no. 800517

First published 2003

ISBN 1 903991 16 1

British Library Cataloguing in Publication Data
A catalogue record for this book is available from the British Library

Cover design by Russell Stretten
Text designed and typeset by GreenGate Publishing Services, Tonbridge
Printed and bound by Page Bros., Norwich

Other Directory of Social Change departments in London:
Courses and conferences 020 7209 4949
Charity Centre 020 7209 1015
Charityfair 020 7391 4875
Publicity & Web Content 020 7391 4900
Policy & Research 020 7391 4880

Directory of Social Change Northern Office:
Federation House, Hope Street, Liverpool L1 9BW
Courses and conferences 0151 708 0117
Research 0151 708 0136

Contents

PART 3 BOARD PROCESSES

PART 4   RESOURCES

Acknowledgements

Permissions

We are grateful to the following for granting permission to reproduce extracts from other relevant governance publications: Bob Garratt, for the table from *The Fish Rots from the Head*; John Wiley & Sons, Inc., New York, for the extract from Christine W Letts, William P Ryan and Allen Grossman's *High Performance Nonprofit Organizations: Managing Upstream for Greater Impact*; the American Council on Education for extracts from *Improving the Performance of Governing Boards* by Richard P Chait, Tomas P Holland and Barbara E Taylor; Minnesota Council of Nonprofits, for an extract from *Management Resources – Responsibilities and Position Descriptions for Nonprofit Board Members*; Volunteer Canada, for an extract from *Recognition Ideas for Volunteers*; National Council for Voluntary Organisations (NCVO), for an extract from NCVO Trustee Board Development Programme Factfile; Directory of Social Change, for an extract from Nina Botting and Michael Norton's, *The Complete Fundraising Handbook*, 4th edn, (London, 2001); Nathan Garber, for extract from Five Models of Governance © 1997.

Contributors

Many individuals have assisted with the preparation of this book. I would like to thank Sean Egan and Myles McGregor-Lowndes for contributing significant sections on legal responsibilities and risk management; Phyllida Shaw and Frankie Airey for preparing case studies; Paul Glenny of Ernst and Young for reviewing my draft on finances; Kitty Carra for undertaking key interviews; Matthew Hunt for facilitating the interview with Barnardo's CEO, Roger Singleton; and Elizabeth Watson for practical support and logistics during the research and drafting process.

Special thanks to my partner, Cathy Hunt, who has been interviewer, contributor, critical reviewer and unfailing supporter.

Sean Egan is head of the Arts and Media Department at Bates Wells & Braithwaite and advises not-for-profit and commercial organisations and individuals in the performing arts, film and television industries. He is a trustee of three arts charities and can be contacted at s.egan@bateswells.co.uk.

Prof. Myles McGregor-Lowndes is currently the Director of the Centre of Philanthropy and Nonprofit Studies at the Queensland University of Technology. His special field is the law and regulation of nonprofit organisations, and he has served on the boards of several nonprofit organisations. He can be contacted at m.mcgregor@qut.edu.au.

Frankie Airey started in development in 1988 with the ground-breaking Campaign for Oxford, which raised £342 million over six years. She then headed the External Relations Office at London University's Royal Holloway College. In 1995, she became director of development at the Victorian Arts Centre in Melbourne, and subsequently established her own consulting business, which she brought back to Britain and merged with Oxford Philanthropic. She has led projects for a wide range of clients including the Sydney Opera House, Imperial College London and the Philharmonia Orchestra. Frankie is a member of CASE and a Director of Sadler's Wells Trust Ltd. She can be contacted at frankie.airey@oxphil.com.

Phyllida Shaw is a researcher and writer in arts policy and management and a facilitator of organisational development. She has a particular interest in the dynamics of smaller organisations and in the impact of research as practice. She has served on the Boards of a wide range of organisations including Artangel, Battersea Arts Centre, Education Through Art, Arts Research Ltd and the National Network for the Arts in Health. She is an advisor to the Baring Foundation and to the National Endowment for Science Technology and the Arts.

Paul Glenny is a senior Partner in the Brisbane office of the international professional services firm Ernst & Young. Paul has a special interest in the not-for-profit sector. For many years he has provided auditing, accounting and related services to a wide range of not-for-profit organisations, both large and small. He serves as a director on the board of a number of not-for-profit entities and understands not-for-profit issues from a director's point of view. He is also a speaker and presenter on governance and reporting in the not-for-profit sector.

Cathy Hunt is the co-director of Positive Solutions. Her previous professional experience was in the management of arts centres, performing arts companies and festivals. Her work in Positive Solutions focuses on cultural policy development for government, and consulting work with non-profits in the sector. Cathy also instigated and manages Investing in Culture, a not-for-profit venture providing interest-free loans and advice to artists and cultural enterprises. She has served on the boards of not-for-profit cultural organisations in the UK and Australia. She can be contacted at info@positive-solutions.com.au.

Interviewees

I would like to extend my thanks to the following who agreed to be interviewed for this book and gave generously of their time:

Anne Mountfield, Board Member, Age Exchange Theatre Company and Chair, Tower Hamlets Old People's Welfare Trust.

Lynette Moore, Executive Director, Alzheimer's Association Victoria.

Jennifer Monahan, Board Member, Asylum Aid.

Roger Singleton, Chief Executive, Barnardo's.

Paul Mitchell, Chief Executive Officer, CARE Australia.

Michael Lake, CBE, Director General, Help the Aged.

Ian Donaldson, President, Leukaemia Foundation Queensland.

Jo-Anne Everingham, National Chair, Oxfam Community Aid Abroad Australia

David Crombie, Chairman, Queensland Rugby Union.

Paul Wright, Chairman, Royal Flying Doctor Service

Jane Holden, Executive Director, Royal New Zealand Foundation for the Blind.

Jonathan Mosen, Chairman, Royal New Zealand Foundation for the Blind.

Lyn Thomas, Chair, RSPCA Queensland

David Keating, General Manager, Surf Life Saving Foundation.

Finally, thanks to Monica Tross, formerly at the Arts Council of England, for starting this ball rolling.

About the Author

David Fishel is Co-Director of Brisbane-based consulting firm, Positive Solutions. He previously managed theatres and arts centres, and has been a board member of four non-profit organisations, and Chair of one. David has provided governance and management training for non-profit organisations in the UK, Europe, Australia, India and Taiwan.

Positive Solutions specialises in providing services for cultural and non-profit organisations and for government and private sector organisations that interact with the non-profit sector. Services include research and policy development, feasibility studies, business planning, organisational development and training. Further details can be found at www.positive-solutions.com.au or by e-mailing info@positive-solutions.com.au.

About DSC

The Directory of Social Change (DSC) aims to help voluntary and community organisations become more effective. A charity ourselves, we are the leading provider of information and training for the voluntary sector.

We run more than 350 training courses each year as well as conferences, many of which run on an annual basis. We also publish an extensive range of guides, handbooks and CD-ROMs for the voluntary sector, covering subjects such as fundraising, management, communication, finance and law. Our trusts database is available on both a CD-ROM and a subscription website.

Charityfair, the annual three-day conference, events programme and exhibition, is organised by DSC and takes place each spring.

For details of all our activities, and to order publications and book courses, go to www.dsc.org.uk or call 020 7391 4800.

PART 1
INTRODUCTION

1 Introduction

Why do we need boards and management committees? What are they there for? How can board and committee members best contribute to an organisation? And what risks are board and committee members exposed to?

Most of the literature on non-profit boards and committees during the last decade, and there was very little before then, has emerged from North America. Much has been produced by academics with an interest and engagement with the sector, some by consultants and trainers, based on their experience of working in the field. In terms of available advice and guidance, the situation is considerably better now than it was up until the early 1990s, when new board members would have been hard-pressed to find any material to guide them, regardless of the existence of thousands of books on different aspects of management in the for-profit sector. Now there is a small but growing number of books on non-profit governance, a few on aspects of non-profit leadership and management, and several websites which provide a forum for discussion of non-profit governance and management issues. Professional and industry lead bodies have also initiated short training programmes for board members from time to time.

There are still significant limitations. Most of the material is based on North American experience and addresses an American audience. There is a strongly prescriptive tone to some of the writing – follow my rules for success – without allowing for the great differences that exist between different types of organisation. Much seems to draw upon and be relevant to larger, well-staffed organisations. There is little recognition of the tight constraints within which so many non-profits operate – volunteer board members with little time to give, and staff fully stretched in meeting the organisation's day-to-day operational requirements. An heroic ideal of board commitment and staff capability is presented – but what does this mean for those of us who live in the mortal world, in command of only modest resources?

This book is addressed to the board members and senior executive officers of non-profit organisations in the UK. Its case studies, illustrations, legal references and contextual information are based on the situation in the UK. It is predominantly concerned with small and medium-sized organisations, although much of the territory it covers will be relevant to larger non-profit organisations also. It is assumed that the organisations have at least one paid professional member of staff, and may have thirty or forty. In other words, the book is not directed at entirely volunteer organisations.

My personal experience results from serving as an executive-level member of staff of four cultural organisations – in each case responsible to the board – and from serving as a board member or Chair of several cultural organisations also; seeing the situation from both sides has been salutary, and is not uncommon. In my first week as the (board-appointed) General Manager of a theatre company I benefited from the generosity and support of two board members, both rather old-fashioned branch managers of banks. They taught me what a nominal ledger was, what double-entry bookkeeping was, and they tried to teach me what a balance sheet was. Then they made it clear what kind of reports they expected to see at board meetings. Later, as a board member myself, I have tried to keep that double role – support and accountability – firmly in mind in my relationships with staff.

In addition to the four questions that opened this chapter, this book addresses one other, key question, which underlies the rest – how do we keep the board motivated and purposeful? Board membership of non-profit organisations is nearly always an unpaid activity. If these organisations are to harness the skills and commitment of the best board members, and society is to benefit from this volunteer generosity, there must be some pleasure and gain for the individual board members. Apart from doing our social duty, and avoiding legal and financial disaster, how do we give ourselves the best chance of enjoying board membership and of being able to look back on our investment of time with a feeling of achievement?

The purpose of this book is to support rather than instruct. For the relatively new board member it is intended to provide a sound induction to the concept of board membership in the non-profit environment. For the more experienced board member it is intended as a resource to exploit as specific issues arise. For the Chief Executive Officer (CEO) it is a stimulus to seeing from the board's perspective and, in so doing, to considering how the board's energies and ability can be harnessed, and what the CEO can do to achieve this. Above all, the book is intended to be practical.

Definitions

Some terms will be used frequently, so here is a brief glossary:

non-profit: independently constituted organisations that do not distribute profits to shareholders, even though it may be desirable for them to produce surpluses to create tomorrow's working capital or judicious reserves. Many of them are limited companies with charitable status, although they may be industrial and provident societies, trusts or associations. There are also public sector entities for which this book may be relevant – for example, those semi-autonomous service-delivery units or agencies established by government, which may, in their values, aspirations and arms-length arrangements from the government emulate independent non-profits. The non-profit sector is variously referred to as the non-profit sector, not-for-profit sector, voluntary sector or third sector.

board: the governing body of the organisation, the group of people who have ultimate accountability for and authority over the organisation, subject to the will of the members. Sometimes called the Board of Management or Management Committee. Here, we will generally use the term 'board', but occasionally we will refer to the 'management committee' to indicate that the book is targeted at both.

charity trustees: similarly, the group of people responsible for the control and management of a charity. For the purpose of this book, trustees are treated as synonymous with board members or management committee members of non-profit organisations (whether or not they are registered charities).

CEO: the most senior paid officer in the organisation, appointed by the board to take overall day-to-day control. The title is often not Chief Executive Officer but General Manager, Executive Director, or even Secretary-General. Exceptionally, some organisations appoint two senior officers: an Artistic Director and a General Manager, for example. Where this is the case the term CEO refers to the joint responsibilities of those two posts, however they may be allocated.

governance: the arrangements for overall control and direction of the organisation, normally in the form of authority conferred by the membership (or key stakeholders) on a board or committee:

> '... corporate governance generally refers to the process by which organisations are directed, controlled and held to account. It

encompasses authority, accountability, stewardship, leadership, direction and the control exercised in the organisation.'[1]

Corporate governance also affects an organisation as a whole, including the agency's purpose, values, culture, stakeholders (including employees) and mode of operation.

A recent report by the Royal Society of Arts described corporate governance as having three components:

1 It is concerned with the accountability of organisations and their personnel to higher bodies or constituencies, which, by inference, have the power to impose sanctions and to require changes in their behaviour.
2 The internal structure and the networks of delegated powers (including authority and responsibility) together make up the internal corporate governance environment and so govern the culture within an organisation, as well as internal accountability of staff and managers to their board.
3 The third component relates to both internal and external governance and is concerned with ensuring that the framework of constraints and incentives lead organisations and their personnel to want to act in a desired manner rather than requiring continual detailed interventions by the controlling authority.

stakeholders: organisations and individuals who have an interest in the success and services of the non-profit organisation – ranging from staff and volunteers to customers, users, funding bodies, sponsors and allies.

programmes, projects and services: the streams of activity undertaken by the non-profit organisation are generally referred to here as 'programmes', although they are sometimes called projects or services.

The non-profit sector

The sector comprises a broad range of organisations across a number of industry 'sectors', including health, welfare, medical research, education, sports, culture, religion and others. The sector has been defined as consisting of private organisations:

■ that are formed and sustained by groups of people acting voluntarily and without seeking personal profit to provide benefits for themselves or for others;

---

[1] Australian National Audit Office, Report No. 6, *Audit Activity Report – January to June 1999*, p8.

- that are democratically controlled;
- where any material benefit gained by a member is proportionate to their use of the organisation.[2]

The sector embraces organisations with no paid staff, organisations with a few paid staff, and organisations with thousands of paid staff (for example, large hospitals and colleges).

In the UK, there are approximately 170,000 registered charities, but these are supplemented by several hundred thousand other non-profit organisations – a total of roughly half a million.

In recent years the environment in which many non-profit organisations operate has been subject to rapid change – especially technological, political and legislative. Expectations of them are higher than in the past and, in many cases, competitive pressures have created entirely new demands of their boards and executive staff.

A number of trends that have influenced development of the non-profit sector merit a brief mention, because they have an impact on the board's business. These include:

- government looking increasingly to the non-profit sector to provide services, and entering into contractual arrangements to secure the service levels expected;
- a growing acceptance of the sector as a key contributor to society's well-being, alongside the private and public sectors;
- heightened expectations, not only from government, but from members, service beneficiaries and users, donors and corporate sponsors or partners. Society's demands for best value rise steadily, and no exception is made for non-profits;
- an increasingly demanding legislative framework, and an increasingly litigious environment;
- the rise of the user-pays philosophy, where at least part of the overall cost is met by the consumer;
- the professionalisation of staff, moving away from the early-retiree from the commercial world or ex-military personnel (though some of them have made excellent non-profit leaders) towards a more dedicated corps of non-profit executives, which is reflected in the launch of specialised training for these executives;
- decreasing volunteer time, linked to two-income families, one-parent families, and a growth in self-employment and 'portfolio' work styles.

---

[2] Professor Mark Lyons, *Third Sector: The contribution of non-profit enterprises in Australia*, Allen & Unwin (Sydney, 2001).

The 'internal' characteristics of non-profit organisations also have implications for their governance and for the board's focus.

- In an organisation not primarily driven by the financial bottom-line it is easy to have imprecise objectives. Consequently, performance can be harder to monitor than in more commercial environments.
- Non-profit organisations are often accountable to many stakeholders – members, users, government, sponsors, as well as to staff.
- Management structures may be complex, especially where national organisations may have board structures or consultative procedures which reflect the range of areas and constituencies they are intended to serve.
- Voluntarism remains an essential ingredient in many non-profit organisations, notwithstanding the comment above about the squeeze on volunteers' time. The day-to-day business of managing and motivating volunteers falls to the CEO and other staff, but the dependence upon a partially volunteer workforce has strategic and board-level implications.
- Values cement the organisation together. Most non-profits were launched by people who shared particular beliefs or aspirations (religious, social, environmental, cultural), and are sustained by like-minded people. However, differing interpretations of how the values should be expressed can generate conflict over direction and priorities, and produce resistance to change that can appear to threaten the organisation's values.
- The relationship between board and CEO is more subtle than in many for-profit or public sector organisations, with a volunteer board overseeing the work of a professional CEO and constrained by the difficulty of agreeing appropriate performance measures.

These external and internal contexts have implications for the work of the board. Increased accountability to government has accompanied the growth in 'contract culture'. Increased accountability to business partners or sponsors has accompanied the maturing of sponsorship. In its monitoring role, the board has to be satisfied that the organisation's obligations are met. But the increasing demands can also present the board with difficult strategic choices regarding the scale and direction of the organisation: what sort of obligations it should enter into, and what kinds of alliances or partnerships are appropriate and desirable. In this and other matters, good quality decision-making is needed.

The rise of the user-pays philosophy both increases the customer/user's expectations and requires some non-profits to become more sophisticated in their marketing and positioning – to ensure they attract customers, and reach the people they were intended to serve.

The professionalisation of senior staff may be a welcome development for many board members, but others may find the process threatening – representing a takeover by 'experts' whom they believe do not fully share the values and ethics of the organisation.

Because of the complex dynamics of board, CEO and stakeholders, less reliance can be placed on relationships being taken for granted. Who is responsible for what (and how) are issues which the board needs to return to periodically and at key points of change in the organisation's life.

The dividing line between for-profit, non-profit and public sector organisations is less clear than it used to be – a by-product of privatisation, contract culture, competitive tendering and best-value procedures in the public sector. As local government has moved away from direct service-delivery responsibilities, both the private and non-profit sectors have moved in to deliver services that used to be the public sector's province.

These shifts have led to the emergence of hybrid organisations that seem to occupy two spheres. Examples of organisations which seem to occupy the territory between non-profit and private sector include some schools and hospitals, which run on quasi-commercial principles, but which do not distribute profits or dividends. Examples of organisations straddling the non-profit and public sector include many tertiary-level education institutions, local-government operated museums, and some statutory bodies, where the board is appointed by and report to the relevant Minister. 'Pure' third sector organisations (but not all of them charitable) include voluntary organisations (e.g. welfare, relief, emergency), many subsidised arts organisations, sports clubs and associations, churches, trade unions and professional associations.

In this slightly blurred situation, board members of non-profit organisations need a heightened awareness of those areas where the organisation may find itself in competition with for-profit organisations. The increasing complexity of the sector, the rise in expectations of organisations and board members, and the relative scarcity of guidance created the stimulus for *Boards that Work*.

Structure of the book

Following the introductory section, the book covers three main areas:

Responsibilities: Part 2 explores what the board is there for, and what its formal and legal responsibilities are. Effective boards do more than fulfil the letter of the law, and this section considers the main areas where the board can add to the organisation's effectiveness, through strategic planning and policy-setting, the appointment of the CEO, coordinated advocacy and performance monitoring.

Processes: Part 3 discusses the processes necessary to keep the board healthy and to optimise the individual board member's contribution – from making the decision to join a board, to contributing positively to meetings, to chairing the meetings. Choices facing the board with regard to board recruitment, induction, board structures, board information, periodic evaluation and planning retreats are also considered.

Resources: The final section, Part 4, includes reference material to draw upon, from examples of policies and role statements to reading materials and useful websites.

Throughout the book, brief illustrations and checklists are provided, with the intention that the reader will adapt the checklists according to their own and their organisation's circumstances. Some of the checklists are identified as evaluative (how are we doing in relation to this issue) and others are action-oriented (10 things we could be doing to progress in this area). There are also a number of case studies, and in-depth interviews with a selection of board members and CEOs.

2 Why do we have a board?

Arriving at a common understanding of the board's function among board members, and between board and staff, is a prerequisite for establishing an overall sense of purpose and direction within the organisation. And because the organisation and its environment change, so the most productive areas of focus for the board may change. The board needs to reappraise its focus on a regular basis. This may lead to a reaffirmation of present practice, or to some changes in priority, composition, structure or meeting arrangements.

While the law establishes a set of common expectations upon the board, there are still a number of views on how the non-profit board should see its broader role or function, beyond legal compliance. The specific calls upon the board vary according to the culture of the organisation, its size and nature, and the overall stage of development in the organisation's history, from fledgling to maturity.

The board's work is most obviously expressed through its regular meetings. But the actions the board takes between meetings may have a greater impact on the life of the organisation, and will influence the quality of discussion and decision-making in the meetings themselves.

Responsibilities

The collective responsibilities of board and management committee members include:

- attending board meetings and organisational activities;
- the approval of the mission;
- participating in the planning process;
- the selection and evaluation of the CEO;
- ensuring legal and financial obligations are met;
- the support and oversight of programmes;
- assistance with fundraising;

- the assurance of board effectiveness;
- community relations and advocacy, representing the organisation.[1]

This may be summarised as:

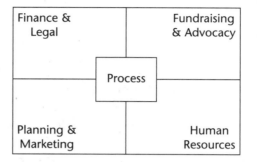

Figure 2a Collective responsibilities of the board

An understanding of the board's role and agenda lays the foundations for a coherent sense of purpose. However, a list of activities is not enough. What should the board be doing within each of the areas of activity identified above? How does that differ from what the board expects the staff to be doing? Is this the same for all organisations, or does it differ from one organisation to another? How does the board articulate these responsibilities, and how does this determine what the board should be doing from one month to the next?

To answer these questions we need to dig deeper than a list of responsibilities, and to address the question of what the board's overall function or purpose is – what the board of a non-profit is there for.

Three perspectives

A starting point is to consider these three different perspectives on non-profit governance:[2]

---

[1] See, for example, Richard Ingram, *Ten Basic Responsibilities of Non-profit Boards*, National Center for Non-profit Boards (Washington DC, 1998); 'Responsibilities of Orchestra Boards' in *A Guide to Orchestra Governance*, American Symphony Orchestra League (New York, 1991); 'The Functions of the Board', in Cyril Houle, *Governing Boards*, Jossey-Bass/National Center for Non-profit Boards (San Francisco, 1997), pp89-94; 'The Role of a Board of Trustees' in *The Good Trustee Guide*, NCVO Publications (London, 1994), p9; 'The Basics of Board Membership' in *Board Member Manual*, Arts Council of England (London, 1995), p5, as well as a number of websites, such as www.mapnp.org/ library/Boards/brdrspn.htm, and www.non-profit.about.com/careers/non-profit/library/weekly/aa011001a.htm. For the diagrammatic summary I am grateful to Madeline Hutchins and other trainers who participated in the Arts Council of England's Board Development Programme.

[2] This summary of the three perspectives is based on C Cornforth and C Edwards, *Good Governance: Developing Effective Board-Management Relations in Public and Voluntary Organisations*, Chartered Institute of Management Accountants (London, 1998), pp11–13.

1 the agency or stewardship model;
2 the political model;
3 the managerial model.

The **agency** view presumes that managers tend to act in their own self-interest rather than in the interest of the 'owners' of an enterprise. In this world, the board members see their main function as being to control the behaviour of managers. They primarily have a stewardship role – making sure that the resources of the organisation are safe-guarded. The occasional public scandals that have surfaced in both the non-profit and commercial worlds serve to reinforce this view of the controlling and monitoring board. Many non-profits have seen the role of the board in this light, especially as organisations move through a process of increasing professionalisation, and increased dependence upon paid staff, which can be accompanied by resistance to letting go of the reins by board members.

The **political** or democratic perspective of the board assumes that board members are there to represent the interests of one or more stake-holders in the organisation, and to express or resolve the differences between those interest groups. Anyone can put themselves forward for election to the board, and no particular expertise forms a requirement for board membership. Pluralism, accountability to the electorate, and the separation of a policy-making elected group from an implementing executive group, are all characteristics of this model. The structure of many membership-based non-profits is influenced by these democratic principles.

In the **managerial** view, the board is regarded as the apex of a management hierarchy. Ideas and practice from management are considered appropriate to governance also – so board members should be chosen on the basis of their expertise and contacts, in order to add value to the organisation's decision-making processes. Like managers, board members will require careful selection, induction and training, and will need to know how to operate as an effective team. Most of the non-profit governance literature of the last 10 years has been based on a managerial view of the board.

Of course, around one boardroom table three board members could each hold one of these views of the function of the board. Indeed, it is possible for a single board member to feel the draw of each of these perspectives at different times, according to circumstances and the matter under consideration. The issue here is not that one view of the board is right and the others wrong, but that each represents a part of what the board is there to do, and that there is often a tension between the three perspectives.

How, then, can the board have a coherent view of what it should be focusing on at any one point in time? How can it reconcile the tensions inherent in these three perspectives?

Reconciling board perspectives

The work of Frederick Herzberg will be familiar to many readers of management literature. Examining the factors that motivate individuals in a workplace, Herzberg drew a distinction between two sets of factors: 'hygiene' factors and 'motivating' factors. Hygiene factors are those basic conditions that need to be satisfied to provide an environment where people can operate positively. These include, for example, a (reasonable) salary, job security and appropriate supervision. Only when these factors have been addressed is it possible to generate higher levels of performance from the individual (and the organisation) through motivating factors. These include recognition, the possibility of personal growth and responsibility.

There is a parallel in board matters. Board members need first to direct their attention to the organisational hygiene, 'caretaker' factors – managed cash flow, legal compliance, a safe working environment for staff and volunteers. Without these basics, the organisation's operations are in peril.

However, 'caretaker' monitoring factors should normally be dealt with speedily through clear, reliable reports, which have been circulated and read in advance of board meetings. This leaves the board free to devote the majority of their time to higher-level issues that make a real difference to the organisation's work. In accepting the task of 'making a difference' to the organisation, and adding value to its work, the board will be adopting the managerial model.

In both monitoring and managerial modes, the well-tuned board, or management committee, will consider the impact of its decisions on key constituencies, which include service beneficiaries or customers and funding bodies. In this way, the political or representational dimension is ever-present. This is not the same as arriving at the boardroom with delegated authority from a specific interest group, which is clearly discouraged in law.

The degree to which the board attends to caretaker or performance-oriented issues will be determined by the organisation's current circumstances. If there are significant financial or personnel problems, the board may choose to devote time and attention to these in detail – in fact, the board would be at fault if it failed to do so. If there are not such problems, the board should be devoting its attention to more strategic matters, and to organisational development and improvement. However, if financial or personnel problems frequently recur, the board should be asking more fundamental questions about the way the organisation is doing business, or the business the organisation is doing.

Accountability

In law, the board has ultimate responsibility for the organisation – the board carries the can. But how can this be expressed?

It would be possible for a board to interpret 'accountability' purely in terms of maintaining a hawkish overview of the cash-flow forecasts. However, accountability implies a great deal more than that, and is part of a chain of relationships. The staff and volunteers are accountable to the board, which, in turn, is accountable to the stakeholders, including clients, members, funding bodies, donors and others.

Accountability also implies accepting a full sense of responsibility for the organisation – in effect, accepting a sense of ownership:

> 'A board needs to know that it owns the organisation. But it owns an organisation not for its own sake – as a board – but for the sake of the mission which the organisation is to perform. Board members don't own it as though they were stockholders voting blocks of stock; they own it because they care.'[3]

This personal sense of ownership calls for the board not only to address the caretaker issues, but also to ensure that the organisation is performing to maximum effect, by addressing a range of higher-level activities, including policy development, advocacy and strategic review.

In short, it is the board's responsibility to take whatever reasonable actions are necessary to ensure the organisation *performs*.

Writing of commercial boards, Bob Garratt describes their function as the 'central processor' of the organisation, which concerns itself with conformance and performance. He presents a model of a Learning

---

[3] Dr David Hubbard, from 'The Effective Board' in Peter Drucker's *Managing the Non-profit Organisation*, Butterworth Heinemann (Oxford, 1992), p135.

Board, which places learning as the pivot around which other board processes revolve. Conformance covers accountability and supervision; performance covers policy formulation and strategic thinking, which drive the enterprise forward. All four tasks feed into each other as part of an annual cycle of board learning. The model seems entirely appropriate to non-profit organisations also.[4]

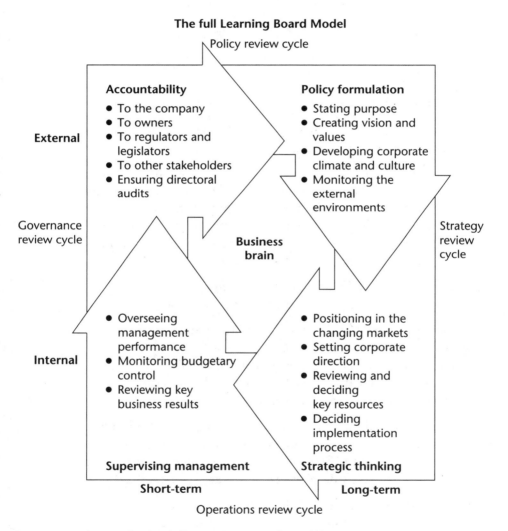

The full Learning Board Model

Policy review cycle

Accountability
- To the company
- To owners
- To regulators and legislators
- To other stakeholders
- Ensuring directoral audits

External

Policy formulation
- Stating purpose
- Creating vision and values
- Developing corporate climate and culture
- Monitoring the external environments

Governance review cycle

Business brain

Strategy review cycle

Internal
- Overseeing management performance
- Monitoring budgetary control
- Reviewing key business results

- Positioning in the changing markets
- Setting corporate direction
- Reviewing and deciding key resources
- Deciding implementation process

Supervising management   **Strategic thinking**

Short-term   **Long-term**

Operations review cycle

Figure 2b The full Learning Board model

Source: Bob Garratt, *The Fish Rots from the Head: The Crisis in Our Boardrooms*, p27.
Reproduced by kind permission of Bob Garratt and HarperCollins Publishers

---

[4] Bob Garratt, *The Fish Rots from the Head: The Crisis in our Boardrooms: Developing the Crucial Skills of the Competent Director*, HarperCollins Business (London, 1997), p27.

For the board to get a grip on the bigger picture – the strategic issues facing the organisation – it will normally need the help of the professional staff. The alternative is a vicious circle, where staff may resist investing time and effort in the board's development and education, leading to a situation where the board is incapable of contributing at a strategic level, which in turn confirms the staff view that the board adds no value, but instead focuses only on petty, operational details which are not their proper concern. This scenario is all too familiar; it is also avoidable.

Because non-profit board and management committee members are drawn from a range of walks of life, many of them do not have a detailed knowledge of the sector to which their non-profit belongs, nor a full understanding of the operations and internal economy of their organisation.

This leads to a problematic paradox.

The board should not be doing the work of the staff, other than in the smallest (or un-staffed) non-profit organisations where they may be obliged to roll their sleeves up and help in very practical ways to supplement the organisation's resources. But to fulfil both its monitoring and more strategic roles, the board needs to develop a keen sense of how the organisation works and of the business or sector it is in. It can only do this by getting close to the organisation and benefiting from a structured process of education and information transfer, which will necessarily be dependent upon the staff.

The paradox is that the board needs to get a close-up understanding of the operation in order to be able to stand back and play a productive role at a higher level. Without some organisational and sector knowledge the board's decisions will lack context, and could be misguided. But the closer the board gets to the everyday operations, the more anxious the senior staff become about unwelcome interference, and the greater the risk that some board members will start seeing only the trees, not the woods. Getting involved in the detail is seductive – it is a lot easier than dealing with the bigger issues.

Later chapters, therefore, will address the issues of how the board secures an understanding of the organisation and how it remains appropriately focused on the big picture.

Governance in changing contexts

The board's focus and mode of operation will be influenced by the organisation's changing circumstances. If there is an effective and experienced senior management team in place, the board may concern itself with aspects of policy development or scenario planning for the future. If there has been a recent change in key senior management, the alert board should move into a different mode. It will need to provide close support, monitoring and supervision until it is satisfied the new management is inducted and familiar with the business. It may revisit aspects of policy to affirm a fresh mutual understanding of organisational direction.

There is no point prescribing one type of board behaviour that fits all organisations. The saying, 'Directors direct and managers manage', is helpful in stressing that the two need to be clear about their respective roles, but in many small organisations, or during times of pressure or crisis, this clear and inflexible division between roles of board and staff is unrealistic. It simply does not reflect the situation that many board members find themselves in. Greater subtlety is called for, requiring board and staff to negotiate their roles according to the periodic needs of the organisation.

> 'Board governance, like everything else is relative. If you manage a multi-million dollar, well established, financially stable organization, your board may fit (although probably not) the picture painted by John Carver, one of the leading board consultants. But if you're the underpaid manager of a $50,000 organisation, most of the received wisdom about boards of directors does not apply. Don't be discouraged because your board does not match the models. You should always keep striving toward the ideal, but you should remember that you are not likely to attain it.'[5]

When to review the board's role

✔ Board members are dissatisfied with their roles or the way the board operates.
✔ Your organisation is experiencing problems that can be traced back to inadequacies in board structure or process.
✔ Your organisation is entering a new phase in its lifecycle.
✔ The CEO has left or is leaving.
✔ There has been a major turnover of board members.
✔ There is a crisis of confidence in the board or the CEO.

---

[5] 'Board Governance for Small Non-profits', Stan Hutton, www.non-profit.about,com/careers/non-profit/library/weekly/aa102898.htm.

The hierarchy of board business

If, beyond the legal fundamentals, governance is a relative matter, this does not change the fact that board members are keen for guidance on what they should be doing. Within the spirit of 'governance in context' it is suggested that the non-profit board should concern itself, in ascending order, with the issues below.

This is offered not as a 'must-do' list, but as an overview of the overall range of board activities. Its objective is to address the 'caretaker' activities to the point where they absorb only modest time and energy, in order to free up time and energy to address those activities that enhance the overall performance of the organisation. The more of the 'performance' activities the board is addressing (in negotiated partnership with the senior staff/CEO) the greater the overall contribution the board will be making to the organisation.

This following is not a procedure to evaluate the board's own performance or effectiveness, which is addressed in Chapter 16, *Assessing and improving the board*, but a tool for stimulating debate about the board's most appropriate short-term focus.

Caretaker activities

1 Legal compliance.[6]
2 Financial monitoring.
3 Personnel responsibilities.

✔ When did we last review relevant legislation?
✔ What level of experience do our senior staff have in our industry sector, and of the legislative framework which affects us?
✔ Do we have risk management policies and procedures in place?
✔ What is the liquidity position of the organisation?
✔ What is the quality (and timeliness) of financial information, including cash-flow forecasts, which the board receives?
✔ Do we maintain full personnel records, including written job descriptions?
✔ Do we have recruitment and equal opportunity policies in place?

---

[6] A more detailed review of legal responsibilities is included in Chapter 4.

Performance activities

Human resource management
1 Appraising the work of the Chief Executive.
2 Establishing parameters for the autonomy of the Chief Executive.
3 Approving appraisal procedures for other staff and volunteers.
4 Team building.
5 Managing organisational change.

✔ When did we last consider the respective roles of board and CEO?
✔ Are there clearly stated guidelines for the CEO's decision-making parameters?
✔ Do we have personnel policies covering recruitment, professional development, leave entitlements and other, discretionary areas?
✔ Does the CEO implement positive leadership and motivation of the staff?

Policy development
1 Reviewing and confirmation of mission, vision and values.
2 Adopting programme policies, personnel policies, financial policies.
3 Adopting strategies to implement the organisation's policies, and performance measures to assess progress.

✔ When did we last re-examine basic purposes of the organisation?
✔ When was our strategic plan reviewed?
✔ Do we have clearly articulated policies with regard to programmes, finances, board processes?
✔ Who is involved in policy setting?
✔ Are we clear on who has to do what to implement our policies?

Resourcing
1 Reviewing income sources periodically.
2 Building an effective development/fundraising function.
3 Making personal and professional contacts available to the organisation.

✔ Have we recently considered the breadth and mix of our income sources?

✔ Have we considered and addressed the risks associated with our current income mix?

✔ Do we have a development/fundraising plan, and supporting strategies?

✔ Are board members actively contributing to the development activities of the organisation?

Networking

1 Maintaining advocacy in the community, adopting an active ambassadorial role.
2 Seeking opportunities for the organisation, through personal and professional contacts and knowledge.
3 Making connections for the organisation, and effecting introductions for the CEO and other staff.

✔ Do we have an advocacy plan to influence our key stakeholders?

✔ Are board members clear about their role and restrictions in implementing such a plan?

✔ When did we last map the organisation's opportunities?

✔ Are board members making their networks and contacts available to the organisation?

Evaluation and improvement

1 Ensuring that appropriate performance measures and evaluation criteria are adopted.
2 Investing periodically in market research, membership surveys or other monitoring mechanisms.
3 Ensuring that benchmarking or other inter-organisational comparisons inform the board's understanding of performance.

✔ How do we monitor progress in the organisation – do we measure against our strategic plan?

✔ What feedback mechanisms do we have in place to ensure we benefit from our monitoring and evaluation processes?

✔ How current is our knowledge and awareness of industry standards and comparable organisations?

Maintaining board effectiveness

1 Reviewing role, scope of activities and procedures regularly.
2 Reviewing composition, skills and knowledge base periodically.
3 Ensuring the board is receiving timely and helpful information.
4 Helping the staff to help the board.

✔ Do we have a process for assessing our own progress?
✔ Do we set annual targets for the board's achievements?
✔ Do we deliver our targets?
✔ When did we last review board structure and processes?
✔ How clear are terms of reference for our sub-committees and task forces?
✔ Are we being provided with the right information at the right time?

Performance and probity

For the board's potential to be realised, there must be support and servicing from the professional staff. Through provision of appropriate and timely information, the staff can ensure that the board do not waste time dwelling on detail that could have been provided in advance. Beyond this, the senior staff have the opportunity to focus the board's attention on critical issues, and to harness the board's expertise and energy in areas that are going to be of greatest help to the staff and the organisation.

In turn, the successful board will recognise that the time of professional staff (and volunteers) is precious to the organisation, and that reporting requirements to the board should be tempered by this knowledge. Consistent with ensuring the organisation is meetings its obligations, routine reporting should be as economic as possible with staff resources.

The overall level of the organisation's achievements will relate closely to the strength and clarity of the relationship between board and staff. And the overall function of the board is to ensure the organisation performs to its maximum potential.

Summary

- Agreement on core functions is a prerequisite for the effective board.
- There are a number of different perspectives on 'governance' and the board's role – they are not 'right' or 'wrong', but need to be explored around the boardroom table to clarify how the board sees its primary focus.
- The board's role should be adjusted according to the nature and scale of the organisation, and its present stage of development.
- The board's attention needs to be devoted both to basic caretaking activity, and to more performance-oriented activities.
- The more time the board can devote to performance activities, the greater its positive effect will be on the organisation.

CASE STUDY: BOARDS IN TRANSITION

This case study describes how the board of a small, artist-led organisation has evolved from a light-touch, hands-off group of 'supporters', slightly uncertain of their role, into a focused and dynamic board that is leading the organisation through an exciting period of development.

Background

Fabrica is an arts organisation operating from a former church in the centre of Brighton. Fabrica was created by four artists from an artists' studio group called Red Herring. Studio groups frequently occupy redundant industrial or retail premises for a few years, in return for a low rent, and move on when the developers move in. For many artists, spotting redundant space with potential is second nature.

It was 1994 when Holy Trinity Church presented a rare opportunity to create a venue for the exhibition of contemporary art. The building, owned by the Church of England, had been leased to the local authority, which had planned to use it as a museum. When the plan fell through, the artists offered to run it as a dedicated exhibition space for contemporary art in Brighton.

The artists knew about raising funds from public sources in particular, and constituted Fabrica as a limited company and a charitable trust. The founding directors/trustees were all friends or colleagues. The unspoken aim was to establish a small board whose members knew and trusted each other, and who shared the belief that the direction of the new organisation should be determined by artists. It is probably fair to say that the board was seen by the artists as a benign necessity, and the board was content to play that role.

In those early days, funds were secured from the local authority, and from other government funding sources. There were four exhibitions per year and an integrated programme of educational and audience development activities. The gallery was closed to the public for four months every winter, because it was too cold, but otherwise things were ticking along nicely.

Then, in 1998, a substantial three-year grant was secured from the Arts Council of England's Lottery Board to develop the programme. This grant moved Fabrica on to a different plane of operation. It could commission more new work and work with more established artists. Increasingly, critics, curators and gallery educators wanted to know how Fabrica operated and what its plans for the future were.

At this point, Fabrica had a Gallery Director, who was responsible for the administrative and financial operation of the organisation, and two programmers (both artists), who shared responsibility for the artistic direction. There was no 'chief executive'. Part-time project staff, freelancers and volunteers supported this core team of three. The board met every few months to receive reports and to make decisions when asked. It was fulfilling all of its legal responsibilities, but its approach remained low key.

Change

It was at the end of 1999 that the board recognised the need to play a more proactive role. Fabrica was facing two challenges. The first was that there was less than a year left to run on the three-year grant from the Arts Council. If it was to maintain the same level of activity, it needed to find new sources of funding. The second was the unexpected resignation of the Gallery Director, due to ill health.

The financial situation was becoming critical. The organisation had been very successful at raising project funds but this had disguised a steady increase in its core costs, which it now had to address. The focus had been on the short term; little time had been spent nurturing contacts with potential funders or developing ideas for generating income.

On the staffing front, the board had to decide whether to appoint a replacement Gallery Director, on a short-term contract, or whether to restructure the organisation. A key funding body was concerned that the departure of the Gallery Director had left the organisation with a major skills gap. It also argued that, while respecting the artist-led ethos of Fabrica, the board should be giving more of a leadership role.

The board agreed to accept a grant from the Regional Arts Board to bring in a facilitator to work with them and the staff, to assess the options and agree a way forward. This process, which was conducted in a spirit of constructive collaboration, achieved the following things.

- It produced a consensus about the organisation's function and longer-term aspirations.
- It addressed staff and board concerns about their respective roles and agreed the terms of reference of each.
- It established a new staffing structure, with new contracts and terms and conditions.
- It provided staff and board members with the renewed confidence to deal with funders and other partners.
- It secured an 18-month grant from the Arts Council of England, which gave the organisation the financial stability it needed to plan for the future.

The board has now expanded from four members to seven. The three new members all bring new contacts, skills and perspectives and potentially valuable local networks to the organisation.

The two programmers now share the role of Artistic Director and Chief Executive. As a result, the board has a greater knowledge of the programming process and the Artistic Directors understand, more clearly, the information needs of the board and its role in securing the future of the organisation.

The Artistic Directors are supported by an Administrator and a Volunteer Coordinator who, in turn, manage part-time project staff and volunteers. The Regional Arts Board's concerns about the administrative and financial capacity of the organisation proved unfounded.

The process that Fabrica went through to secure Recovery funding from the Arts Council of England was a positive one for the whole organisation and highlighted areas in which the board needed to take action, including setting job descriptions, terms and conditions, training provision, health and safety procedures and access policies.

The board has adopted a training and professional development plan for the staff and board and it is overseeing health, safety and access works on the building that will improve conditions for staff, visitors and artists.

Conclusion

The manner in which Fabrica was created clearly influenced the composition and style of the board. The board members were friends and colleagues and when everything was going well, the board saw no need to take a more proactive role in what everyone referred to as an artist-led organisation. In turn, the staff were wary of the board becoming too demanding and too involved in the day-to-day operations. These concerns and uncertainties were only addressed when Fabrica faced decisions that only the board could take.

The role of the facilitator, paid for by the then Regional Arts Board, was essentially to empower the board and the two Artistic Directors, first to define and then to be more assertive in their respective roles.

The respect of the board for the programming skills of the Artistic Directors and for the efforts of staff and volunteers to make Fabrica a critical success, despite the difficult working conditions, meant that once the board's role had been clarified, the board and staff found it relatively easy to establish a productive working relationship.

Key points

- A small board of friends and allies, expanding to incorporate a wider range of knowledge and skills and taking on a more proactive role.
- A programme that is attracting national, critical attention, with the result that more people have expectations that this is an organisation that will deliver and an organisation from which they might learn. This places pressure on the organisation to have plans and processes that it can articulate.
- A tradition of part-time employment, enabling those staff who are artists to continue to make their own work.
- A building that presented exciting programming opportunities, but had to overcome health, safety and access shortcomings.

Case study prepared by Phyllida Shaw

AN INTERVIEW WITH JENNIFER MONAHAN, BOARD MEMBER OF ASYLUM AID

Asylum Aid is a national charity which assists refugees in the UK by providing free legal advice, and representing them in their asylum applications. Asylum Aid also campaigns for the fair treatment of refugees in the UK. In 2001 the organisation assisted people from 104 countries. Over 90 per cent of the cases handled by Asylum Aid resulted in the asylum seekers being granted leave to remain in the UK.

Jennifer Monahan became a Trustee of Asylum Aid through an interest in human rights issues developed during her career as a journalist.

What is the story of Asylum Aid?

Asylum Aid grew out of a small group, 'Rights and Justice', which fought for the rights of minorities overseas. The needs of asylum seekers arriving in the UK led to the establishment of Asylum Aid in the early 1990s. One of the caseworkers with Rights and Justice, Alasdair Mackenzie, subsequently became the Coordinator of Asylum Aid. Legal aid was not available for asylum seekers at appeal, so the aim was to provide advice and representation that refugees could not otherwise afford.

Until 1999 we operated out of a small office in Islington, North London. Then we moved to larger offices in East London. In 1999 Asylum Aid launched the Refugee Women's Resource Project, in response to the lack of specialist advice and support for women asylum seekers. We trebled in size, and now have 17 staff.

After 12 years at the helm, Alasdair Mackenzie moved on during 2002, and a new Coordinator, Morris Wren, was appointed.

How did you become involved?

I had been living in Paris, working as a freelance journalist in the field of human rights. When I came back to the UK I had difficulty getting established again. I worked as a volunteer for the Refugee Council, and the post of acting press officer came up. This brought me into contact with asylum seekers and, after the job ended, I continued helping individual asylum seekers and campaigning for asylum rights. Alasdair Mackenzie invited me to put my name forward as a member of the board. That was seven years ago.

INTERVIEW

Where does Asylum Aid's income come from?
Out of a total of about £500,000, we received a grant of just over £300,000 from the National Lottery Community Fund in 2002, and a grant of £52,000 from London local authorities. The trend seems increasingly towards project-oriented grants: this year, just over £50,000 was donated from various sources as unrestricted donations. For the first time, this year we receive a small proportion of our income from public funds, which are now available for asylum appeals, but we will not compromise on standards.

What do you see as the key issues facing Asylum Aid?
First, the context within which we work has become more antagonistic and restrictive, both from a political and media perspective. We have to continue providing high-quality advice, and the level of demand has risen because of hasty and ill-informed first decisions by the Home Office. This has led to a huge backlog of appeals, and a doubling of the number of adjudicators to handle these appeals.

Secondly, there has been a growing pressure to provide all-round support for asylum seekers, because of the shortcomings of government measures, and notably dispersal outside London. Asylum seekers are being placed wherever there is available housing – and this is often in areas that are remote from support services. Our caseworkers have found that practical humanitarian problems hinder clients in pursuing their legal claim for asylum. One member of staff now concentrates on practical support, and we're helping community groups to respond to the demand, for instance through offering training. But our core function remains high quality legal help.

There are also some internal issues we need to deal with. Communication has to be more systematic, now that we are bigger. We need to maintain both fundraising and lobbying functions – but because of resource constraints we have had to make a choice between having either a Fundraiser or a Press and Publicity Officer. (Both roles had previously been filled by one person, which was too much.) We decided to appoint a full-time Fundraiser.

What is the composition of the board?
The board is made up of people who have been involved in the issues. There are nine elected members and up to four co-opted. Three of the current board members are former Asylum Aid

clients. The board also includes former staff and volunteers.

There is only one sub-committee, devoted to fundraising. The Refugee Women's Resource Project has a steering committee, which includes some members from the board.

How would you describe the nature of the board's engagement with the organisation?

The board is very involved in setting strategic directions, and in making submissions to Government to influence policy developments. The board is also very hands-on – everyone tries to help. With the development of the Refugee Women's Resource Project, alongside our core service, we are stretched.

The board helps with fundraising. We aim to increase membership and plan to hold future events, with the participation of prominent people.

How would you like to see the board develop?

We probably need more fundraising expertise at board level. We also must maintain a strong focus on external communications.

Some of our board processes would benefit from being more systematic perhaps – and we need an induction pack for new members.

Regarding the composition of the board, I would like to see some members from the community groups who have to deal with the sharp end of Government asylum policy.

What advice would you give to a new board member?

There are no passengers here.

3 Recruitment: the new board member

I don't want to belong to any club that will accept me as a member

Groucho Marx

A board's eye view

What power does the board have to appoint new board members? Some boards have the freedom to co-opt new members, subject to ratification of their appointment at a subsequent Annual General Meeting (AGM). In many membership-based organisations, the Constitution (or Memorandum and Articles of Association) determines that all board-member appointments are subject to election by the membership. In others, a majority may be member-elected, but some may be co-opted by the board, subject to confirmation by the membership at the next AGM. In some statutory bodies, the relevant Government Minister makes the appointment. This does not necessarily mean that the board has no influence over the nature of the choice, but the board's capacity to build or re-build itself is ultimately beyond its control.

Whether there are constitutional constraints or not, the board has some level of influence over its composition, either directly through formal powers of co-option, or indirectly, through influencing those who make the appointment decision. Even by signalling board needs to the general membership, it may be possible to encourage more useful nominations at election time.

3.1 Influencing the nominations

When a second local government agreed to become a significant funder of the organisation, it saved our skins. The additional funding enabled the Centre to get through a difficult first phase of its independent life (it is still operating, over 20 years later). But, just as our first local government funding body had the right to appoint three board members, so did the second. There was a danger that we would end up with a group of board members who regarded their role only as keeping us honest on behalf of their political

---

masters, and not contributing in any real sense to the effectiveness of the organisation. Boldness seemed to be the best response.

I waited in the corridors of power while the Chair of the relevant Committee was in a meeting. When he left the meeting I secured a two-minute walk down the corridor to his next meeting, during which time I put our position, stressed the importance of having a strong board to champion the organisation, and explained our need for experienced board members with commercial nous or particular community connections – and the desirability of gender balance. He came up trumps. We were the fortunate recipients of three capable, motivated and appropriate board members.

The board may identify the need for new members because:

- board retirement procedures require current board members to step down;
- new challenges or directions require new skills at board level;
- some board members are not pulling their weight;
- there is too much pressure on a small group of active board members;
- one or more board members' personal or work circumstances result in their having to resign from the board.

Where the board has some control over the process of identifying and approaching potential new members, the following is suggested as a structured process for board recruitment.

1 Produce a profile of the board in relation to its current composition. It may be useful to adapt the Board Recruitment Grid (p33) to help with this audit.
2 In the light of recent strategic planning, and the organisation's major goals, identify what skills would be most useful to the board. Discuss with current board members, and the CEO, what the priority needs are in terms of professional, commercial, educational or other experience. Bear in mind that an effective board is a team. The most successful commercial or professional individuals are not always team players – in some cases they are too goal driven, or accustomed to independent action, to have the patience for committee meetings. There are some additional, personal qualities, therefore, which do not feature on the Recruitment Grid.
3 Invite both board and staff to suggest potential board members in the light of the needs identified. Then, with their help, draw up a list of 'people who may lead to people', so that the scan of potential

board members is not confined to the board's own networks. These sources of suggestions might include:

- existing board contacts
- staff suggestions
- funding body suggestions
- friends of the organisation
- key clients
- board members of other organisations
- relevant professional societies
- business associations
- sponsors or donors

4   Having approached some of these contacts for ideas and suggestions, draw up a long list (keep it for future reference – you don't necessarily need to go through this process every time the need for a new board member arises). Review the list, perhaps with a temporary sub-group of the board (sometimes referred to as a Nominating Committee).

5   Develop a Board Member Information Sheet for prospective new board members. The sheet should pull together information about the potential new member, including biographical information, why they want to join this particular board, what they hope to bring to the board, what they would like to get from their board membership and any questions they might have. Protocol may determine that the prospective board member does not complete this, but that you complete it on their behalf – if you are approaching a busy (or senior) person, asking them to complete an application form may not be the most appropriate first step in the relationship.

6   Contact the list of potential candidates to recruit for board membership and ask to meet with them. This is likely to be a task for the Chair, or a member of the board who has been allocated this specific role.

7   If they are willing and show initial interest, prospective board members should meet with the board Chair and the Chief Executive, hear an overview of the organisation and receive relevant organisational materials describing the organisation's services to the community, and a board member job description. The prospective new member should hear about how the organisation orients new members. Provide names of several board members whom the prospective new member might contact with any questions. In turn, find out more about the prospective member's interest, motivation and experience. Are they interested in serving

a cause, raising their visibility, developing personal skills, improving their networks?

8 Identify if there are any potential conflicts of interest with the candidate, e.g. is he or she on the board of a competing organisation, or a supplier of the organisation.

9 Feed back information to the current board, and if there is any short-listing to do, decide who your priority potential members are. Obviously, to minimise embarrassment, you should know enough about a potential member to avoid contacting them unless they are a serious contender. Nevertheless, there may be occasions when there are more names than places.

10 Invite the prospective new member to a board meeting. Notify current board members that a potential new member will be attending. Consider name tags to help the potential new member become acquainted with board members. Introduce the member at the start of the meeting and, at the end, ask the potential new member if they have any questions. Thank them for coming.

11 Shortly after the meeting, call the prospective new member to hear if they want to apply to join the board or not. If so, solicit their completed board member application and provide all applications to the board for their review and election.

12 Notify new members (those who have been elected) and invite them to subsequent board meetings and the board orientation.

This may seem over-formal and structured. But, apart from the benefit of following a thorough and coherent process, a signal is being sent to the potential board member that their involvement is taken seriously; and the amount of information they receive prior to joining the board will make a substantial difference to their capacity to contribute productively at an early stage.

Board recruitment grid

The chart is designed to record the profiles of current and potential board members. It assumes that you currently have six members (numbers 1–6) and have identified a further three potential members (letters A, B, C). Go through the chart ticking the boxes that describe each actual and potential member. When you have done this for your first board member, you should have a series of ticks in column one. When you have done the same for the second board member, you should have a series of tickets in column two, and so on. It is intended as a model for adaptation.

Profile	Existing Board Members						Potential members		
	1	2	3	4	5	6	A	B	C
Age									
18–25									
26–35									
36–45									
46–60									
Over 60									
Gender									
Female									
Male									
Ethnicity									
South Asian									
African									
Caribbean									
European									
Geographic location									
Urban									
Rural/Regional									
Expertise									
Administrative									
Industry-specific									
Business									
Finance									
Information Technology									
Fundraising									
Legal									
Marketing									
PR									
Personnel									
Constituency									
Business									
Government									
Community									
Other									

In addition to the demographics and professional experience which this grid records, there are other factors to consider:

1 What is the prospective board member's record of achievement?
2 Do they have the capacity to cooperate with others? Some highly intelligent individuals are excellent at challenging, probing, and refusing to accept things at face value – but in a board meeting these attributes can come across as abrasive and disruptive if they are not tempered with respect for others' opinions.
3 Are they genuinely interested in the organisation's work? Without this motivation they probably will not stay the distance.
4 Are they sufficiently available to give the time needed?

Beyond networking

Some boards go beyond the networking process to identify prospective members, using open advertising to solicit nominations, or even engaging the services of a recruitment agency to search out prospective board members. In both cases this may serve to create contacts that go well beyond the range of the board's networks, and send a signal to the wider community that the organisation is keen to establish and maintain links with the community and be open and accountable. In politically fraught environments this may protect the organisation from the tendency towards (or charge of) factionalism.

In the case of using a recruitment agency, this may be a highly targeted exercise, seeking out specific skills or attributes – effectively undertaking the work that a board nominating group might carry out, when there is not the time or resources for the board to take this on or, as in the case of the 'Rescue' Foundation (see p43), when there is no board, because the organisation is being established from scratch.

3.2 An appointments committee

When the Royal Flying Doctor Service of Australia (RFDS) (Queensland Section) was looking to strengthen the board with new members, they created a Remuneration and Appointments Committee of the main board; its role being to develop the terms of reference for new members. Initially, the committee considered the ideal board for the organisation, in terms of skills and attributes required. It then undertook a skills audit of existing members to determine the weaknesses and gaps that needed to be filled.

Together with the main board, the committee subsequently compiled a list of potential new members who had the skills required. This was supplemented through 'word of mouth' beyond initial board contacts. As and when vacancies occur the board approaches those now on the database with the skills required at the time.

The Chair of the RFDS (Queensland Section) believes that the use of a recruitment agency is appropriate for 'non-profits' in many cases, to ensure that new contacts are identified beyond the professional and personal spheres of existing board members. He also believes that in some cases it is appropriate for such boards to offer some form of remuneration. For both board members and the organisation, this creates a different sense of relationship, one that has a stronger contractual basis, and recognisable value that can be measured and assessed.

The prospect's viewpoint

It is always flattering to be asked to join a board, but before you make a decision to do so, you want to know what you are letting yourself in for. How frequently will you be expected to attend meetings and other events? How much time per month and over a year will you be expected to contribute? Are there specific reasons why you have been asked to join – issues which the board believe you will help to address because of your expertise? Is this an approach which has been discussed by the board as a whole, or is it a more individual (or maverick) approach by a single board member or the CEO? Have you got the time, given your professional and personal commitments? Are there any potential conflicts of interest with regard to other non-profit organisations you are involved with?

If the approach made is rather informal, or even unprofessional, be wary. You may be highly motivated to want to help this organisation – you may even decide that it is your mission in life to bring professionalism to their board processes – but this is a major commitment, and not guaranteed to end in success.

If the approach comes from an organisation with which you are not very familiar, ask a few direct questions:

- What are the main issues the organisation is facing?
- What is expected of the board as a whole, and the individual board member?

- What stage of development has the organisation reached?
- Is there a strategic plan?
- What is the state of the organisation's finances?
- How often does the board receive financial reports?
- How is the board structured?
- Who are the other board members?
- How often does the board evaluate its own performance?
- How often does the board evaluate the effectiveness of the CEO?

Ideally, the approach from the organisation will be accompanied by something like this information sheet:

What you need to know about the Board of the Anywhere Community Association

Term of office	3 years. Elected at Annual General Meeting. Board members may serve a maximum of 6 years. Board members may be appointed by the Board to fill vacancies until the next Annual General Meeting.
Time requirements	We require a time commitment of about 88 hours per year, or an average of 7 hours per month for board meetings, committee meetings, orientation sessions and special events, including preparation time.
	We do most of our work in meetings. We cannot do a good job or meet deadlines without full participation from members.
Board meetings	The full board meets at least 10 times per year, usually on the last Thursday of each month, from 5 p.m. to 7 p.m. See below for meeting schedule.
Committee meetings	Sub-committees meet at the discretion of committee members to accomplish certain tasks by established deadlines. Attendance is essential for the committees to do their work.
Orientation sessions	The membership committee will arrange orientation sessions as needed.
Other time requirements	*AGM*: We hold an Annual General Meeting, which includes the presentation of community service awards.
	Social events: We normally have at least one or two social events per year where staff, friends of the organisation and board members can interact.
	Fundraising: At present, we are funded primarily from fees-for-service, and a Government operating grant. Board members have had little involvement in fundraising. It is reasonable to expect this to change. Next year, we will be starting a capital campaign in which board members will play a prominent role

Strategic planning: We are completing the update of our strategic plan. There will be several meetings and one day-long retreat (on a Saturday) over the next 3 months.

Selection process	Board members and staff identify prospective board members.
	Prospects receive information package. If still interested, they are invited to attend a board meeting.
	If board and prospective member agree, prospect is interviewed by Nominating Committee.
	On recommendation of Nominating Committee, name is placed on the slate for election by the membership at the next AGM. If the recruitment is to fill a vacancy on the board, the candidate may be appointed by the board to serve what remains of the term.
Approach to governance	We believe that the board's role is to ensure that ACA establishes and maintains the trust of the community by being clear in its mission, prudent and ethical in its activities, and accountable for its actions. We try to implement effective and principled governance, in keeping with our adopted Code of Ethics and Board Duty Statement.
Our mission and goals	*Mission*: [your mission statement] *Goals*: [your annual goals / objectives]
Values and beliefs	The board of ACA subscribes to, and acts in accordance with the following values and beliefs [your values statement]
Directors' Code of Ethics	Our board members sign this code of ethics:

As a board member of ACA, I will:

- be committed to the mission of ACA

- act in a manner consistent with the mission and values of ACA

- focus my efforts on the mission of ACA and not on my personal goals

- accept responsibility and share power in order to work as a productive, cooperating member of the Board of Directors

- avoid conflicts of interest between my position as a board member and my personal and professional life

- support in a positive manner all actions taken by the Board of Directors even when I am in a minority position on such actions

- never exercise authority as a board member except when acting in a meeting with the full board or as I am delegated by the board

- keep confidential matters confidential
- be accountable to the 'moral ownership' with the rest of the board members for competent, conscientious and effective accomplishment of the obligations of the Board
- ensure that discrimination is never practised at ACA
- act in a manner consistent with this Code of Ethics despite personal opinions, values or differences.

Upcoming meetings and events	*Regular board meetings**	*Annual General Meeting*	*Board evaluation*
	■ January 28	■ June 22	■ April 29
	■ February 25		*Social Events*
	■ March 25	*Orientation*	■ Summer picnic TBA
	■ April 29 (Board evaluation)	To be arranged	■ End of year open house TBA
	■ May 27	*Committee meetings*	
	■ June 24 (Auditor's report)	■ Board Development TBA	
	■ July/August TBA	■ Personnel TBA	
	■ September 30	■ Strategic Planning TBA	
	■ October 28		
	■ November 25		
	■ December 16 ** normally held last Thursday of month*		TBA = To Be Arranged

© 1997. Reproduced with kind permission of Nathan Garber (Nathan Garber & Associates; e-mail: nathan@GarberConsulting.com)

Finally, before agreeing to join, the potential board member should ask:

- Is this the right organisation for me?
- Is this the right time?
- What contribution will I be able to make?
- What do I want to get out of board membership?

An increasing number of boards have developed a role statement or job description for board members. This is simply produced, and highly desirable – the Information Sheet above provides a basis for such a statement, which makes clear to the current and prospective member what is expected from them. It also provides the Chair with a benchmark against which to measure individual board members' commitment.

Role descriptions for specific Officers of the board are included at Resource 5 (pp284–90), along with a more detailed role statement for the ordinary board member.

Induction

On joining, the new board member should expect a structured induction process, to bring them up to speed as quickly as possible. This increases their value to the organisation, and minimises the risk of feeling like an outsider for months after they have joined.

3.3 Six years, then an induction

Possibly the most depressing conversation I had with a board member of the theatre was during the first board retreat. If there had been retreats previously in the history of this 75-year-old organisation they were lost in the mists of time. This was the first retreat any of the present board members had attended. On the first evening of the retreat a board member confided that she had been on the board for six years but this was the first time she had understood her role, and the first time she felt able to make a practical contribution. A very late induction.

Dependent upon the information and processes that have preceded the board member's appointment, the induction procedure could include some or all of the following:

- a meeting with the Chair to clarify board roles, particular expectations of the new board member, strategic issues;
- a meeting with the CEO to learn about the key personnel, the range of operations, issues currently facing the organisation;
- a tour of the organisation's premises, however humble, along with an opportunity to meet some of the staff;
- an invitation to see the organisation's activities and programmes in action;
- the receipt of an Induction Pack (see below);
- a follow-up meeting with either Chair or CEO for clarification of any of the material in the Board Manual.

At the end of an induction process the new board member should be informed, motivated and ready to engage with the organisation and the other board members.

Induction Pack

The Induction Pack, or Board Manual, should contain, amongst other things:

- the organisation's annual report;
- the organisation's Constitution (Memorandum and Articles);
- the most recent audited financial statement;
- the strategic plan and financial projections;
- a list of current board members, titles and affiliations;
- a board organisation chart;
- a staff organisation chart;
- a brief biography of the CEO, and of other board members;
- two or three recent sets of board Minutes, and supporting papers relating to any key issues currently under discussion by the board;
- the Code of Ethics/Code of Conduct;
- board role descriptions;
- a list of key forthcoming dates (meetings, events);
- the organisation's newsletter, brochure, or other publications;
- recent press cuttings relating to the organisation's work.

Given this information at the outset, most board members will feel far more confident about the context within which they will be contributing, and about the current issues facing the organisation. And while the initial assembly of an Induction Pack is clearly rather time-consuming, it is relatively simple to keep it up to date.

New board member's induction checklist

- ✔ Have you had a meeting with the Chair?
- ✔ Have you had a meeting with the CEO?
- ✔ Have you visited the organisation's premises, and met the staff?
- ✔ Do you know the history of the organisation?
- ✔ Do you have copies of:
  - the organisation's annual report?
  - the organisation's Constitution (Memorandum and Articles)?
  - the most recent audited financial statement?
  - the strategic plan and financial projections?
  - a list of current board members, titles and all affiliations?
  - a board organisation chart?

- a staff organisation chart?
- the organisation's newsletter, brochure, or other publications?
- a brief biography of the CEO?
- two or three recent sets of board Minutes, and supporting papers relating to any key issues currently under discussion by the board?
- the Code of Ethics/Code of Conduct?
- board role descriptions?
- key policy documents?

If the board member is entirely new to non-profit governance, their induction may need to include some further guidance on legal and fiduciary responsibilities, and some encouragement to feel free to contribute to board meetings and ask questions, in order to develop a fuller understanding of the organisation and the issues involved. If the board member is new to non-profits, they may benefit from a discussion about some of the differences and similarities between commercial boards and non-profit boards.

Board members schooled in the commercial world can find the priorities and processes of the non-profit world mystifying. Enhancing shareholder value is often the driver of the for-profit organisation, while delivering services to specific constituencies is usually the driver of the non-profit. Financial performance will be a key element in for-profit decision-making, while financial performance is often balanced with other factors in the non-profit. At first, even the concept of an operating loss (met by Government grants) goes against the grain for a commercial board member, for whom operating loss is equal to failure. Some commercial firms, concerned to address the 'triple bottom line' of financial, social and environmental results, are perhaps moving closer to the performance criteria familiar to non-profit organisations.

The degree of consultation and debate that precedes decisions in a non-profit can be highly frustrating for anyone used to working in an entrepreneurial environment. *Why are we spending so much time on this? Let's just make a decision!* Of course, the reason so much time is being spent is that, in the absence of simple financial drivers, achieving commitment from those around the table, or from the organisation's stakeholders, is essential for long-term success. It takes time to appreciate this.

Summary

- The board is a team. It needs the right mix of skills, experience and personalities to operate effectively.
- Even where the board is elected by a membership, it is possible to signal to 'the electorate' what the needs of the board are, to encourage appropriate nominees or candidates.
- The approach to a potential board member should be clear, structured, and professional.
- For co-options the board should not rely on its personal contacts, but should network widely to identify prospects.
- Potential board members should satisfy themselves that this is the right organisation for them.
- A structured induction process will help to harness the energies of new board members more quickly.

CASE STUDY: RECRUITMENT OF NEW BOARD MEMBERS

The 'Rescue' Foundation (not its real name) is a non-profit organisation that grew out of the 'Rescue' Club established in the early 1900s. The concept of a Foundation emerged as a way of addressing the limitations of the Club's focus on service delivery and training, to the detriment of marketing and fundraising.

This was a unique position as the board had to be built from scratch and, due to circumstances at the time, fairly quickly. The General Manager (appointed by the parent Association) decided to use a recruitment agency for the purpose, with the costs being absorbed within the recruitment and professional development budget. A mid-sized private agency with experience of senior managerial recruitment was briefed. Of the two staff in the agency responsible for the contract, one had considerable personal and professional contacts with senior executives within the community.

The agency assessed the nature and needs of the organisation with the General Manager, and together they drew up a list of significant criteria. The task of the agency was to identify those people who might be interested in such a position and who were 'well connected' into different networks in the community. The Foundation was looking to recruit individuals who would also bring specific skills such as legal, financial and personnel. The necessary characteristics of the Chair were determined to be someone who had a generosity of spirit, was a potential donor to the organisation, and could demonstrate leadership.

The initial step was for the agency to present a long list of names to the organisation, which were scanned to ensure that the individuals being considered had no apparent conflicts of interest, for example in relation to any positions they held on other boards in the community. The organisation gave approval to the agency for potential board members to be contacted and interviewed, from which 10 names emerged of interested people with the skills required. Starting with the Chair and other Office holders these members were then approached and interviewed by the organisation – and the board of the 'Rescue' Foundation came into being.

The same process was chosen some years later by the Foundation when the board needed to recruit additional new members.

The benefits of using an agency were perceived to be:

- finding people other than friends and colleagues of existing board members who could bring with them new networks and contacts;
- finding new people in the community who are willing to serve but had just never been asked – 'shaking the tree';
- lessening the chances of particular external 'friendships' and 'professional alliances' influencing the decision-making processes of the board – preventing schisms and cliques.

An Interview With Jo-Anne Everingham, National Chair, Oxfam Community Aid Abroad Australia

Oxfam Community Aid Abroad is the Australian affiliate of Oxfam International and has been operating in Australia since 1953. It is a secular aid agency that supports long-term development programmes in over 30 countries across the world. It also provides emergency relief specialising in clean water and sanitation in disaster situations, such as the Mozambique floods and East Timor relief. Oxfam Community Aid Abroad's third programme intervention is to campaign and advocate for changes in policies and practices that cause or perpetuate poverty and injustice. In common with the other Oxfams around the world, Oxfam Community Aid Abroad has signed up to three basic promises:

INTERVIEW

INTERVIEW

1   We will work to put economic and social justice at the top of the world's agenda.
2   We will cooperate in strengthening the merging global citizens/movement for economic and social justice.
3   We will significantly improve the quality, efficiency and coherence of our work.

Jo-Anne Everingham is National Chair of Oxfam Community Aid Abroad Australia (OCAA) and has served on the board for 11 years. She lives in Maryborough and lectures in Asian Studies at the Wide Bay Campus of the University of Southern Queensland.

What are the key issues the board has had to face in the recent past?
The decision whether or not to make a name change and a brand change from Community Aid Abroad to Oxfam Community Aid Abroad was an example. We have had some major organisational decisions to make over the years, including the decisions to merge with Freedom from Hunger and then to affiliate with Oxfam International. These decisions led to other decisions about autonomy, independence and organisational processes.

The board has become better at making these big decisions over the years. We now try to define: what decision we have to make, what criteria it should meet, and who we should talk to about this. Then we gather the information and identify options, and test them against the criteria. This process has been tested and evolved over time through hard experience.

We used this process most recently in deciding whether or not to phase out our programme in some of the regions we work in overseas. We felt uncomfortable about this decision, and it was very difficult to make, since the programmes were all high quality and we had strong relationships with the partner organisations. However, we gathered the right information, measured against agreed criteria, and in the end felt able to stand by our decision as a good one for the organisation and our partners in the long run. We are sure our impact on global poverty will be increased by focusing more like this.

We also recruited and appointed a new Executive Director last year. That was an intensive responsibility for the board and significant for the future of the organisation.

What changes have you seen in the board over the years?

I have been on the board around 11 years, since the merger with Freedom from Hunger in the early 1990s. This is my final year on the board and I will be moving on.

The board has changed a lot since I first joined. The board doubled in size with the merger and then halved again when the merger was complete. The latest change to the board is that our board will no longer be a State-based board but is moving over to a nationally elected, skills-based board.

We started out like any other community organisation, and we have evolved. Roles have needed to be clarified and there has been increasing pressure to be accountable.

The change in focus has been evolving over time. At first we changed our focus to policy rather than operations, but having adopted the Carver Policy Governance model [see p264] we have defined this even more as a distinction between 'ends' and 'means'. We now express our mission as 'ends' and focus on what we have to achieve and for whom. We are more 'ends' focused. The board only deals with operations to the extent of saying what would be an unacceptable means to achieve goals. We set the limits to the ways of operating and we set the goals, but we do not focus on the how to achieve those goals – just how not to do so.

An example of this change in focus is that when I first joined we used to go through the budget line by line and approve things like the stationery budget, but now we just state broad principles including that the budget must be in surplus and that the organisation must meet legal requirements in spending the money, that it should achieve certain ratios of income to be spent on our programmes. We also say that financially the organisation needs to achieve a certain cost ratio for fundraising, and then the staff go about achieving these goals.

Any further board changes planned?

The big decisions have already happened and the new system is being implemented, with our first national elections currently under way. We will also be developing the structure of the Community Reference Committee in order to get supporter input into our policy directions. There will be a period of consolidation of the governance system now.

The shift to a Policy Governance model and a professional board has been driven internally by staff and board members, and externally by our increasing profile nationally and internationally. Ausaid is one of our major funding bodies and it has tightened its management and reporting requirements. Our Oxfam International affiliation has put further pressure on us to be more professional and efficient.

How has the board been involved in planning?
We see the strategic plan as being led by the Executive Director. The board needs to set criteria for the plan to meet and things that must be delivered or observed, including that the plan should be developed by a participatory process, and that it should:

- enhance OCAA's integration with Oxfam International;
- increase the agency's income – particularly untied community support income;
- maximise effective community involvement in the agency's work;
- ensure we maximise our impact and achieve the strategic changes outlined in our Ends policies;
- be cost-effective; and
- respond appropriately to key trends in Australia and globally.

However, it is a staff-led process. A starter debate is used to launch the strategic planning process, and the board is one of the groups who input into that debate. When the initial draft of the strategic plan is completed we hold a full-day meeting to review it. This meeting is additional to the normal meetings, and this year we made some significant changes at that review stage.

We do not use the strategic plan as a routine board guide. We tend to use the Ends statements as our progress measure. We examine reports against Ends policies at our meetings, to see how far operational activities are fulfilling our intentions. We get a comprehensive summary report against the plan once a year.

Does the board get involved in fundraising?
We aren't closely involved in fundraising. It is seen as separate from the job of being a board member. Board members get involved in fundraising as volunteers with the organisation rather than as board members. In this way some of us played an active role in the capital appeal to purchase our national office building.

We do expect that people will express their commitment in some form of giving but it is not the focus of the board. There have been major projects where a board has been set up with a more specific fundraising intention, such as the International Youth Parliament.

What do you see as the role of the Chair?

The main job of the Chair is to make sure that the board is doing its job well. It's about keeping a finger on the pulse, mediating and facilitating the board processes – ensuring they are open, thorough and orderly. The board is a team, so the Chair has no extra rights to information or decision-making.

The Chair is sometimes the spokesperson for the board – not for the organisation, but for the board. A good Chair needs skills in facilitation, communication and organisation and needs to be able to think in terms of systems rather than details. They also need to have a fair bit of passion for the cause.

What sort of demands does Oxfam Community Aid Abroad make on the individual board members?

We meet four times per year, and we are pretty strict about meeting attendance. If someone misses more than two meetings without giving cause we ask them to explain why they should remain on the board. We have reduced the amount of time the board meetings take. They used to take all day Saturday and Sunday but now we meet Friday night and all day Saturday. The meetings have shortened but the work between meetings has increased. During meetings we set up processes to be followed between meetings, such as preparation of discussion papers, proposals or conferring with other people. Decisions are still made in the meetings but most of the work is done outside the meetings now.

Almost all the papers are prepared by the board's members now – in the past they were prepared by staff. This has happened as a result of defining the role of the board more precisely in relation to the organisation, and giving board members responsibility and a sense of ownership over decisions and processes. The agenda is also set by board members, whereas it used to be set by staff. With the board taking ownership and responsibility it has also meant being on the board is more work. But all of these processes have made decision-making much quicker.

INTERVIEW

What relationship is there between the board and the Executive Director?

We have increasingly reduced potential friction between the Executive Director and the board by drawing clearer lines about roles and responsibilities. If there is friction it is usually caused by a board member deviating from policy focus to operational focus. Our mutual expectations are much clearer now and the board's role is to support as well as performance-manage the Executive Director. I think there is an amicable understanding of that. As long as the Executive Director implements a reasonable interpretation of the board's instructions we will stand by his actions and decisions. It is both a monitoring and mentoring role with the Executive Director.

For the board the Executive Director is one of our main sources of information – he either has the information we need or will gather it for us so we can make decisions. He is also the organisational spokesperson and gives the organisation the profile necessary to have a real impact.

What strategic choices and challenges face the board in the next few years?

We have just changed the way board members are elected onto the board. It used to be that representatives from each State committee sat on the board. We have now moved to nationally elected members. The numbers won't change but the makeup of the board will. A key challenge for the board in this new system will be to deliver skilled and community-connected people. Two of the office bearers will be changing and that will raise issues of continuity and organisational memory.

Another ongoing challenge is to focus on the debate around our policy objectives – debate about what a development organisation needs to be doing in order to really change the world.

The board needs to listen to the owners and supporters of the organisation and improve ways of hearing what they are saying. This will be especially important without State members on the committee, so we will need to make sure everyone is being heard.

There is also the challenge of delivering an integrated one-programme approach. In the past the different programme sections of the organisation focused on different issues as they saw fit – long-term regional development, emergency work and advocacy work might have different emphases. The one-programme approach is where all parts of the organisation will focus on the same core issues, e.g. Fair Trade, Indigenous Rights, Gender and Development. This is going to be primarily a staff responsibility, but the board will be involved.

What advice would you give to a new board member?

■ Realise that a plurality of ideas is advantageous, so don't be afraid to contribute to the overall diversity of debate.

■ Foster connections with supporters, so you know the values of a large group of people.

■ Before bringing something up, test it against policy – put it into context.

■ Know how policy governance works.

We are planning a half-day board induction for new members. They are also invited to a staff induction day – these are held regularly throughout the year. We run a buddy system so another board member talks to them before, through the meeting and afterwards at a de-briefing with them. We sometimes run refreshers, e.g. on budgets – how we read them and how we look at them.

INTERVIEW

PART 2

RESPONSIBILITIES

4 Letter of the law

Chapter contributed by Sean Egan

Ignorance of the law excuses no man

John Selden

All non-profit organisations are regulated by the law to a greater or lesser extent. There are specific rules and general obligations affecting their areas of operation, which may be daunting for a new board member but should be seen as promoting board probity and responsible action rather than being an unnecessary interference.

There are many similarities in the underlying legal requirements of the UK and other jurisdictions; it is the mechanism of regulation that contains the major differences. In England and Wales the impact of charity law, and the position of the Charity Commission as the principal regulator, is the distinctive characteristic of the non-profit sector. Other jurisdictions, such as Scotland and the USA, prefer to focus regulation on the requirements needed for an organisation to qualify for tax benefits, and as a result the tax authority has the primary regulatory role.

This chapter outlines the laws most relevant to board members of non-profit organisations and shows how these laws act to promote a coherent notion of proper conduct, which should form the basis for all board activity for charities and non-charities alike.

Understanding the constitution of the organisation is the starting point for board members to appreciate their obligations. This chapter looks first at the different types and constitutions of organisations, then the resulting obligations, and finally practical issues for board members to consider.

The reference to 'board member' refers to an individual who is a member of the governing body, irrespective of the legal structure of the organisation.

Types of organisation

Most charities and other non-profit organisations fall into one of the following categories.

- **Companies limited by guarantee.** These are separate legal entities, run by a board of directors for the members who, like shareholders in a company limited by shares, have limited liability. The members guarantee a maximum contribution to the company in the event of its winding up, even if the company is insolvent. This sum is usually £1. Members of charitable companies limited by guarantee cannot receive dividends or other distributions of profit. The members of the company are owners only in the sense of exercising voting rights, since they have no entitlement to a share of the net assets on winding up.
- **Trusts and unincorporated associations.** These are not incorporated (i.e. they do not have the status of companies) and do not have limited liability. They are governed under the terms of their constitution by a governing body and have no separate legal entity. As a result, obligations entered into on behalf of the organisation are the personal liability of the individuals comprising the governing body. In principle, therefore, these individuals have unlimited liability for the obligations of the organisation. Unlike a trust, an unincorporated association is usually a membership-based organisation. The individuals of the governing body of an unincorporated association can be protected against unlimited liability if the members agree to provide an indemnity against any losses of the association.
- **Other incorporated bodies.** Industrial and Provident Societies are becoming less common. They are governed by the Industrial and Provident Societies Act 1965, and are incorporated organisations that are either bona fide cooperative societies or voluntary organisations carrying on an industry trade or business for the benefit of the community.
- Organisations incorporated by Royal Charter or by special Act of Parliament are by their nature rare, and are wholly governed by the terms of their individual constitution.

Constitutions

The constitution of the organisation will be determined and interpreted by the relevant law – principally company law and/or charity law.

Company law

The principal statute is the Companies Act 1985, which prescribes the form of company constitution, dividing it into the Memorandum of Association and the Articles of Association – commonly shortened to 'the Memorandum' and 'the Articles'. The Memorandum deals with the fundamental elements of the company, the most important of which is the objects clause – the aims of the organisation – and the statement as to the nature of the company – i.e. whether it is limited by shares or by guarantee. It also deals with arrangements on dissolution. The Articles deal with the mechanisms of operating the organisation – how members' and directors' meetings are held and how the members and directors are appointed.

The *constitution* of a charity which is also a company, will be governed by company law, and the *operation* of the charity will be governed by both charity law and company law.

Charity law

The decision to become a charity is of fundamental importance and will affect most aspects of an organisation's activities. The major advantages of being a charity are the seal of approval this lends when seeking funding, and a host of tax advantages. These need to be set against the disadvantage of additional regulation and legal restrictions on the organisation's operations.

The most recent major charity legislation – the Charities Acts of 1992 and 1993 – confirmed the Charity Commission's position as the regulator and adviser to the charity sector, with extensive powers to investigate and take over the operation of charities.

Charity trustees are under a general duty to register the charity with the Charity Commission if the charity has income of more than £1,000, occupies land, or has a permanent endowment. Some organisations such as industrial and provident societies, grant maintained schools, some universities and other institutions have specific exemptions from registrations.

Unincorporated charities have their constitutions in the form of a trust deed, association rules or other document which specifies the organisation's objectives (which need to be exclusively charitable), the powers to achieve the objectives, how the governing body is composed, how trustees are appointed and how the organisation can wind itself up.

Responsibilities and liabilities

This section focuses on the obligations arising from the nature of the organisation rather than the obligations an organisation may decide to incur. For instance, the obligations of a non-profit organisation by virtue of being an employer will be the same as those for with-profit employer organisations. It is crucial that the governing body understands the nature and extent of all such obligations, whether under (for example) consumer protection legislation – for the sale of goods; property law – for premises; or copyright and trademark law – for intellectual property.

Many of the duties of board members are broadly similar irrespective of the legal structure of the organisation, and are referred to below as the '*general duties*'. Duties that are dependent on the legal structure are referred to as the '*special duties*'.

General duties have developed over many years across the various forms of non-profit organisation, and can be seen as a reflection of what society considers the minimum standards of good governance.

There is a common perception that the duties on charity board members are heavier than for directors of non-charity companies and that charity board members are more at risk of personal liability. However, that perception should be reversed once you have allowed for the fact that paid company directors are more prepared to take risks, and are considered to have more expertise in the nature of their business (they are usually full-time employees), and also recognise the reluctance of courts to penalise individuals acting honestly for charities. In reality it is rare for board members of charities to face personal liability unless the wrongdoing is obvious. As was said in a leading charity case (*Scargill and Cave v Charity Commission and HM Attorney General*, High Court, 2 September 1998):

> 'The court should not, in principle, be anxious to find fault with charitable trustees who, while doing their best, make honest, even stupid, mistakes.'

Who are the board members?

Companies

Identifying the directors of a company is normally easy, as directors are appointed and the appointment is recorded at Companies House. Individuals acting as directors can be treated as though they were appointed, and can be subject to the same duties as if they had been appointed. In addition, individuals or organisations that are exercising such control over the company that, in effect, they are making decisions for the company can be treated as directors. They are called 'shadow directors' and are subject to directors' duties.

Charities

The Charities Act 1993 defines the trustees as 'the persons having the general control and management of the administration of the charity'. All directors of charitable companies are trustees for the purposes of charity law. For other charities it should be clear who has these powers, prior to any delegation, and as a result who are the trustees. Patrons, for instance, can be helpful in fundraising but 'patron' should be a purely honorary title.

General duties of board members

Duty to act in the interests of the organisation

Board members have a wide duty of honesty and good faith and must exercise the powers vested in them by the constitution properly. Board members must do the best for the organisation irrespective of their own interests. Breach of this obligation can lead the board member to having to make good any loss incurred by the organisation through his or her actions.

A board may delegate authority in accordance with the constitution of the organisation, provided that the delegation is appropriate and monitored. However, a charity trustee has limited ability to delegate, as there is a positive obligation to retain discretion as to how trustee powers are exercised.

Duty to act for the proper purposes of the organisation

Even though a board member may subjectively be acting honestly in the belief that actions are in the best interests of the organisation, there is an additional obligation to exercise powers in accordance with the constitution – an objective test. If a court finds that the board member acted contrary to the powers expressly or impliedly provided for in the constitution, there might have been a breach of duty, even though the action was believed to be in the best interests of the organisation.

Duty of skill and care

Board members can face legal proceedings for the quality of their decisions, if they ought to have performed better, but not for mere errors of judgement. The more sophisticated a board member's skills, the higher will be the expected level of performance. But this does not excuse total ignorance as, in effect, there is a requirement for every board member to obtain a reasonable understanding of the duties owed and to have a minimum level of competence. In practice, the minimum expected level of competence for full-time directors will be higher than for trustees who are unpaid and can devote only a portion of their spare time to the charity.

Duty to avoid conflicts between personal interest and duty

The duty as a board member must take precedence over personal interest. In general terms non-charity directors may sanction the entering into contracts in which they have an interest, so long as the director complies with the constitution, fully discloses the circumstances, and does not vote on or influence the decision to enter into the contract. Charity trustees, on the other hand, are generally prohibited from being personally interested in contracts as a result of their duty not to profit from their office. Non-charity company directors may under specific circumstances receive loans from the company, but charity trustees may not – exceptions can be made but only in extreme circumstances. A sample conflict of interest policy statement and board member declaration is included at Resource 2 (pp268–9).

Board members therefore need to consider whether they have any involvements that in any way may conflict with the business of the organisation. The most difficult issues arise where a body, such as a Council, funds an organisation and a member of the Council or one of its officers is a board member. Whilst the advantages for both funder and organisation are clear, the individual is vulnerable should, for instance, there be a dispute relating to the funding. If the funder contemplates cutting or ceasing funding, the individual would be under a duty to disclose the information to the organisation and as a result could breach duties owed in turn to the funder.

The degree of performance

Board members are not obliged to perform their obligations continuously, and are under no obligation to come to every board meeting. However, non-attendance is unlikely to be an excuse if the board member fails to be involved over a period when there were failures by the board, and certainly not if he or she had minutes of the relevant meetings.

Where there is wrongdoing by another board member and if the board member is unaware of it (and is not culpable for being unaware), he or she will not be liable for any loss to the organisation. But if the board member is, or becomes aware of the wrongdoing, then he or she must consider what steps could be taken to prevent the wrongdoing, and should at least record his or her views, or consider resigning. These are important safeguards to ensure the board as a whole acts with propriety.

Special duties of board members

Charity trustees may not profit from their office and no payment may be made for charity trustees' services as trustees. Genuine altruism is a key principle in charity law. Payments of expenses and for the professional services of charity trustees (as distinct from services as trustees) can be made, if they are reasonable and are allowed for in the constitution. Usually this relates to so-called 'charging clauses' for solicitors and accountants. Charities sometimes wish to reimburse trustees for lost earnings – any such payment can only be made if the constitution so provides and should be carefully considered. Best practice would be to clarify the position with the Charities Commission, even though it is reluctant to sanction such payments.

Employee duties
Directors of non-charities who are employees will be subject to the express obligations in their employment agreements, the implied duty of good faith as employees, and will have statutory employment rights.

Specific offences arising on the winding-up of a company
In addition to possible claims against a board member for any breach of the general duties, there are three statutory offences that apply when companies are wound up. These are of the utmost importance to every director, who should bear them in mind whenever there is the possibility of insolvency.

Delinquent actions – if a director (or other person) misapplies or retains property of the company, or is in serious breach of duty towards the company and its creditors, then the director may be personally liable to make good the loss. This offence principally relates to directors knowingly diverting assets of the company.

Fraudulent trading – this is a criminal offence and can result in a director being personally liable for compensating the loss arising from the wrongdoing. Court cases are rare, as to be successful specific allegations of fraud or dishonesty (usually defrauding creditors) must be proved, and this requires proving the individual's intention.

Wrongful trading – wrongful trading is not a criminal offence but, like fraudulent trading, it can lead to a director being personally liable. It applies only when a company is wound up and has insufficient assets to meet its creditors' demands, and where a director ought to have known that the company was unlikely to avoid that fate and yet the company did not minimise the loss to creditors – usually by continuing to trade.

This is the most common source of concern to directors, as it will often determine the decision to cease trading and wind up the company. It does not prevent companies that are in difficulties continuing to trade, but the onus is on the directors to be able to demonstrate that a decision to continue was reasonable. The directors therefore need to be continually aware of potential financial difficulties, record the discussions and concerns they have, and record the basis for decisions to continue – taking professional advice as necessary.

Good governance can help directors protect the company and themselves from any dishonesty or fraud within the company, but it will not be able to prevent these sorts of issues arising. However, good governance will prevent claims for wrongful trading and ensure creditors are properly treated.

The authority to enter into obligations

Board members need to be clear as to the rules governing who can take legally binding decisions on behalf of the organisation.

Ostensible authority

Persons contracting with the organisation are not under any obligation to check whether a particular person has authority to bind the company to any agreements, so long as it is reasonable to expect they have the requisite authority.

Actual authority

The board must be clear who is authorised to enter into obligations on behalf of the organisation. For a company to be properly managed, it is essential that the board members consider and decide this issue and record their decisions in minutes of the board meetings.

Directors of non-charities may be paid for their services and are more likely to execute the day-to-day decisions, and therefore need to be clear between themselves of the obligations each individual can enter into without reference back to the board. All significant decisions made outside board meetings should be notified to the board.

For charities the day-to-day operation of the company will be undertaken by senior employees who are not directors under company law, though their job title may include the term – such as 'administrative director'. The board should ensure employees have appropriate job titles and are clear as to what obligations they can and cannot enter into on behalf of the company. This is not just a question of protecting the directors; if there is transparency in decision-making power, this will lead to a greater sense of cooperation and teamwork within the organisation.

Ratification

Where there is the concern that a board member has or may be in breach of his or her duties, such breach may, in some circumstances, be ratified. For non-charity companies the members of the company would need to pass a resolution approving the action. For charities applications may be made to the Charities Commission. In neither case can board members escape liability for acts of dishonesty, or acts that the company could not lawfully do.

Other criminal offences

These mainly relate to the failure to comply with reporting requirements, such as persistent default in submitting Charities Commission annual returns or accounts, or the failure to submit company documents such as accounts, or the failure to comply with specific rules such as those applying to charities for public collections and fundraising.

Are we being diligent?

✔ Are all board papers supplied in advance?
✔ Do board members read their papers in advance?
✔ Do we receive regular and clear financial reports?
✔ Do we have full and frank debate?
✔ Have we defined policies in relation to areas of greatest risk or significance for the organisation, including conflicts of interest?
✔ Do we check on the implementation of board decisions?
✔ Do we have a thorough induction process for new board members?
✔ Do we have a duty statement for board members?
✔ Do we have a Code of Conduct for board members?
✔ Do relevant managers attend board discussions related to their area of responsibility?

Practical tips for ensuring legal compliance

- Introduce an induction pack for new board members which includes the items referred to in Chapter 3, and also copies of the last three years' audited accounts; banking arrangements (including details of overdraft facilities and cheque-signing rights) and a summary of the last three years' cash-flow requirements and budgets.
- Agree the roles of board members and identify any specific responsibilities.
- Keep and circulate board minutes.
- Consider training for staff who have day-to-day responsibility for satisfying reporting requirements.
- Hold regular risk assessment reviews to ensure risks are identified.
- Review insurance – levels and type of cover (see Chapter 5 and Resource 3).
- Hold regular board meetings and agree arrangements to deal with issues that arise between meetings. It may be agreed that any decisions are notified to the next board meeting for ratification.
- Clarify with staff the authority of individuals to enter into obligations with third parties.
- Identify particular skills of board members to enable expertise to be identified and gaps in skills to be addressed.
- Identify committees and branches and their roles and responsibilities – minutes of those meetings to be submitted to the full board.
- Unincorporated organisations should review arrangements for investments particularly in respect of the Trustee Act 2000.
- Identify circumstances that may lead to conflicts of interest; regularly review and ensure that there are adequate procedures in the constitution and elsewhere for dealing with conflicts should they arise.
- Keep a register of board member interests.

Summary

- Board members need to understand the legal framework for their organisation, and be familiar with their Constitution (Memorandum and Articles).
- The boards of non-profit organisations, including charities, need to be aware of their general duties (which affect boards of all organisations), and the special duties that apply more specifically to charitable organisations.
- The board should establish clear lines of authority with regard to who can enter into obligations on the organisation's behalf, and what arrangements there are for taking decisions between board meetings.
- Through some simple and practical steps, the board can protect itself and the organisation from the danger of non-compliance.
- It is rare for the board members of non-profit organisations to be found personally liable – the courts are reluctant to punish individuals who have been acting honestly.

5 Keeping to the straight and narrow

Chapter contributed by Myles McGregor-Lowndes

The board is responsible for ensuring that the organisation does not break the law, and for optimising organisational performance. The challenge for boards and senior management is how to implement legal compliance and risk management planning in order to protect the organisation from adverse risk or breach of the law, but in a way that does not dampen the inspiration, enthusiasm or the vision brought by volunteers, staff or board.

These plans need to be more than mere policy manuals, little used in the day-to-day life of the organisation. Legal compliance and risk management planning can lead to solutions that enhance a non-profit organisation's mission. Once the fundamental principles are understood, wisdom and creativity are needed to craft the most appropriate strategy for the organisation.

Legal compliance

Legal compliance planning is necessary when legislative offences are involved and you wish to prevent any breach or minimise the penalty in the event of breach. For offences which require negligence or an element of intent you can seek to avoid or minimise any penalties by demonstrating that all practicable steps were taken to prevent the offence occurring. The primary aim of legal compliance planning is to comply fully with the law and eliminate all risk of breaching the law.

A typical legal compliance process will:

1 identify the offences to which the organisation and its officers are exposed;
2 determine how the organisation could breach the provisions, and the likelihood of such a breach;
3 design a programme to eliminate the risk of breaches;
4 ensure that the programme is implemented, is working and is regularly revised.

A compliance plan differs from a risk management plan (discussed below) in that the benchmark is set by the law, not the organisation, and the system is designed to completely eliminate breaches of the law. Moreover, measures to prevent a breach occurring cannot be compromised on the basis of cost.

Essential elements of a compliance plan

Structural elements

The structural elements that a compliance programme will embrace are:

- **Commitment:** there needs to be a dedication to effective compliance with the legislative requirements at all levels of the organisation. An example should be set by the full commitment of the board and senior management.
- **A compliance policy:** a clear written policy that includes a statement of the organisation's commitment to compliance with legislation.
- **Managerial responsibility:** all managers need to understand, promote and be responsible for compliance with the relevant laws within their day-to-day responsibilities.
- **Resources:** adequate resources are necessary to implement the compliance policy.
- **Continuous improvement:** a philosophy of continuous improvement in compliance performance should be adopted.

Operational elements

The operational elements that should be covered by a compliance programme are:

- **The identification of compliance issues:** the compliance requirements of the organisation need to be specifically identified and managed.
- **Operating procedures for compliance:** the legal requirements need to be integrated into the organisation's day-to-day operating procedures and systems.
- **Implementation:** the compliance programme needs to be consistently enforced and provided with remedial measures and continuous training.
- **Complaints and failures handling system:** there needs to be a clearly defined system for detecting and recording compliance failures by the organisation.

- **Record keeping:** the components and applications of the compliance programme need to be systematically recorded.
- **Identification and rectification:** all compliance failures need to be classified and investigated to determine their cause and enable their rectification, particularly systemic and recurring problems.
- **Reporting:** internal reporting arrangements are needed to ensure that all breaches are reported in an appropriate way to those with sufficient authority to correct them.
- **Management supervision:** the compliance programme should include appropriate supervision at all levels to ensure compliance with the organisation's policy and operating procedures.

Maintenance elements

The maintenance elements that a compliance programme will cover are:

- **Education and training:** appropriate induction and ongoing training about the workings and relevance of the compliance plan is necessary.
- **Visibility and communication:** the organisation's commitment to compliance needs to be well publicised to staff, volunteers, stakeholders and other third parties.
- **Monitoring and assessment:** compliance can be promoted and maintained, and compliance failures identified, by appropriate monitoring and assessment.
- **Review:** the compliance programme needs to be regularly reviewed to ensure its effectiveness.
- **Liaison:** ongoing liaison with the regulatory authorities is necessary so that the organisation is aware of current compliance issues and practices.
- **Accountability:** there needs to be appropriate reporting on the operation of the compliance programme against documented performance standards.

Risk management

The range of risks facing an organisation vary according to its activities, and according to the specific programmes and developments it is planning.

5.1 Some typical risk areas

- Property loss
- Chattels or contents loss
- Motor vehicles (own or use by volunteers)

- Interruption of business or services
- Company records loss
- Computer records loss or corruption
- Fraud and theft
- Product liability
- Professional negligence
- Negligence in delivery of services
- Contractual liabilities
- Compliance with Government grant conditions
- Volunteers
- Nuisance, such as excessive noise and activity

A more complete list of risks is included at Resource 3 (pp271–80). Perhaps the most obvious physical risks relate to medical and healthcare organisations (accidents or unsuccessful surgery), and to sports organisations (injury of participants). But even a small non-profit organisation embarking on a new venture may find itself exposed to risks that had previously been dormant or improbable. For example, a fundraising activity that includes the sale of food (e.g. a 'bring and buy' cake sale) brings into play food hygiene issues and the possibility of injury to patrons eating infected food. An organisation expanding its premises faces all the risks of a construction programme, cash-flow problems, disruption to its business, and the question of whether the current management and board can cope with the demands of the future, expanded operation.

Risk management is the process of managing an organisation's potential exposure to liabilities, preventing them, or providing for funds to meet the liability if it occurs. Liabilities are not limited to physical risks, but also include risks arising from legal requirements, financial, and moral or ethical issues.

Risk management is an increasingly common management strategy in the commercial sector.[1] It is not to be confused with an insurance portfolio: that is merely transferring certain selected risks at a predetermined cost to another entity. Insurance is an important part of a risk management strategy, but a risk management strategy is more encompassing, proactive and cost effective than insurance.

---

[1] Some standard business references to risk management are Kenneth MacCrimmon and Donald Wehrung, *Taking Risks: The Management of Uncertainty* (The Free Press, New York, 1986); Neil Crockford, *An Introduction to Risk Management*, 2nd edn (Woodhead-Faulkner Limited, Cambridge, 1986); H. Borowka, 'Understanding Risk Management', *Occupational Hazards*, November, 1991, pp57–60; Robert Baxt, 'Risk Management, a New Development in Legal Practice', *Company Director*, September, 1994, p45; Ian Glendon and Eugene McKenna, *Human Safety and Risk Management*, (Chapman & Hall, London, 1995).

Choosing between legal compliance planning and risk management

How do you choose when to use risk management and when to use legal compliance planning?

Legal compliance planning is necessary when legislative penalties and offences are involved and you wish to prevent them occurring, or, if they do occur, you wish rely on a 'due diligence' mitigation (i.e. you did everything reasonably practicable to prevent the offence occurring, and you can prove that you did so). The primary aim of legal compliance planning is to fully comply with the law and eliminate all risk of breaching the law.

You need to follow risk management principles when you wish to manage the organisation's exposure to risks, and to reduce their impact if they occur.

The differences between the two concepts are:

■ risk management *reduces* and *manages* risks; compliance planning seeks to *eliminate* or *prevent* them completely;
■ risk management undertakes a *cost–benefit* approach (if cost exceeds the benefits from control, then reduce control); compliance must prevent a breach occurring *regardless of cost*;
■ the benchmark for the compliance standard for risk management is *set by the non-profit organisation*; the benchmark for legal compliance is *set by the law*.

5.2 Risk management or legal compliance planning?

The failure to comply with the food hygiene laws at a fête would be a breach of the law and lead to a penalty being imposed on the organisation. Legal compliance planning should be used to eliminate the risk of this event occurring. If it did occur, then your legal compliance plan may assist in demonstrating 'due diligence' in order to seek a lesser or nil penalty.

The failure to include VAT in your prices at the same fête may result in the non-profit organisation still being liable to pay VAT to the Government. This does not result in a penalty or offence being committed – there is no law that says you have to collect VAT from a person. You just have to remit an appropriate amount of VAT to the Government, whether it is collected or not!

A system of formal checks to completely eliminate this event occurring at a fête may be too expensive. The non-profit organisation may decide on a risk management system for such a possible event that is less costly to introduce and maintain (e.g. information and advice to stallholders), and which will reduce the possibility of the event occurring to an acceptable level. In this situation they do not have to ensure that the risk is completely eliminated, because there is no legal obligation that prohibits the conduct, unlike the failure to comply with the food hygiene laws in the first situation.

Risk management strategy

The 2000 Statement of Recommended Practice (SORP) issued by the Charity Commission applies to all charities in relation to accounting periods ending after 1st January 2001. It provides that 'all charities must include in their annual report a statement confirming that the major risks to which the charity is exposed, as identified by the trustees, have been reviewed and that systems have been established to mitigate those risks'. This requirement has rather put the cat among the pigeons and raised the profile of risk management for charities.

SORP does not of itself impose legal obligations but is regarded as best practice for charities. The Charity Commission guidance on charities and risk management makes it clear that all charities are encouraged to make a statement regardless of their income. Charities whose gross income is over £250,000 must include in their annual reports 'a statement as to whether the charity trustees have given consideration to the major risks to which the charity is exposed and systems designed to mitigate those risks': (Charities (Accounts and Reports) Regulations 2000). There is a slight difference between the wording of SORP and the Regulations. Good governance dictates that trustees should be undertaking these sorts of risk assessments. Neither SORP nor the Regulations deal with how the risk assessment is to be undertaken but merely require a statement as to whether the assessment has been undertaken.

This section outlines the process for establishing and maintaining a risk management strategy. Like many management processes it is continual and cyclical. If an organisation has adopted a strategic planning process, risk management planning can be absorbed into such a process.

The following outline will need to be varied depending on the size, activities, internal environment and management structure of the particular non-profit organisation. Some boards, because of their organisation's size and complexity, will delegate the task to the CEO who may seek external professional assistance; other boards, with few or no paid employees, will do it themselves or form a volunteer task group to assist them.

Another common variation is the scope of the risk management plan. While large organisations may have the need and resources to embark on a comprehensive risk management exercise, in smaller organisations particular discrete areas of activity can be chosen for risk management.

The choice of appropriate persons to lead the process will be important in the development of a comprehensive and appropriate risk management plan. The individual or team need to have an excellent knowledge of the activities, dynamics and history of the organisation; an awareness of the law, and a knowledge of insurance. Where a volunteer task group is required, past Chairs, lawyers, insurance brokers or agents and auditors or accountants may all be particularly suitable for appointment to such a committee. Past office holders are often useful because of their long experience with the organisation. The choice of the Chair of such a working party is crucial. They must have the drive to see the project through the first cycle of implementation and review, which can be a demanding task.

Non-profit organisations that have organisational links to national bodies may be able to seek assistance from those bodies. Many industry lead bodies have collected and assessed information needed in the risk management process. It makes good management sense for peak bodies of churches, service clubs, sporting codes and other interest groups to provide information on common issues to all member organisations, and assist in the formulation of a risk management plan.

The risk management strategy consists of several logical steps, which are much the same for commercial or non-profit organisations. They are:

1. **Identification of risks:** what are the possible liabilities or hazards that face the organisation, its officers and members?
2. **Evaluation of risks:** what is the probability of a loss and the severity of such a loss? How much danger, how soon, how often and who is exposed?
3. **Designing a risk management programme:** what are the most effective and cost-efficient controls to prevent or minimise the probability of a risk's occurrence and the cost of a loss? What methods and to what benefit?
4. **Implementation and review of the strategy:** the strategy must be implemented and reviewed regularly by the board. Is the plan working and what changes are needed?

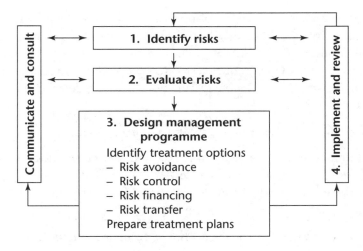

Figure 5a The steps in a risk management programme

Step 1: Identify risks

Identifying risks involves the systematic assessment of all hazards that could affect the non-profit organisation arising from its activities. This part of the process needs to be as complete as possible for the plan to be effective, and it can be a time-consuming task.

It is important to establish accurately the organisational context in order to focus attention on pertinent matters. There will be a legal context. Is the organisation a company, a trust, or something else? Will overseas jurisdictions be involved? Accurate identification of the association's legal context is crucial to ascertaining the possible liability issues.

If the organisation is large or has diverse activities, other identification strategies may need to be employed. A risk identification survey form might be sent to key persons in the organisation to aid in producing the inventory of risks.

Step 2: Evaluate risks

Not all risks identified by the previous step will be significant, but some may have a good chance of developing into a liability. For example, a childcare centre may identify the potential risk of defamation in their newsletter as well as physical injury to their clients through their negligence. Probably the negligent injury has a higher probability of happening than the defamation. This piece of information can then be used in the third step, to allocate scarce resources most effectively in controlling potential risks.

Instead of a statistical ranking of the risks, which may be near impossible, a simple qualitative risk classification may be adequate. An organisation assigns qualitative values to the likelihood of an event happening, and the consequences or impact to the organisation if it does, to construct a qualitative risk analysis matrix to describe the level of risk.

The risk could also be classified in terms of *likelihood* as:

A (almost certain)	The event is expected to occur in most circumstances.
B (likely)	The event will probably occur in most circumstances.
C (moderate)	The event should occur at some time.
D (unlikely)	The event could occur at some time.
E (rare)	The event may occur only in exceptional circumstances.

The following risk *consequences* or *impact* could be defined and used for classification purposes:

Trivial	No action required, low financial loss.
Minor	No further action is needed at present, but monitoring will be necessary to ensure that controls are maintained.
Moderate	Efforts need to be made to reduce the risk, but the costs of doing so need to be carefully considered.
Substantial	The activity should be halted until the risk has been reduced or sufficient control measures are in place.
Intolerable	The activity that gives rise to the risk should be prohibited – this may indicate that it needs to be part of a legal compliance plan.

The two measures of likelihood and consequences can now be brought together in a level of risk matrix.

Example of Qualitative Risk Analysis Matrix – Level of Risk

Likelihood	CONSEQUENCES OR IMPACT				
	Trivial	**Minor**	**Moderate**	**Substantial**	**Intolerable**
A (almost certain)	S	S	H	H	H
B (likely)	M	S	S	H	H
C (moderate)	L	M	S	H	H
D (unlikely)	L	L	M	S	H
E (rare)	L	L	M	S	S

H = high risk: detailed research and management planning required at senior levels
S = significant risk: senior management attention needed
M = moderate risk: management responsibility must be specified
L = low risk: manage by routine procedures

While this may not give the precision of statistical tables, it does permit a prioritisation of risks facing the company.

An organisation may consider it sufficiently important to construct a risk register that records all the identified risks, their likelihood of occurrence, consequences and risk priority.

Step 3: Design a risk management programme

Once the activities of a non-profit have been systematically identified and prioritised, it is possible to begin to consider how these risks may be best managed. This step will result in the formal production and adoption of a risk management strategy. It is likely to be prepared by staff, but should be approved at board level. If there are board members with risk management experience, or relevant industry knowledge, their expertise may be harnessed in the preparation of the strategy.

The identified risks should be prioritised from those that threaten the existence of the company to the trivial. The processes in the last two steps should have identified the risks and evaluated them. The main problem will arise in risks that have the attributes of high severity and low frequency. These are the most unpredictable and embody the greatest threat to the existence of the non-profit organisation.

Several strategies are commonly used to minimise risks.

Risk avoidance

It may be that the company avoids the risk altogether by consciously not entering into the activity at all. An example might be that a childcare organisation believes that there are grave risks for itself, its staff, its management committee and clients in administering medicine to children. It may deal with this risk by refusing to be responsible for administering medicine to children in its care. Children must either not come to the centre when requiring medication or their parent must arrange for some suitable qualified person to attend to administer the medicine.

Another example is the use of trampolines in youth sports centres. The rate of injury amongst users, despite upgraded supervision and training, may lead the organisation not to include the activity in its programme. Or if an organisation is sponsoring a 'fun run' it may consider cancelling the event unless the appropriate standard of first aid care is available at the event.

Risk avoidance is the most overlooked strategy option. It may not be an available option for certain activities that form the core of a non-profit organisation's existence, and there is a danger that it may marginalize particular constituencies, such as disabled people, by depriving them of services. By the same token, it can also be used as a political lever to persuade governments to alter the legal or funding environment.

Risk control

If it is not appropriate to avoid certain activities, then the question is what can be done at an economic cost to reduce the risk. The risk may be controlled by reducing the probability that it will happen or, if it does happen, limiting its severity. Often a combination of the two is possible.

Such controls are merely good practice. Examples are the training that the company may give to its staff and board, minimum qualifications of staff, and setting up policies to minimise liabilities arising from the activities of the company. However, it is not enough just to have a board policy on a matter – it must be recorded, communicated and understood by those who can prevent the liability.

An example in a childcare centre may be a policy on safe play equipment. The board may have developed a procedure to ensure that only safe equipment is purchased and existing equipment is inspected and maintained. This procedure needs to be implemented and clearly understood by those concerned. Further examples are security and fire detection alarms, covering locks and other such precautions for physical assets, to fire evacuation drills for staff, clients and the public.

An area not to be overlooked is the quality of the board. A board of committed, capable and qualified persons, who provide complementary skills such as accounting, law, management and professional expertise appropriate to the organisation's activities, is a good risk control measure.

5.3 Risk action plan

Risk: Playground equipment

Recommended Response: Transfer risk by insurance, managing the risk by playground safety inspections, supervision of play and complete removal of dangerous equipment.

Action Plan
Proposed Action: Administrator to seek insurance cover for accidents in playground, secretary to engage health and safety expert to assess playground safety, volunteer parents to supervise play at all times, and the old swings are to be removed immediately (and until removed are to be made inoperative as well as posted with warning signs).

Resource Requirements: Administrator to be given discretion to engage professional assistance of up to £500 to acquire a safety inspection and £1,000 for the insurance.

Responsibilities: Administrator.

Timing: Safety inspection report to be delivered within 2 weeks, insurance cover note within 24 hours, immediate removal of old swings and immediate supervision of the playground.

Reporting and Monitoring Required: Matter to be put in General Business on Board Meeting Agenda until resolved. Once resolved, an annual self-assessment of playground equipment and safety will be undertaken.

Person Responsible: Administrator, Mr Imma Slick   **Date:** 1/1/03

Reviewer: Chair, Glenda Checkup   **Date:** 1/7/03

Risk financing
This entails estimating the cost of a risk over a period of time and building financial reserves to cover the cost of an eventual liability. It is like a self-insurance scheme. It may involve non-profit organisations banding together to finance combined risks in insurance pools.

Risk transfer

This usually entails the transfer of the risk to an insurer. However, there are other ways of transferring risk to others, by means of exemption of liability clauses or sub-contracting the activity to an independent contractor.

In recent years exemption clauses have not been very effective legally, but they still have a role to play in discouraging small claims.[2] Often an exemption clause is used in tandem with an accident insurance policy, which can be purchased by a member, parent, participant or client. Such a policy has set entitlements on the occurrence of a specified event, for example, up to £2,000 compensation for a broken leg during a football match. While the injured person may be entitled to sue for a greater amount, they will accept the accident insurance payout and take the matter no further.

Risk may be transferred by contracting out the particular activity to an independent contractor. The sub-contractor takes on the risk and liability for the particular activity. For example a childcare centre may obtain parental consent for a nearby medical practitioner to administer medication to children. The risk is thus transferred to the professional medical practitioner. There is less chance of injury given the professional training of the practitioner, and if negligence does cause injury it will usually be the burden of the doctor (see Box 5.4).

Insurance is available for risks of all kinds, but it is important to insure the right risk at the right price. Insurance brokers and agents can be very helpful in providing assistance in such matters. Be aware though that their job is to sell insurance, and if you are not happy with their advice, it should be independently verified. In recent years it has become more common for Charity Trustees (i.e. the board members) to consider also taking out Trustee Indemnity Insurance, as the Charity Commission appears to have adopted a more accommodating attitude to charities changing their constitution to allow this.

Step 4: Implement and review the strategy

The risk management plan should finally be considered and approved by the board. It is critical to identify who in the organisation is responsible for implementation of the strategy. This will differ with the organisational structure of the non-profit organisation.

---

[2] Refer to John Livermore, *Exemption Clauses and Implied Obligations in Contracts* (The Law Book Company Ltd, Sydney, 1986); Berna Collier, *Romalpa Clauses: Reservation of Title in Sale of Goods Transactions* (The Law Book Company Ltd, Sydney, 1989).

5.4 Risk transfer

Kids Child Care Ltd was concerned about the safety of its playground that adjoined its centre. The playground was built by the local service club on land owned by the Council many years previously. The Council gave the land to the organisation for use as a playground, provided it was available to the public for use too.

The playground was not only used by the organization's own children, properly supervised during the day, but also by the public at other times. Kids Child Care felt that the risk of unsupervised persons injuring themselves and liability attaching to the organisation was growing. They had been informed by their insurer that the insurer would no longer cover the organisation for unsupervised members of the public injuring themselves on the playground equipment. Kids Child Care could neither effectively exclude members of the public from the equipment's use, nor afford to have the park fully supervised.

The organisation gave the land back to the Council and used the playground as members of the public. The risk liability has been transferred back to the Council.

Successful risk management strategies are built into the culture of an organisation. It becomes not solely a board function, but everyone connected with the organisation is expected to play a part in the control and minimisation of risks. For example, new board members and employees are made aware of risk management as part of their induction, and employees and volunteers may be encouraged to report potentially dangerous physical assets.

The strategy should be reviewed at least annually, and immediately on changes in the law or the organisation's activities. It is imperative that the board check that the strategy has been implemented.

- New board members, volunteers, and employees will need to be made aware of playground risk management policies, procedures and systems as part of their induction training.
- The playground equipment will need to be regularly inspected before use for visible damage and also more intensively at a set period to ensure the equipment is still in good order and safe.
- If new games or equipment are introduced into the playground, then attention should be given to altering the risk management plan accordingly.

Risk is a part of living in our society, but strategies may be developed to minimise and finance its resultant liability. As non-profit organisations, their individual board members and senior manages face greater liability risks, more systematic strategies are required. The challenge is to treat the risks in an appropriate and cost effective manner so as to protect the organisation and its stakeholders without snuffing out the inspiration of volunteers or social entrepreneurial spirit of employees with the deadening hand of inflexible bureaucratic rules and procedures.

Summary

- Risk management reduces and manages risks; legal compliance planning seeks to eliminate or prevent breaches of the law completely.
- Risk management benchmarks are set by the organisation; legal compliance benchmarks are set by the law.
- A typical legal compliance process will identify the offences to which the organisation and its officers are exposed, determine how the organisation could breach the provisions and the likelihood of a breach, design a programme to eliminate the risk of breaches, and ensure that the programme is implemented and working.
- A risk management strategy will identify the possible hazards or liabilities, evaluate their probability and impact, design a programme to minimise the probability of their occurring, while still remaining economically viable, and ensure the strategy is implemented and reviewed.

INTERVIEW

AN INTERVIEW WITH MICHAEL LAKE, CBE, DIRECTOR GENERAL, HELP THE AGED

Help the Aged was set up in 1961 to respond to the needs of poor, frail and isolated older people at home and overseas. As a national organisation Help the Aged campaigns with and on behalf of older people, raises money to help pensioners in need, and provides direct services where gaps in provision have been identified. Help the Aged commissions research into the achievement of better quality living, and devotes significant resources to the needs of disadvantaged older people in other countries.

Michael Lake joined Help the Aged in 1996, following a military career.

What are Help the Aged's principal objectives during the next few years?
We intend to become a major player in the field of ageing research. We want to help older people's organisations to flourish throughout the UK, to strengthen our roots in local communities, and to deliver the best UK-wide information service for older people and their carers.

Our strategic direction recently has been away from service delivery and more strongly towards advocacy and lobbying, and the research needed to underpin this. For example, Help the Aged used to operate sheltered housing, but divested itself of its homes 15 years ago, with the establishment of the Anchor Housing Association, one of the largest providers in the country. This was a traumatic change. It seems extraordinary now, but immediately afterwards we started the process again, following a specific legacy. We are just about to complete the transfer of our current portfolio of residential and care homes to a consortium of Friends of the Elderly and Hanover Housing Association, set up for the purpose. This change will enable us to focus on our core objectives and ensure that the charity benefits the many, rather than a few. I believe our role is to question, test the boundaries and be prepared to identify and try new things. We do not want to get locked into service provision.

What are the distinguishing characteristics of Help the Aged?
We are always seeking to be innovative, and to retain our independence. There are a relatively small number of charities that are truly independent from Government.

There are more than 200,000 charities in the UK – this proliferation dissipates their public impact – the public are tired of charities falling over each other and Government regards the sector as inefficient, so we don't hesitate to use the tools of the commercial sector to improve our methods of operating.

Collaboration is important to Help the Aged – for example there is a strong cooperative relationship with the Age Concern network, even though this might normally be considered a competitor organisation.

Another example of finding a distinctive way of achieving our goals is the recent merger with Research Into Ageing. This was an independent charity, occupying a field of work that Help the

Aged wanted to develop: biomedical research. Rather than set up an alternative organisation and spend years maturing it, we absorbed Research Into Ageing into our own organisation. This also had the effect of doubling their budget, and retaining their board. Both organisations are winners.

Change is now recognised as normal in the organisation. We've been raising more money, doing more, having a greater impact in recent years. Our public profile has also risen.

What do you regard as the key issues facing Help the Aged currently?
Internally, I would say the main issues are:

- efficiency and professionalism within the organisation;
- recruiting the best people;
- well-targeted training;
- ensuring staff understand our values and purpose;
- clear and systematic processes throughout the organisation;
- the need to develop clear structures.

Externally, the main issues are:

- people don't really know what we do, although we are well known;
- growth is important to us, to increase our impact;
- we need a strong fundraising function;
- we need to demonstrate our mandate in order to be credible politically – we must show the public we represent their views (we use opinion polls to help with this);
- regionalisation and devolution – we need to respond to these forces and adopt a more devolved structure, but not a federated structure.

The last is a major challenge – how do we remain fast-moving and efficient if we adopt a more complex and decentralised structure?

Some operations can't be devolved. For example, it wouldn't be appropriate for the shops – the retail operations are most efficient run as a single entity, not split along geographical lines. We also need to retain strategic thinking at the centre.

How is Help the Aged's income made up?
Forty per cent of our income comes from retail and merchandising activities (we have 370 shops), 25 per cent from donations and gifts, and 15 per cent from legacies. The rest comes from a

range of sources, including community fundraising, housing, community transport and grants.

The main growth recently has been in corporate fundraising. This used to be largely philanthropic, but is now much more firmly based on contractual relationships. We look for real synergy with our corporate partners.

Legacies are also a growing area – mainly because we are putting more effort into this. Our direct commercial activities are also growing. Overall, our income has risen from £40 million to £74 million in the last five to six years.

What recent developments have there been at board level?
We have largely eliminated subsidiary committees, and now operate with a single tier board, although we have a Remuneration Committee and an Audit Committee, which is responsible for overseeing finances, efficiency and risk management (covering all aspects of the business, not just financial issues). There is a sub-committee for our activities in Northern Ireland – it is possible this may become a model for England, Scotland and Wales in the future.

Five years ago board meetings were very report-oriented; now we have checks and balances in place which prevent the board needing to engage at this level of detail. Trustees are more involved in proactive, forward thinking, predicting the risks.

We have cut from board activity anything that can be done by working groups or by direct mentoring between trustees and senior staff members (Directors), e.g. Director of Retail. And we leave them to find their own way of implementing this – we don't lay down prescriptive approaches.

We had a review of our governance processes and structures two years ago – but we are looking again at governance needs in the light of the increasing complexity and pace of development of Help the Aged. The latest review addresses not only structures and reporting arrangements, but standards of attendance and formalising our induction and training procedures for board members.

How is the board involved in strategic planning?
Strategic planning comes from the bottom up. We have an agreed board paper that confirms strategy. Any changes require a

briefing to the board. However, such changes don't come out of the blue, they'll have been discussed with the Chair.

There's a two-day annual conference where we discuss blue-sky issues – this involves both trustees and senior staff.

Managing the board is one of the most important aspects of my job. I treat the members as individuals within a collective. The Chairman and I seek to provide an atmosphere that generates healthy and constructive debate.

How many are on the board?

The board is currently 23, although we aim to reduce this number. There is no problem recruiting board members, people are flattered to be asked. We identify gaps, usually on a skills basis, then network to identify potential recruits. We took on a couple of board members as a result of the takeover of Research Into Ageing, and a couple as a result of redefining our relationship with Help Age International.

Do you think board members should be paid?

There are pros and cons. I would like to see board members remunerated, to strengthen the sense of contractual obligation. Although the legal responsibilities are the same as for other corporations, if board members don't turn up to a meeting it's very difficult to do anything about it. However, there is much to say for a volunteer board.

6 Cheques and balances

If money be not thy servant, it will be thy master

Proverb

Some board members experience a high anxiety level when it comes to the finances of the organisation. This may be linked to a fear of the personal consequences of financial failure by the organisation. It may reflect a lack of confidence in the information being presented by staff, or even a lack of confidence on the board member's part with regard to his or her own financial literacy.

It is true that there have been a few notorious cases where an organisation's finances have gone pear-shaped and the finger has been pointed at the board – but it is also true that these are rare and exceptional cases, where the staff were behaving fraudulently or very unwisely, and where the board took its eye off the ball. Whilst it is true that Government is far from keen to 'trap' unwary board members and trustees, the finances of the organisation are, nevertheless, ultimately and unavoidably the responsibility of board members. Some commonsense precautions and control systems can help to keep the board and the organisation on the straight and narrow.

This chapter comments on three aspects of finance that concern the board: financial responsibilities and procedures; financial monitoring and management; and adding value to the planning processes.

The aim is to illustrate how extra value can be extracted from the organisation's financial processes once the basics have been dealt with – and to encourage board members to use financial information dynamically. Necessarily, the chapter runs through some of the rudiments of financial procedures first, for the benefit of those who may be new to non-profit boards or less familiar with the subject. It does not attempt to provide a complete guide to accounting.[1]

---

[1] Those who need more assistance will find the brief run-through of a set of charity management accounts in Mike Eastwood's *Charity Trustee's Handbook*, Directory of Social Change (London, 2001), pp98–105 helpful. Other sources of advice are provided in Resource 12.

The board is responsible for ensuring that the non-profit organisation operates in a financially sound manner, and is financially accountable. The board should:

- make sure that a realistic budget is developed and that the underlying assumptions that drive key budget items are understood and are realistic;
- ensure the budget is developed early enough so that the entire board can be involved in its review and approval before the beginning of the fiscal year;
- expect management to produce timely and accurate income and expenditure statements, balance sheets and cash-flow projections, and expect to receive these in advance of board meetings;
- require periodic confirmation from management that all required filings are up-to-date and that tax deductions, insurance premiums and such like are being paid when due;
- consider the value of maintaining standing Audit and/or Finance Committees;
- use financial reporting mechanisms to inform strategic planning and review of the organisation's efficiency and effectiveness.

Reporting procedures

There are differing recording and reporting requirements for differing legal entities –companies, associations, friendly and provident societies, for example. Those entities which are registered charities share a set of requirements laid down in the Charities Act, which requires, amongst other things, that:

- organisations with income greater than £100,000 have their accounts professionally audited;
- organisations with income from £25,000 to £100,000 have their accounts examined independently;
- organisations with income of less than £25,000 have their (simplified) accounts examined independently.

Charitable companies, whatever their income, must have their accounts professionally audited and meet the annual reporting requirements of the Companies Acts. Other charities can elect to have their accounts audited, regardless of their turnover. More detailed specifications on how accounts should be kept are provided in the Statement of Recommended Practice (SORP), which is updated periodically.

Transparency and reliability in the organisation's finances are essential to maintaining the confidence of key stakeholders – donors and Government funding partners. Non-profits are responsible for the public money they receive, and must be in a position to provide a clear picture of how it is being used.

Other legislative frameworks under which organisations are incorporated (e.g. religious bodies, or a special Act of Parliament) may provide guidance as to the financial reporting obligations of the organisation.

Basic procedures

- ✔ A receipt is issued for all money received.
- ✔ Receipts are in duplicate and numbered consecutively.
- ✔ All money is banked promptly without deduction.
- ✔ Originals of cancelled receipts are retained and accounted for.
- ✔ Each bank deposit is reconciled with the relevant receipts issued.
- ✔ The chequebook is kept in safe custody.
- ✔ Two cheque signatories are required.
- ✔ No blank cheques are signed.
- ✔ All expenditure is fully documented.
- ✔ Vouchers and supporting documents are filed in cheque number order.
- ✔ Cash payments and receipts are recorded on a regular basis.
- ✔ Bank reconciliation is performed on a monthly basis.
- ✔ Records are kept for seven years or as otherwise required by law.

Financial controls

The Charity Commission provides helpful advice on precautionary financial control procedures, which are just as relevant for other non-profit organisations as for charities.[2]

It is a fundamental duty of all charity trustees to protect the property of their charity and to secure its application for the objectives of the charity. In order to discharge this duty it is essential that there are adequate financial controls over the charity's assets and their use.

[2] CC8 'Internal Financial Controls for Charities' (Version May 2001), available at www.charitycommission.gov.uk/publications

Three principles underpin this advice:

1 Segregation of duties Both with income and expenditure transactions, dividing duties between different people increases the degree of protection against fraud, error or oversights.

For example, if the person who checks that incoming cash has been reflected in the bank statements is not the same person who records the incoming cash, it will be easier to detect dishonesty.

Segregation of duties is one of the fundamental tenets of robust control systems. Whilst limited resources may limit smaller organisations' ability to segregate duties, every opportunity should be taken to do so within existing resource constraints.

2 Qualification of staff and advisers Board members need to ensure that their staff and volunteers are competent and properly trained. The board, accountant and external auditor should maintain an ongoing dialogue on systems improvements and other issues arising, rather than trusting to an annual exchange of views and information.

3 Budgetary controls Organisations must work within agreed budgets, which should be discussed and approved at full board/management committee meetings.

Policy and probity

- ✔ All money and assets are used solely to pursue the objects of the organisation as set out in the constitution.
- ✔ Full, accurate accounting records are kept and stored securely for at least seven years.
- ✔ Bank accounts are operated and cheques signed by more than one person.
- ✔ Cheques are not signed without details of the amount of the payment and purpose for which it will be spent.
- ✔ Funds given for different purposes are kept separate in the accounts.
- ✔ Property is under the control of the trustees.
- ✔ Tax is paid when due and tax reliefs collected in full.
- ✔ Money is not accumulated for its own sake; if there are surplus funds, they are earmarked for a specific future use.
- ✔ VAT registration occurs if 'taxable turnover' exceeds or will exceed the threshold level for registration; if registered, VAT returns are submitted as required.

✔ A record of wages is kept to satisfy PAYE National Insurance requirements.

✔ Payroll deductions and taxes have been deducted as required before making payment to staff or for casual labour.

Monitoring and management

The board has three main roles in relation to financial monitoring and management of the organisation.

- **Planning:** the board needs to plan the financial structure and activity of the organisation through approval of annual or longer-range budgets.
- **Monitoring:** the board needs to monitor the financial operations of the organisation to ensure that targets are being met and that there is no misappropriation of funds.
- **Decision-making:** the board needs to respond to financial indicators and figures with strategies (normally proposed by staff) and decisions which maintain the financial health of the organisation, e.g. approve the arrangement of an overdraft if cash flow falls below a certain amount.

The organisation's accounting system should enable the board to see clearly:

- where the organisation's money is coming from and going to;
- whether the organisation is in surplus or deficit;
- what the income, expenditure and cash-flow expectations are for the future;
- what assets and liabilities there are;
- what return on investments is being secured.

See Box 6.1.

The budget

When developing the budget it is important for the board to understand and confirm the assumptions that underlie the figures, e.g. donations, earned income percentages, special project income, government grant levels – and to make sure they are clearly expressed. No board member's question aimed at clarifying the assumptions or the risk exposure should be considered too naïve. This is the board fulfilling one of its core responsibilities.

6.1 Improving information incrementally

When I took over as Chair, financial information was being tabled at the board meeting, without supporting notes or summary. It was impossible to absorb, and led to considerable disquiet – even if the staff in this small organisation had the finances under control, there was no way the board could know.

Over a period of several months, step by step, improvements were implemented which led to annotated management accounts/financial reports being circulated a week ahead of the board meetings, in a form which made it easy to compare actual performance against budget, and the accumulated position in the year to date. The small business accounting software package made this relatively straightforward, once it was set up properly, and the addition to the board of a capable accountant from one of the major firms provided a back-up resource for the (financially unqualified) staff to draw upon as needed.

'The budget construction process can be seen as a strategic function, in which boards, free from the detail of operational management, can identify overall organisational priorities.'[3]

Once developed the budget may be compared to last year's figures and any changes fully understood. Also each month or quarter should be compared to one another, and the reasons for any significant changes understood.

In addition to the annual budget, the board will require:

1 monthly or quarterly income and expenditure accounts (management accounts), comparing actual results against the budget for that period, and for the year to date against the budget for the year to date;
2 balance sheets, particularly to check on the organisation's liquidity position, and solvency (see below). Larger organisations, and those with a volatile income/expenditure pattern may require these monthly – others would expect to review them less frequently;
3 cash-flow forecast for the next 6–12 months;

---

[3] C Cornforth and C Edwards, *Good Governance: Developing Effective Board-Management Relations in Public and Voluntary Organisations*, Chartered Institute of Management Accountants (London, 1998), p64.

4 for some organisations, project-based accounts as well as time-based accounts.

Management accounts

The management accounts can be layered into different levels of detail, and annotated. This gives board members the opportunity to see the big picture at a glance, but to explore further detail if they wish. By drawing attention to material variances from the approved budget, and explaining these in annotations or a brief covering report, the staff (or Treasurer) can avoid the board devoting time to points of clarification and explanation in its meetings. Conversely, the covering report may set the scene for necessary discussion of a significant matter, such as dealing with a potential deficit or allocating the fruits of an unexpected wind-fall. The more the board is helped to focus on strategic issues the more it will be able to add value.

Most board members will have their own views as to what level of financial detail should be presented to the board, in what format, and with what frequency. There are no hard and fast rules. But it is important for the board to discuss periodically, with the CEO, what their expectations and needs are, in the light of:

- the board's desire for significant management information;
- the board's need for reassurance that income and expenditure are on track, or awareness if they are not;
- the discouragement of board focus on petty detail (does it matter if the stationery budget is 2 per cent over or under, when there are bigger fish to fry?);
- a sense of economy with the staff's time.

The table opposite provides an illustration of quarterly management accounts, or income and expenditure statement for a three-month period, indicating the actual result, the budgeted result and the variance between the two, both for the most recent quarter, and for the year to date.

The inclusion of the results for the same quarter in the previous year will be helpful in an organisation that has a similar pattern of work from one year to the next.

Most organisations prepare their management accounts on an accruals' basis, some on a cash basis. Accruals-based accounting adjusts the figures presented to allow for expenses which have been incurred during the accounting period but not yet paid (such as a fuel bill which

Same Qtr Last Year		Second Quarter			Year to Date		
		Budget	Actual	Budget Variance	Budget	Actual Variance	Budget
INCOME							
41,770	Fees	45,900	44,068	-1,832	104,500	90,850	-13,650
4,914	Other income	5,400	6,625	1,225	13,050	14,850	1,800
86,450	Grants	95,000	95,000	0	190,000	190,000	0
133,134	TOTAL	146,300	145,693	-607	307,550	295,700	-11,850
EXPENDITURE							
52,689	Salaries (projects)	57,900	55,600	2,300	114,000	106,575	7,425
33,215	Salaries (admin.)	36,500	36,500	0	73,000	73,000	0
4,100	Production Costs	4,500	4,200	300	25,500	16,500	9,000
3,458	Marketing	3,800	5,800	-2,000	13,580	14,580	-1,000
34,030	Admin/Overheads	37,400	39,500	-2,100	71,400	78,965	-7,565
500	Depreciation	1,600	1,600	0	2,100	2,100	0
127,992	TOTAL	141,700	143,200	-1,500	299,580	291,720	7,860
5,142	*Surplus/deficit*	*4,600*	*2,493*	*-2,107*	*7,970*	*3,980*	*-3,990*

has been received for fuel already used); and also adjusts for prepayments (such as an insurance bill which has been paid, the cost of which should be spread across the year as a whole). Cash-based accounting reflects the cash that has gone into and out of the bank account.

Balance sheet

The balance sheet and cash-flow forecasts are of particular importance to help board members identify whether the organisation is in financial difficulty. The balance sheet indicates the relationship between current assets and current liabilities. If current assets are insufficient to cover current liabilities, or are even close to that position, there may be a danger of insolvency.

Cash-flow forecast

The organisation is insolvent if it is unable to meet its (payment) obligations as they fall due – hence the importance of cash-flow forecasting, which will show if incoming cash during the next few weeks or months is expected to be adequate to cover the payments which have to be made during that time. If the organisation continues to operate during a period of insolvency, there is a risk that the directors may be guilty of 'insolvent trading' and may be personally liable for the debts of the organisation.

- If there is a danger of insolvency the company must be run in the creditors' interests.
- When in financial danger, seek expert financial advice.
- Wrongful trading occurs if there is no reasonable prospect of avoiding liquidation.
- All creditors must be treated fairly depending upon their security and legal preference.

The implications of this are clear. The board must have confidence in the financial information presented, must be aware of the asset—liability position, and particularly the future cash flow position, and should seriously consider bringing in specialist advisers in the event of solvency problems.

The table opposite summarises the difference between the income and expenditure statement, the balance sheet and the cash flow statement.

Other reports

The precise annual reporting requirements will be determined by the organisation's legal framework. In all cases the board is likely to be required to ensure that an annual statement of income and expenditure and a closing balance sheet are prepared, and in many cases an audit will need to be undertaken by a qualified accountant or other approved individual. The audited statements are then generally required to be presented to the members at an AGM.

In addition to the routine financial reports, the board may develop specific financial performance indicators, which assist it in understanding the health of the organisation at a glance. An advanced version

Income & Expenditure Statement (Statement of Financial Performance)	Balance Sheet (Statement of Financial Position)	Statement of Cash Flow
A summary of the income and expenses from the first to the last day of the reporting period	Your organisation's 'net worth' (what it owns less what it owes) at the last day of the reporting period	A summary of cash flows in and out from the first to the last day of the reporting period for your business operations, investment and financing activities
Revenue (income)	Assets	Cash in from operations
less	Current	
	Non-current	less
Expenses		
	less	Cash out from operations
= Operating Surplus (Deficit) before Income Tax	Liabilities	
	Current	= Net Cash Flows from Operating Activities
	Non-current	
less		Cash in from investing
	= Net Assets (Accumulated Funds)	
Income Tax (not usually paid by non-profits)		less
		Cash out from investing
= Operating Surplus (Deficit) after Income Tax		= Net Cash Flows from Investing Activities
		Cash in from financing
		less
		Cash out from financing
		= Net Cash Flows from Financing Activities
		The three cash flows added together give: Net Cash Flows

of this is the 'Dashboard', described in Chapter 15, *Monitoring Our Progress*.

If relevant, a budget report for a particular project that is germane to the decision-making process may be worth examining. Such reports can be long and involved to produce, so it is wise to be frugal with requests for these so that the staff do not become overloaded. It is better to keep a handle on the overall budgets and reports and let the Treasurer or Finance Committee deal with the detail.

The board may also occasionally ask for operating reports on debtors and creditors and possibly a copy of the bank statements once in a while, although again, this level of detail may well be better left to the Treasurer and Finance Committee to deal with.

6.2 A glossary of financial terms

Accounting Period
That period of time covered by a set of financial statements.

Accounts
A summary of the transactions (payments in, payments out) over a period of time, and of the balances at a point in time. Most organisations will prepare monthly or quarterly accounts showing progress over the year, and annual accounts.

Accruals' Basis of Accounting
The accounting convention where income and expenditure is recognised in the period that it is earned or incurred, rather than when received or paid.

Assets
Everything your organisation owns that will give an economic benefit at some point in the future: money, money owed to you, equipment, property, land, stocks, investments, and so on.

Audit
A yearly report on the financial accounts prepared by your organisation, carried out by an independent, qualified auditor.

Balance Sheet (Statement of Financial Position)
A financial statement summarising your organisation's assets and liabilities on a particular day (such as the last day of your financial year).

Bank Reconciliation
A check that the figures entered in your cash book match those on your bank statement – a basic and fundamental accounting control procedure. Generally performed monthly.

Cash Basis of Accounting
A method of accounting under which revenues and expenses are recorded only when cash is received or paid out.

Company Limited by Shares
A legal entity whose membership is made up of shareholders whose money helps finance the company.

Company Limited by Guarantee
A legal entity with no shareholders, but whose members pledge an amount in the event of its winding up.

continued

Cost-Benefit Analysis
A process comparing the benefits which may arise from a particular course of action to the costs of performing it.

Creditors
People or organisations to whom you owe money.

Current Assets and Liabilities
Assets due to be converted into cash or obligations due to be paid during the normal business cycle or within a year, whichever is longer.

Debtors
People or organisations who owe you money.

Depreciation
The value of larger items of equipment (assets) declines each year. Depreciation is a method for showing how much the value has declined over the year. It is, in effect, the cost of using the asset. For example, a computer costing £2,000 has an expected life of four years. It will be depreciated by £500 each year. At the end of four years its value will have reduced to zero.

Financial Accounts
The annual or statutory report of the organisation's income, expenditure, assets, liabilities, cash flows and accompanying explanatory notes required to be prepared and presented to members or regulatory authorities.

Liabilities
Everything your organisation owes to third parties as a result of past transactions or events.

Management Accounts
Regular reports on income and expenditure, prepared for purposes of management control.

Management Audit
Examination and appraisal of the quality of management action in an organisation.

Income and Expenditure Statement
A financial statement showing the amount of accounting profit earned by an entity over an accounting period.

Solvency
Maintenance of a sufficient level of liquid assets by a company to meet its obligations. 'Liquidity' also relates to the ratio of current assets (cash, or

investments/savings that can be quickly converted into cash) to current liabilities.

Turnover
The total annual income of the organisation.

Variance Analysis
The process of identifying and explaining differences in actual results from those in the budget.

Finance committees

Should there be a standing Finance Committee? The advantages are that there will be a group of board members (normally selected as a result of their expertise) who scrutinise the finances more closely than the board as a whole, who provide support and constructive criticism for the staff concerned, and who may preclude the need for devoting much time and energy to discussion of financial details in the board meetings. As a result the board as a whole should be more confident that they are receiving accurate, reliable and relevant information and can focus on the higher-level and strategic aspects of managing the financial affairs of the organisation. Spending board meeting time enquiring into detailed aspects of financial reports and establishing the accuracy or otherwise of the reports that are presented is not a good use of board time and energy.

The disadvantages of a standing Finance Committee are that important decisions, even decisions with policy consequences, may be taken unwittingly or 'on the hoof' by members of the Committee, abrogating the board's responsibilities. The shifting sideways of financial discussion may result in the majority of the board never coming to grips with the economy of the organisation, and consequently feeling ignorant or disempowered. The best financial brains on the board may be sucked into consideration of operational detail rather than strategic overview – and by the same token, the staff may not develop their financial reporting skills because the board members on the Finance Committee are doing their job for them.

Many non-profit organisations specify the office of Treasurer in their constitution, but many are not entirely sure what the Treasurer's role should be, especially if there is a Finance Committee or a professional Finance Officer in the organisation. A role description for the Treasurer is included at Resource 5 (pp284–90). Generally, the stronger the professional finance infrastructure, the less hands-on the Treasurer's role should be – checking periodically that procedures and reporting processes are operating smoothly, but not undertaking the detailed activity. Where there is a Finance Committee, the Treasurer might be expected to chair that group.

Audit committees: guardians of the faith?

Commercial organisations are increasingly being encouraged to establish an Audit Committee. This is not concerned purely with the annual audit of the organisation's accounts but with:

- improving the quality of financial reporting;
- ensuring the board is in a position to make well-informed decisions regarding accounting policies and procedures;
- reviewing the scope and outcome of external (and internal) audits;
- potentially, contributing to other improvements in governance.

The critical faculties of an Audit Committee's members will determine whether the committee adds real value to the organisation. The committee's duties may include:

- overseeing the monitoring of controls in place to ensure the effective and efficient operation of all significant business processes;
- reviewing the company's accounting policies and reporting requirements;
- recommending the appointment and remuneration of the external auditors;
- following up the implementation of recommendations made by the auditors;
- ensuring that reports issued by auditors to management are those being received by the board;
- assessing the risks, internal and external, affecting the business and ensuring the risks identified are being appropriately managed;
- organising a presentation by the insurance broker as to the organisation's insurance plans for the next year;
- assessing the adequacy of management reporting;
- reviewing company behaviour and compliance with the law.

Some of these duties continue throughout the year whilst others become necessary only at certain times, for example, when the auditors have a matter to raise with the committee. Clearly, the scope of the committee's work can extend beyond audit and other financial matters to include risk assessment, and issues of probity and conflict of interest.

Interaction of responsibilities

The responsibilities of the board, the Audit Committee and the external auditors do interact:

- The board is primarily responsible for the preparation of true and fair financial statements, and the establishment and maintenance of a system of internal controls.
- The Audit Committee assists directors in the fulfilment of their duties by, amongst other things, overseeing the financial reporting process and interacting with management and the external auditors on behalf of the board.
- The external auditors express an independent opinion on the financial statements prepared by management and the board.

Larger organisations may see value in establishing a standing Audit Committee. Smaller organisations may combine the Audit Committee with the Finance Committee, or cover the Committee's functions in the form of an annual 'task force' or review.

6.3 Eye off the ball

The centre had been in operation for 12 years. The Chief Executive and Finance Officer were experienced and capable, and their reporting to the board was of a high calibre. Their last joint activity was to plan for a significant expansion of the organisation's premises, and secure the finance for this to occur. Having built the organisation from its very early days to this important milestone, both felt it was time to move on, and both secured high-level jobs elsewhere within the sector.

The new Finance Officer came from a different sector. He was anxious to prove himself. When the organisation encountered cash-flow problems during the construction process – caused by the construction payment schedule, not by trading or profit and loss difficulties – he tried to deal with it without consulting the CEO or board. His principal technique was to defer payment of the payroll tax deduction to the Inland Revenue. Within a few months, nearly £100,000 had been withheld, at which point the Inland Revenue paid a visit, demanding the back payment.

The board soon found itself on the receiving end of a prosecution by the Inland Revenue. Shortly before the matter was due to come to court, an agreement was reached between the Inland Revenue and the organisation's main funding partner – but part of the arrangement involved winding up the organisation. (Fortunately the assets were transferred to a new organisation, with a new board, which was able to complete the premises developments and continue the operations.)

The board had taken their eye off the ball. At a time when key members of staff left the organisation they failed to recognise that an incoming Finance Officer, especially one lacking experience in the sector, would require closer monitoring and support than his predecessor. Effectively, the board needed to revert temporarily to the more hands-on role that it had played in the organisation's early life.

Ultimately, both the board and the organisation escaped lightly. It might have been different.

Adding value through expertise and strategic input

To add maximum value to the organisation the board's involvement in the finances needs to be at the highest level possible. Where there are financially experienced staff in the organisation, the board's time on monitoring may be reduced and correspondingly more time invested in considering more strategic questions:

- To what degree are our policy priorities reflected in our financial priorities? Are we putting our money where our policy mouth is?
- How can we improve our long-range cash-flow forecasting and management?
- What level of liquidity is necessary for the organisation?
- What should our reserves policy be?
- What is an appropriate cost-benefit analysis framework to assist us with major capital expenditure decisions, or decisions about launching new programmes of work?

Financial expertise

In the small non-profit organisation where specialist financial expertise may be thin on the ground, and where the financial reporting may be part of a generalist (or multi-skilled!) administrator's time, the board may have to be closer to the day-to-day finances. But even here, it will be in the organisation's best interest to embark upon a programme of education and training, to try to ensure that the daily finances and regular financial reporting are largely handled by the staff, in order to move the board to a level of financial debate which harnesses their intellectual capital more productively.

Although board members are not all expected to be experts in finance, the effectiveness of the board's contribution to financial issues will depend upon some financial expertise amongst the board members and the managers who report to them. Where boards lack this expertise, managers may be obliged to devote time simply to explaining financial information.

The most useful contributions from board members are likely to occur where managers welcome challenging questions from board members. Board members need to feel free to request and understand information about the relative costs and intended performance outcomes of expenditure options. In so doing they keep a focus on the overall effectiveness of the organisation – are we investing in those areas which will achieve best results? Are we investing in those areas which most help to fulfil our mission and achieve our agreed objectives?

Budget setting

Involvement in the budget-setting process places the board in a stronger position to make a strategic contribution to the organisation. The discussion and challenging of budget assumptions in detail prior to the budget's approval is an educative process (for all concerned), and can establish a shared knowledge base that will raise the level of subsequent financial discussion through the year, including the consideration of priorities and options.

Board members who understand the essential cost structure of their organisation – whether through their reading of figures or their access to the organisation's operations – can make more useful, better-informed contributions, though they constantly need to guard against the risk of being drawn into inappropriate discussions about operational details. When the board has an understanding of the economy of the organisation, they are in a position to turn their attention to higher-level financial issues, such as:

- selecting and considering ratios and other indicators which relate the consumption of resources to the quantity of outputs or to the quality of outcomes;
- identifying what value is added at different stages of the organisation's service processes, by quantifying the cost and benefit of the different activities undertaken;
- analysing the costs and benefits of different options available to the organisation;
- benchmarking: identifying and comparing key resource/performance ratios with relevant organisations (described in *Monitoring Our Progress*, Chapter 15).

In other words, using accounting-based information to assist performance evaluation at a strategic level.

How are we doing?[4]

- ✔ Does the person responsible for preparing the financial reports for the board attend that part of a board meeting at which finance is discussed?
- ✔ Does the Chief Executive personally check all financial reports before they are distributed to the board?
- ✔ Is the person who prepares the financial statements free to discuss with the board any matters relating to the accounts?
- ✔ Is a standard format used for all financial reports?
- ✔ Does the board receive:
  - monthly financial statements prepared on an accrual basis of accounting?
  - monthly or quarterly cash flow statements?
  - all reports on a timely basis?
- ✔ Does the board receive a regular written report from the administrator or Treasurer highlighting any exceptional items in the financial statements?
- ✔ Is a regular comparison made of budgeted income and expenditure with actual income and expenditure?
- ✔ Are detailed budgets prepared for all activities?

---

[4] Adapted from the exemplary Scottish Arts Council publication, *Care, Diligence and Skill*, edited by Graham Berry and Paul Pia (Edinburgh, 1995).

✔ Does the board insist that:
- detailed budgets, including cost—benefit assumptions, are prepared for all substantial capital expenditure?
- feasibility studies are carried out and circulated to the board showing how all capital expenditure will be paid for before any final decisions are taken?
- at least three quotations are obtained from potential suppliers before considering any major capital expenditure?

✔ Does the board ensure that actual capital expenditure is compared with budgeted capital expenditure on a regular basis?

✔ Are detailed working papers prepared and kept by staff to support figures in all financial reports prepared for the board?

✔ Are all questions asked at a board meeting properly answered or, if not, deferred to the next meeting?

✔ Does the board ensure that the investment of the organisation's funds 'at call' (i.e. readily available) or otherwise with an institution is in line with the organisation's policy?

✔ Does the board ensure that the organisation has an adequate system of internal control over all financial transactions and takes control of assets?

✔ Does the Chair of the Board or Chair of the Audit/Finance Committee meet the organisation's auditors at least once a year?

✔ Does the board review all management letters from the external auditor?

✔ Is the board satisfied with the quality of financial information provided for board meetings?

Summary

- Board members cannot afford to ignore the organisation's finances, but they should not be obsessive either.
- The board has three main roles in the area of finance: planning, monitoring and decision-making.
- Involvement in the budget-setting process places the board in a stronger position to make a strategic contribution to the organisation, using accounting-based information to assist performance evaluation.
- The board should ensure that basic procedures and controls are in place – poor financial procedures should never be allowed to undermine your organisation's hard work and achievements.
- Audit or Finance Committees provide a means of focusing relevant expertise of selected board members on a more detailed examination of financial processes, and other compliance and conduct issues.

7 People matter

Policies and procedures

People matter. Non-profit organisations are established to meet their needs and like many for-profit and public sector organisations, they depend on capable and motivated staff to deliver their services. Unlike such organisations, non-profits often also depend on the contributed time and expertise of volunteers, including those on the board. They are often not in a position to remunerate their staff as handsomely as for-profit organisations would for similarly demanding work. This is partly because the absence of a bottom line driver precludes a link between individual performance and financial outcomes. It is also because of a continuing tension between devoting resources to infrastructure and administration, and devoting resources to visible service delivery. Perhaps, too, there is a continuing resistance to paying non-profit CEOs and other staff the proper rate for the job – on the basis that they 'want' to do the work.

The board's people (or 'human resources') responsibilities are:

- to appoint the CEO;
- to support the CEO and monitor his or her progress;
- to establish personnel policies;
- to provide advice and, potentially a 'Court of Appeal' within the organisation's disciplinary, grievance and appeal procedures;
- to provide leadership, in conjunction with the CEO.

And, of course, there are some basic legal requirements:

- to comply with employment law;
- to maintain employer's liability insurance;
- to have a statement of terms and conditions of employment;
- to avoid discrimination against potential or actual employees;
- to observe health and safety requirements.

Policy Development

The appointment of the CEO, establishment of a working relationship and evaluation of the CEO's progress are covered in Chapter 14, *Recruiting the CEO*. This chapter deals with policy development, personnel procedures and some of the challenges of volunteer-based organisations.

A dispute over a claim of unfair dismissal is not the time for the board to be waking up to the need to establish disciplinary procedures. These need to be discussed and adopted in calm waters, not under the pressure of resolving a current and pressing problem.

In many organisations the board will wish to take a practical hand in the development of personnel policies – there are likely to be board members who have some previous relevant experience, from their professional, commercial or other spheres of work. Moreover, personnel policies will find their way into the statement of terms and conditions of employment, and form the basis of the contractual relationship between board and staff. The board needs to be familiar with their obligations, and satisfied that the policies provide a rational, equitable and workable framework for day-to-day management.

Examples of policies that the board should consider establishing, include:

- Equal opportunities
- Recruitment
- Pay policy
- Maternity/paternity and other (e.g. compassionate) leave
- Arrangements for sick leave
- Health and safety
- Training and staff appraisal
- Disciplinary and grievance procedures

Beyond these policy frameworks, the board will also be concerned with the following.

- Staffing structure, and number and nature of posts.
- Rates of pay and job descriptions (this will be partly covered by pay policy).
- Terms and conditions of employment not covered by the policies listed above.
- Systems for the appointment of the CEO.

This is no picnic. It can represent a lot of detailed work, and much of it may seem to be of a low priority. Under operational pressure at management level, and short of time to address strategic issues at board level, why should the board be focusing on these arcane policy matters?

The price for inconsistency in handling specific issues may be greater than irritated or demotivated staff – it could end in front of an Industrial Tribunal. So, there are positive as well as negative reasons for investing in good personnel frameworks: assisting the establishment of a motivated and harmonious workforce and volunteer force, and avoiding damaging and time-wasting disputes or litigation.

The development of an adequate personnel framework is a prime candidate for a temporary Task Force or Working Group, given the workload for the board that has few of these policies in place. This Working Group might comprise a couple of board members, a couple of staff members (including the CEO) and, possibly, the temporary co-option of a willing outsider with relevant experience – especially if the board lacks personnel expertise or senior management experience. The Working Group should be given a realistic timeframe, and a set of priorities as to which areas of personnel procedure to tackle first. If they do not already exist, grievance, disciplinary and recruitment procedures should be given priority.

7.1 Different rules

Sally was ill. The CEO felt strongly that staff should be kept on full salary throughout the duration of the illness. There was no Sick Leave Policy. A decision to pay full salary and to hire a temporary replacement would add to existing budget problems. The board's advice was sought. Instead of being able to refer to an established policy applicable to all staff, the board had to decide quickly how to address the particular case at hand. In such situations, it is often difficult to avoid discussions of the merits of the individual staff member or this year's budget situation ('doesn't Sally's husband have a job?', 'how many weeks will it be before she's back?', 'can we afford to be humane?').

Instead of providing the CEO with clear directions on how the organisation should provide support to its employees, the board may find itself drawn into providing advice 'in the heat of the moment'. A thoughtful discussion on the principle of fair treatment of all employees and the merits of one policy option over another may not occur.

After 45 minutes of heated emotional discussion, Sally got sick leave with pay. Her case was decided on an individual basis. No policy was ever developed.

Three years later, the board composition has changed and there is a new CEO. Neither knows what previous boards did (or why). Joe is a long-term employee who is now ill. He doesn't get sick leave with pay. When the rest of the staff learn about this, they are (justifiably) angry that the board and senior management have 'different rules for different people'. The negative feelings of staff towards the organisation because of ad hoc, inconsistent board/staff decision-making can seriously jeopardise its development over the longer term.

Employment legislation[1]

The organisation's employment practices will need to comply with a number of pieces of legislation, covering for example:

- Disabled Persons
- Race Relations
- Sex Discrimination
- Health and Safety at Work
- Employment Protection

Individual board members are not expected to be experts in employment legislation – but there are some specific obligations and some broader equity principles enshrined in employment law, which need to be reflected in the organisation's policies and procedures. When these policies and procedures have been drafted and discussed by the board, it would be wise to put them in front of an appropriately qualified lawyer (and/or experienced union official) for a second opinion on whether they are sufficiently robust to deal with issues that may arise in the future.

---

[1] In this and in other parts of this chapter I am indebted to Madeline Hutchins, who has played a significant role in disseminating good personnel practice through her training for arts and other non-profit organizations.

7.2 Statement of terms and conditions

Sample contents

- Official name of Employer
- Employee's official job title
- Who can give Employee directions and to whom Employee reports
- Details of Employee's pay, pay period and hours of work. How salary is to be paid and when it is to be reviewed
- Details of Employee's holiday entitlement
- Details of pension schemes
- A notice provision enabling either Employer or Employee to terminate employment, and specifying the period of notice
- A provision specifying whether the contract applies for a continuous period or a fixed term
- Full job description of Employee's position
- Appraisal procedures
- Health and safety regulations and procedures
- Sickness absence and sick pay entitlements
- Details of maternity/paternity leave entitlements
- List of disciplinary rules and grievance procedures
- Reimbursement procedures for Employee's out-of-pocket expenses
- Any confidentiality requirements binding Employee
- Redundancy procedures
- Termination of employment procedures
- How the contract may be officially revised by both parties

While the board may be closely involved in the development and adoption of personnel policies and procedures, implementation will be delegated to the CEO and, through the CEO, to other staff. Periodically, the board may wish to audit personnel processes, to ensure that:

- they are being implemented;
- they are consistent with current legislation;
- any problems or gaps in procedure are identified and put right;
- they are helping to create a positive workplace, not just dealing with problems as they arise; and
- each person in the organisation knows
  - who they are responsible to;
  - the boundaries of their job description and any overlaps with others;

- team decision-making requirements;
- where responsibilities have been delegated;
- what meetings or officers do they report to, and whether they make decisions and report these, or make recommendations to the officers/meeting.

Beyond policy

The board demonstrates its leadership responsibilities by providing the organisation with a clear sense of direction, and through establishing effective structures and processes for the staff and volunteers. When there is conflict within the organisation, the board must act – either by clearly backing the CEO's handling of the situation or, when necessary, intervening to resolve a conflict which involves the CEO or has exhausted the organisation's normal channels.

Providing the policy frameworks is only the start. They cover the 'hygiene' factors, without which it is difficult for staff to operate effectively. But beyond the hygiene factors lie the motivational tools and structures: clear target-setting, appraisal of staff, feedback mechanisms, rewards and recognition. While the board should consider these issues in its dealings with the CEO, the motivation of other staff falls to the CEO – the board's role is limited to ensuring that the systems are in place, and occasionally participating in 'ceremonial' activities that recognise the efforts of staff and volunteers. The fact that they are ceremonial does not diminish their importance. Recognition is a powerful motivator.

Appraisal procedures

An appraisal process is the critical link between the organisation's Strategic Plan and day-to-day operational processes. It provides the opportunity to align individual staff members and volunteers with the organisation's broader agenda. A regular system of appraisal, taking place annually or twice-yearly, that allows for a review of the individual's performance, would normally be conducted by the staff member's or volunteer's line manager. Between these formal meetings there should be regular, informal feedback and supervision.

An appraisal agenda

1 Has the staff member or volunteer done what he or she undertook to do?
2 What has gone well or badly? Have support and resources been adequate?
3 Review and assessment of achievements, and setting targets for the next work period. Wherever possible, targets should be set by the individual as well as for the individual.
4 Training and development needs, and future training plan.

For senior staff members, it may be appropriate to use one member of the board as a support figure, or a staffing sub-committee. Personalities should be considered, and the allocation of the support figure should, wherever it is felt appropriate, allow for a woman to be supported by a woman.

The appraisal and support system should operate all the time, not only in probationary periods or crises. Access to it should be easy.

Volunteers

Some non-profits operate with few or no volunteers. Others would find the work of volunteers indispensable. Even without the contractual obligations that are brought into play as a consequence of a wages system, most volunteers and the organisations they work for benefit from the role clarity, appraisal and communications that characterise good staff management.

Volunteers will range from those helping to deliver the day-to-day operations of the organisation, to those providing advice, to board or management committee members. While their motivations vary, they fall into three broad categories:

1 **Ideological** – resulting from a belief in the importance of the organisation's work.
2 **Personal** – resulting from the need to make use of time, acquiring skills, needing social contact, adding a leisure activity.
3 **Collective** – resulting from enthusiasm generated from a joint effort towards a particular event (school fete, festival).[2]

The common sense of reward is satisfaction in a job well done, and 'making a difference'. In some cases, the privilege of being more closely

---

[2] Sue Kay explores these motivations in 'Understanding Volunteers', *Arts Business*, 28 September 1998.

involved in the organisation's work – seeing behind the scenes – is itself an additional motivation.

Not all non-profits will want to manage and organise their volunteers in the same way. The degree of formality, and the nature of the rewards, will be affected by the scale and nature of the work. What is appropriate for a volunteer front-of-house in a theatre may be very different from what is appropriate for a volunteer in a health or welfare organisation. What is common, however, is the need for a systematic approach that recognises the needs of the individual volunteer. Some ways of helping to optimise performance from volunteers include the following:

- Set annual goals for increased volunteer involvement and commitment.
- Help volunteers understand the problems in the field and the role and work of the organisation.
- Be certain that your organisation operates a competent information and referral programme. The basic service activity of a voluntary agency is to serve as a channel between those who need help and those who can provide it.
- Keep the dream alive! Don't let yourself be so concerned with the problems you face that you fail to recognise that volunteers look to you to keep the goals in sight.
- Provide all possible credit and thanks for volunteer activity.

Apart from the fact that board members are nearly always volunteers themselves, the board's concern should be to ensure that there is clarity in the organisation's interaction with volunteers. This starts with vision – why are we engaging volunteers? What do we hope to add to our organisation as a consequence? It includes commitment – a conviction that volunteers are important to organisational performance: this is a message that must be reinforced from the top to ensure that volunteers are not marginalized. The board should ensure there are policies and procedures in place, and will want to be involved in any strategic decisions in relation to volunteer usage or development – for example, the decision as to whether there should be a paid volunteer organiser, or whether volunteers should be assisting in specific aspects of the organisation's work.

Resource 4 includes a range of ways in which volunteer involvement can be recognised and rewarded. Many of these will be for the staff (or volunteer organiser) to implement – but there will often be occasions when the board member, or board collectively, can add its voice and its weight to volunteer recognition.

Personnel procedures: a health check

DO YOU HAVE THE FOLLOWING ?	Yes	No	Don't know	Needs work
A clear understanding of the board's role as employer				
A clear understanding between the board and senior staff of each other's responsibilities				
An understanding of the organisation's management ethos				
A diagram showing the staffing structure of your organization				
A recruitment and selection procedure				
Signed contracts for all staff				
Job descriptions for all staff				
A pay policy and structure, and a system for annual pay reviews				
Leave procedures (maternity, paternity, compassionate)				
An induction system for all staff, board members and volunteers				
Comprehensive terms and conditions for all staff				
A system for personnel records for all staff				
An equal opportunities policy				
A training policy				
A system of monitoring and appraisal for all staff				
Disciplinary rules and procedures				
Grievance procedures				
A redundancy policy				
A health and safety policy				
Recruitment, appraisal, reward and appropriate grievance and disciplinary procedures for your volunteers				
A communication system including a company handbook				

Summary

- People are at the heart of all non-profit organisations – providing appropriate and equitable policies and procedures is essential for organisational harmony and motivation.
- Compliance with employment law, adopting terms and conditions of employment and avoiding discriminatory behaviour are amongst the board's legal obligations.
- The board's expertise should be harnessed in the development of personnel policies.
- Implementation is largely a matter for the CEO, although the board would be well advised to audit personnel processes periodically, to ensure they are up-to-date and being properly implemented.
- Through appraisal processes the board can help to motivate the CEO, and ensure that others in the organisation are motivated.
- Recognition and praise are prerequisites of volunteer motivation.

AN INTERVIEW WITH LYN THOMAS, PRESIDENT, RSPCA QUEENSLAND

RSPCA Queensland aims 'to be a proactive and compassionate advocate for all animals'. In 2001 the organisation benefited from over 85,000 hours of volunteer time, investigated over 10,000 reported cases of cruelty, and launched nearly 100 prosecutions. Agreement was also reached with the State Government on significant new legislation to be introduced into Parliament, increasing penalties for offenders.

Lyn Thomas has been President of RSPCA Queensland for three years, and on the board for five. She had previously been President of the Cat Protection Society of New South Wales. When she arrived on the RSPCA board there had been a succession of CEOs and Acting CEOs in a short space of time.

What were your first steps in these circumstances?
A succession of CEOs and Acting CEOs in a short period exposed weaknesses in the Society's personnel procedures. Putting that right became a priority issue for me as the new President.

INTERVIEW

Like many non-profits, personnel procedures were not the only aspect of the Society's systems and infrastructure to require attention during a period when expectations of the Society were increasing. Before the RSPCA could significantly enhance its impact across the State, a number of steps had to be taken, including improved office and administration systems, and increased attention to developing cooperative relationships with stakeholders.

The hiring of an appropriate CEO was effected with the help of a recruitment consultant. With 150 responses to the advertising, sifting down to a final short-list was a demanding task. But I and the other board members were clear there had to be a professionalisation of the senior management function of the Society, and the conditions, remuneration and rigour of the selection process would need to reflect this. RSPCA Queensland has 120 paid staff and approximately 650 volunteers – a skilled CEO was needed to provide people leadership, and to re-establish (and then maintain) productive relationships with Government departments, donors and others.

What other organisational changes have occurred?
Amongst other developments, the Society has incorporated in recent years, requiring a constitutional change to comply with Incorporated Association requirements. A downsizing from 16 to 11 board members was effected at the same time, and there were significant changes in the composition of the board during this period.

The board members now have position descriptions. They are expected to give between eight and ten hours a month to the Society, a good deal more time is required of the President. A high level of attendance is expected. Board terms are for two years, but office bearers are elected annually.

How has the board's role developed?
Being drawn into the day-to-day operations is all too tempting for board members who are passionate about animal protection but, increasingly, the board is focused on strategic rather than operational issues. Temporary task forces are being adopted to tackle specific issues. When the job is done, the working party is disbanded. Board members seem happier to contribute their time

and energy in this way, knowing that the task forces have a limited shelf-life.

Of course, board members want to help animals – and they can, but only in the context of the Society's policies and structure. They represent the organisation, not themselves.

What is the make-up of the RSPCA's income?
Of the RSPCA Queensland's $6 million annual income needed to provide its functions, 30 per cent comes from bequests, and roughly 3 per cent from inspectorate services provided to State Government. Other income comes from kennel services, dog obedience classes, product and merchandise sales, and donations generated from specific campaigns. The Society's board is not, at this stage, an active fundraising board.

What is the board's role in planning?
Strategic planning is a relatively young discipline for the Society. Without a formally adopted plan, however, there was a tendency for ideas to be generated too whimsically, and previous ideas discarded too lightly. Following a more thorough-going planning process, new ideas are now tested against a consistent yardstick – is it in the Plan? Is it in the Budget? If it is not in the Plan there have to be very cogent reasons to run with a new idea. If it is not in the Budget, something else has to drop before a new initiative is adopted. I believe this discipline makes life easier for the CEO and management. The board has one or two planning meetings each year, and one meeting focusing on the budget.

It's very easy to get bogged down with the dog-of-the-day issue. But we're here to help 40,000 animals, not just to save one, because that doesn't fix the problem.

I see a key part of my role as liaising between the board and the CEO. The board is responsible for the strategic direction of the organisation, the CEO for delivering the goals and objectives through his management team.

Communications between board members are largely by e-mail, although this has meant there is a danger that the less wired-up can be left out of the loop. Teleconferencing is also utilised. The flow of information around the board, and between the board, CEO and staff, is the oil that keeps the engine moving.

INTERVIEW

What are your personal priorities?

Having worked for years with animal charities, I recognise that long-term public education is necessary to generate positive attitudes to animals, and wider concern over animal welfare. De-sexing of pets should be compulsory, to limit the number of unwanted pets: animals that are in danger of being mistreated and, tragically, may face euthanasia due to a serious lack of good homes.

What is your advice to a new non-profit board member?

- Focus on the strategic level, not the operational.
- Accept majority decisions.
- Be prepared to lobby – we work in a political environment.
- Be willing to operate in a committee framework.
- Represent the organisation, not an issue or faction.

8 Policy and planning toolkit

Plans are nothing, planning is everything

Dwight D Eisenhower

Policy development

An influential publication in the non-profit world has been John Carver's work on Policy Governance.[1] Carver places the business of defining policy as the highest responsibility of boards. By focusing on policy articulation, Carver argues, boards can avoid the temptation of becoming entrapped in the operational detail, which is not their proper concern, and can provide a clear and comprehensive framework within which the CEO operates. The Carver 'model' identifies four areas of policy:

1 **Ends:** mission-related policies – what outcomes are to be achieved, for whom and at what cost.
2 **Executive limitations:** boundaries for acceptability within which the staff undertake their responsibilities. These policies apply to the process (or the 'means') of achieving these outcomes.
3 **Board-staff linkage:** the manner in which the board delegates authority to staff, how it will evaluate staff performance (i.e. on achieving the identified results – 'ends' – and within the executive limitations policies).
4 **Governance process:** the board determines its philosophy, its accountability and the specifics of its own job.

See Box 8.1.

Focusing the board strongly on policy, and on the processes necessary to implement policy, represents an important step forward. However, there has subsequently been reaction by some against Carver's model, largely for three reasons.

---

[1] John Carver, *Boards That Make A Difference*, Jossey-Bass Inc. (San Francisco, 1997).

1 It appears to assume a non-profit organisation where there is enough staffing infrastructure for the CEO to fulfil any policies the board defines (to be a 'real' CEO). In the one- or two-person organisation, the model smacks of too many bosses (thinking of grand plans) and not enough workers (to implement them).

2 It is unrealistic to suppose that the board will not interpret its role as requiring other levels of involvement and overseeing of the organisation. For some Carver's approach resembles an inflexible 'one-size-fits-all' solution to the board function, which conflicts with the real world.

3 The amount of time that the board will need to devote to the policy-development process: spread over a series of meetings, it can take as long as a year for the policies to be discussed and agreed. In the non-profit world where board members seem to be increasingly time-poor, this is a great deal to ask.

8.1 Carver in a nutshell

■ The Trust in Trusteeship – being clear who the 'owners' of the organisation are, to whom the board are responsible.

■ The board speaks with one voice or not at all.

■ Board decisions should predominantly be policy decisions.

■ Boards should formulate policy by determining the broadest values before progressing to more narrow ones.

■ A board should define and delegate, rather than react and ratify.

■ Ends determination is the pivotal duty of governance.

■ The board's best control over staff means is to limit, not prescribe.

■ A board must explicitly design its own products and process.

■ A board must forge a linkage with management that is both empowering and safe.

■ The performance of the CEO must be monitored rigorously, but only against policy criteria.

Placing policy centre-stage can produce the benefit that the board speaks with one voice. By devoting time to discussing aspects of organisational policy, differences are brought to the surface and resolved, making it far more likely that the board will act as effective advocates, understanding the key directions of the organisation, and communicating them coherently to stakeholders and the community. Whether the Carver approach is adopted fully or not, the board will benefit from time devoted to policy articulation.

Policy debate can occur at different levels of significance for the board. Some relate to fundamental choices of directions for the organisation, others relate to administrative processes:[2]

Policy level	Issues
Major	■ Merger with another organisation ■ Expansion of programme into new area
Secondary	■ Establishment of an outreach programme ■ Programme outcomes (local, national, international services) ■ Constituency development outcomes ■ Major equipment or facility acquisition ■ Basis for compensation (e.g. performance-based, equity-based, tenure-driven)
Functional	■ Budgeting process, finance and resource outcomes ■ Fee schedule ■ Criteria for personnel evaluation ■ Collaborative purchasing (e.g. bulk purchasing, purchases through a cooperative) ■ Communications and liaison processes ■ Board processes
Minor	■ Selection of contract services
Standard Operating Procedures	■ Payroll distribution
Rules	■ Requests for leave of absence ■ Parking ■ Smoking on premises ■ Dress code

Policy initiatives or suggestions can arise from anywhere – the board, CEO, staff, members, or stakeholders. Most often it will be the CEO or an active board member who initiates policy discussion. In some cases it will be triggered by a problem, with both the board and CEO wanting to establish a coherent and consistent approach to dealing with that problem should it arise again. Wherever the policy arises, it is the board's prerogative and responsibility to adopt (or amend) the policy. The imaginary dividing line in Figure 8a suggests where responsibilities may lie in the business of developing and adopting policy.

---

[2] Diane Duca, *Non-profit Boards, Roles, Responsibilities, and Performance*, John Wiley & Sons Inc. (New York, 1996), p71.

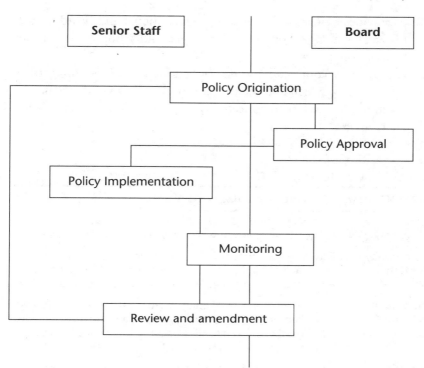

Figure 8a Who is responsible for policy?

It is in the articulation of the Strategic Plan (or Business Plan – the terminology varies from one organisation to the next) that policy is translated into practicalities and assigned priorities. It is here, in the objectives, strategies and action programmes, that the realisation of policy is mapped out.

Strategic planning

The planning process also creates an opportunity for aligning the board, CEO and others behind a common sense of direction – it can be an invaluable component in team building. It can also flush out differences which have remained below the surface, creating friction and conflict, and which will need to be resolved.

From the board's perspective there are four practical benefits from the planning process.

1 It helps to focus the board on those issues that are of highest importance to the health and success of the organisation.

2 It provides a means of measuring organisational and board performance, by laying out a range of strategies and action plans that can be monitored.

3 It provides a 'contract' between the board and CEO with regard to the priorities, which become the basis of the CEO's performance.

4 It filters information, by concentrating the board's attention on what really matters.

Sample contents of a strategic plan

PART 1: CURRENT SITUATION (business diagnostic)

Anywhere Community Association in context	What Anywhere Community Association is and does, when founded, relationship with other agencies or organizations
Anywhere Community Association's external environment	External environmental scan, including brief comments on political, economic, industry, competition, technological, international and possibly other headings (see below)
Anywhere Community Association's internal environment	Internal environmental analysis (strengths and weaknesses) including brief comment on products and services, people, structures, systems, facilities, technology, finances and possibly other headings (see below)
Implications of the external and internal analysis (and Anywhere Community Association's overall progress to date)	Brief summary of issues arising from the previous three sections which have implications for future action by Anywhere Community Association

PART 2: FORWARD PLAN

Vision	The world we wish to create – how it will look in five or ten years' time
Mission	The purpose of our organisation, why it exists
Values	Principles and drivers that inform the way we work
Aims or Goals	Top-level statements (or Goals) for our activities and for organisational functions
Performance indicators	How we will measure progress towards these Goals
Objectives	Three or four key achievements necessary to fulfil the Goals
Strategies	How these key achievements will be reached
Action programmes	Practical steps to implement the strategies (this level of detail is often relegated to an 'operational' plan)
Risk analysis/management	Probability and impact of main areas of risk, and how these will be mitigated
Financial projections	For the period of the plan

The Strategic Plan is a board document, just as policies represent board decisions and parameters. However, the board's role in the strategic planning process can range from relatively modest input at key stages, to almost full engagement in all aspects of the plan's development.

The board's role in the strategic planning process

At a minimum	At a maximum
In an organisation where the CEO is experienced in planning and has adequate staff support, and where perhaps the board and CEO have worked closely on planning previously, the board's active involvement could be limited to the following:	In an organisation where there are only one or two staff, where board members have planning expertise (and the time), their contribution could comprise most of the following:

At a minimum

1 Confirming the planning and consultation process

2 Attending a planning retreat or away-day

3 Reviewing the mission and vision

4 Reviewing the situational analysis

5 Determining key Aims, Outcomes or Strategic Intents

6 Confirming the preferred strategies and risk mitigation plan

7 Defining key results areas and performance indicators

8 Adopting the plan

At a maximum

1 Planning the plan – preparing the schedule for the planning process

2 Confirming who will be consulted

3 Attending a planning retreat or away-day

4 Reviewing the mission

5 Analysing the current situation:

- review of the last plan, what progress has been made?
- key achievements of the last few years
- strengths and weaknesses (services, products, personnel, systems, premises, finances, reputation)

6 Implications for the future

7 Defining the Vision

8 Determining key Aims, Outcomes or Strategic Intents

9 Possible strategies

10 Evaluation of possible strategies, and selection of preferred strategies

11 Risk analysis and mitigation

12 Action plans/programmes

13 Defining key results areas and performance indicators

14 Financial projections

15 Adopting the plan

The 'minimalist' eight steps of board involvement are based on the board's irreducible planning responsibilities:

1 To establish the mission and values which guide organisational direction.
2 To confirm the assumptions made about the organisation's environment.
3 To determine the level of risk which is acceptable to the organisation.
4 To ensure that the core business of the organisation is maintained.
5 To accept the plan as a key board working document.

The external and internal environment scan will pool the knowledge and opinions of both board and staff on the organisation's current situation. Where a thorough-going review of the Plan is taking place, other input may be brought to bear. For the external environment scan, the views or expertise of one or two specialists in the industry may be sought, or brief papers commissioned from them on specific topics. For the internal environment scan, a facilitator might be brought in to steer discussions – or a human resources specialist might be asked to examine aspects of organisational communication and structure, or personnel procedures.

Internal environment review

The internal environment review will include commentary on the strengths and weaknesses of different aspects of the organisation's services and infrastructure culled from group discussion at different levels of the organisation, including the board or management committee.

The areas it should cover include:

- **Services:** quality, reputation, range of programmes, outreach, special events, publications
- **People:** volunteers, board members, experience/skills, effectiveness, customer relations
- **Physical factors:** premises, atmosphere, access, facilities for the public, security
- **Goodwill:** friends' organisations, local government, community organisations, local businesses, media
- **Knowledge, market data:** locality, customers, industry developments
- **Income:** grants, earned income, sponsorships, donations

External environment review

Not all elements of the external environment will necessarily be significant for each non-profit organisation. But this framework can stimulate debate, leading to an understanding of those external issues and changes which are most likely to have an impact on the organisation in the next few years. This is the crux – not to write a detailed prognosis on the future of Britain or the world, but to identify the most pertinent external factors, and consider their implications.

- **Economics:** flow of money, goods, services, information and energy – what economic trends are most likely to affect us?
- **Politics:** allocation of power, laws, policies, taxes – are there any policy or legislative changes in the pipeline?
- **Demographics and social trends:** the way people live and what they value – what lifestyle changes will affect our work in our main geographical locations?
- **Technology:** the development of machines, tools, processes, materials, equipment and know-how – how will our work benefit from or change as a result of technological development in our industry?
- **Culture:** the beliefs and values of the wider market place, including cultural elements of language, religion, history, customs – what developments in the broader cultural environment are likely to affect our services or communications?
- **Natural environment:** location, space, topography, climate, pollution and natural resources – if our work is related to or affected by environmental contexts, what trends do we predict?
- **Industrial environment:** awards, legislation, union politics, industrial relations – what broader changes are happening in our industry sector?
- **International environment:** trade agreements, politics, economies, diplomatic relations, culture, growth – what impacts do we predict on our links with colleagues, markets and beneficiaries abroad?

Vision, mission and values

The organisation's *vision* can either be expressed as a world which you want to realise, or a description of how you want your organisation to look in five or ten years' time. The former visualises briefly how the environment will have changed as a consequence of your organisation's work. The latter might more formally describe the change in your organisation in terms of services, structure, systems, beneficiaries and finances. An externally focused vision statement, describing the world you want to see, can be highly motivational.

The *mission* is the purpose of the organisation, the reason it exists, but it also encompasses the values that underpin the organisation. The mission statement focuses on organisational purpose, but is often accompanied by a statement of values or principles.

The process of generating and confirming the statements of vision, mission and values can be a powerful way of digging into the heart of the organisation, and reminding board members, staff and others why they are doing the work. The mission and values also become an important litmus test for specific strategies and projects – to what degree does a proposed strategy or project help to fulfil the mission we have confirmed?

The process can also be very time-consuming if it is not facilitated effectively. Hours and days can be wasted going around in circles trying to refine an acceptable form of words – and there is an inverse ratio between the time spent doing this and the inspirational, motivating impact of the words that emerge. The process needs discipline, and a guillotine.

Organisation	Vision	Mission	Illustrative Values
Help the Aged	A future where older people are highly valued, have lives that are richer and voices that are heard	To secure and uphold the rights of older people everywhere	■ People matter ■ Passionate about combating disadvantage ■ Relevant ■ Collaborative ■ Accountable ■ Setting standards
Barnardo's	The lives of all children and young people should be free from poverty, abuse and discrimination	To help the most vulnerable children and young people transform their lives and fulfil their potential	Derived from Christian faith, and shared by people of other faiths, Barnardo's seeks to: ■ respect the unique worth of every person ■ encourage people to fulfil their potential ■ work with hope ■ exercise responsible stewardship
Alzheimer's Association Victoria (Australia)	A society committed to the prevention of dementia, while valuing and supporting people living with dementia.	Providing leadership in policy and services for people living with dementia, their families and carers.	■ The worth of every individual ■ Strength and unity with respect for diversity ■ Cooperative relationships ■ Organisational integrity ■ Responsiveness, innovation, creativity and flexibility ■ The contribution of all people involved with our work

Figure 8b provides a simple overview of a typical strategic planning process.

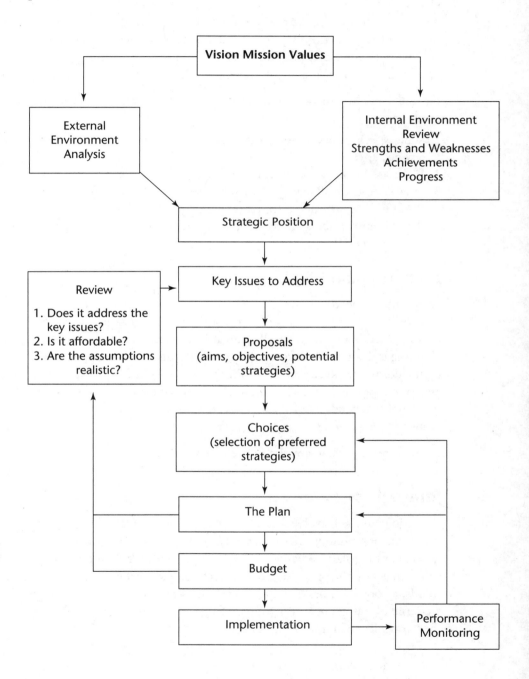

Figure 8b Planning process overview

Some planning tools

Even where the board does adopt a minimum intervention approach, and there are some who object to this on the philosophical grounds that the strategic plan is the board's business and no-one else's, there are a number of tools and approaches that the board can bring to the planning process which will add to the quality of strategic thinking in the organisation.

First, the board can raise and structure debate around five strategic questions:

1 What specifically does our organisation want to achieve in the next few years?
2 What are the key choices facing us?
3 How should we allocate resources between our different objectives?
4 What have we learned from past experiences?
5 What improvements are required to enable us to make better use of our resources?[3]

Scenario planning

Secondly, the board can draft, commission or ask the CEO to prepare several distinct scenarios in order to consider possible situations which the organisation might find itself facing in five or ten years' time. Strategic planning is distinguished from other levels of planning (e.g. operational) by including the possibility of alternative futures and either making an assessment of the most likely future the organisation will experience or, more positively, envisioning the preferred future that the organisation wishes to realise, and setting out to make that future happen.

'We cannot work to create a future which we do not first imagine.'[4]

Strategic questions

Scenario planning involves assembling a possible market environment, which the organisation may experience. This may be based on assumptions about legislative changes, competitor growth (or disappearance), shifts in labour supply, medical or technological advances, cultural trends, or other factors. Having created the scenario, which may cover a couple of paragraphs or a couple of pages, the board and CEO can then consider the implications of this for the organisation. How would

---

[3] Mike Hudson, *Managing Without Profit: The Art of Managing Third-sector Organisations*, Penguin (Harmondsworth, 1995), p90.

[4] Peter Ellyard, Executive Director, Preferred Futures Pty Ltd.

we prepare for such an environment? What are the potential dangers and benefits for us? What implications does it have for the nature of our services and how we deliver them?

Strategy evaluation

Thirdly the board can require that proposed strategies be subject to rigorous analysis, to ensure that only the most appropriate strategies find their way into the plan that is adopted. The testing of potential strategies may include risk analysis or impact analysis, amongst other tools.

Risk analysis

More detailed consideration of risk assessment and mitigation is provided in Chapter 5, *Keeping to the Straight and Narrow*. With regard to considering proposed strategies, the board will be most concerned with three principal areas – financial risk (can we afford it, what is the level of exposure?), operational risk (can we actually make this change?) and management risk (do we have the expertise to manage a new field of work?).

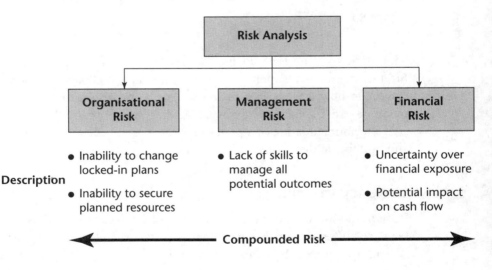

Figure 8c

Impact analysis

Impact analysis plots resources required for a specific programme, initiative or strategy against the impact that the programme is likely to have on fulfilling the organisation's mission, as with the range of strategies facing a theatre shown in Figure 8d.

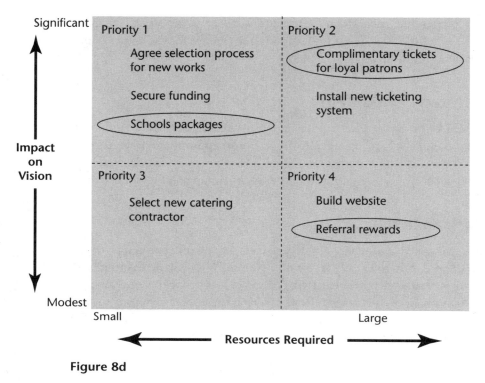

Figure 8d

Those proposed initiatives which achieve the greatest impact for the most economic investment of resources should be allocated priority, subject to how feasible it is to implement them within the short- to medium-term. The circled items in the diagram above are the theatre staff's recommendations on preferred strategies for enhancing income and building audience loyalty.

Urgency matrix

Perhaps the simplest, if most subjective, tool for determining priorities between different possible strategies or programmes is the Urgency Matrix. In a group discussion, the board and staff visually plot (on a flip-chart or whiteboard) what they view as the most urgent and the most important initiatives. Those that fall into the top right-hand corner will be given priority, subject to affordability and some of the other tests highlighted here.

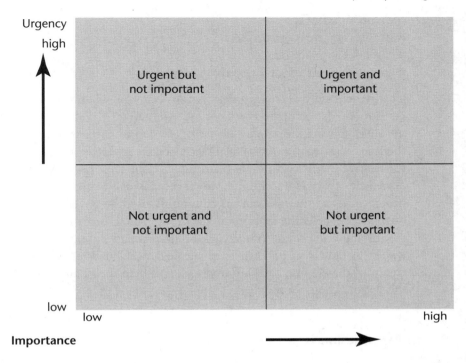

Figure 8e Urgency matrix

Whether the board uses any or all of these tools for prioritising strategies will depend on the range of alternative courses of action that have emerged, the degree of involvement in planning that is customary for the board, and the staff capacity to undertake this level of analysis independently.

Cost-benefit analysis

In the case of a major investment decision, or a programme which necessitates a significant reallocation of resources, a more fully structured cost-benefit analysis will be called for. This requires identifying and weighting the financial, environmental and other costs associated with the development, and the social, cultural, environmental and other benefits which may accrue from it.

Indicative costs
- Financial
- Other resources
- Environmental

Indicative benefits

- Impacts on our core markets
- Broader social impact
- Impact on our organisational capacity

Cost-benefit only assists as a decision-making tool when the proposed investment is compared with any alternatives (including doing nothing). By weighting and allocating 'scores' to each of the positive (benefit) and negative (cost) factors the board may arrive at a view as to the relative merits of different courses of action. This thumbnail sketch does little justice to a technique which is capable of being quite sophisticated in its application, and is commonly used by governments and businesses in reaching investment decisions. The secret of success lies in identifying an accurate framework of criteria and a rational basis for weighting and scoring. But even applied fairly unscientifically, the rigour of developing such a framework will help the board to explore the options more thoroughly.

8.2 Drucker on strategies

There is an old saying that good intentions don't move mountains; bulldozers do. In non-profit management, the mission and the plan – if that's all there is – are the good intentions. Strategies are the bulldozers. They convert what you want to do into accomplishment. They are particularly important in non-profit organisations. One prays for miracles but works for results, St Augustine said. Well, strategies lead you to work for results. They convert intentions into action and busy-ness into work. They also tell you what you need to have by way of resources and people to get the results.

I was once opposed to the term 'strategy'. I thought that it smacked too much of the military. But I have slowly become a convert. That's because in many businesses and non-profit organisations, planning is an intellectual exercise. You put it in a nicely bound volume on your shelf and leave it there. Everybody feels virtuous. We have done the planning. But until it becomes actual work, you have done nothing. Strategies, on the other hand, are action-focused. So, I've reluctantly accepted the word because it's so clear that strategies are not something you hope for; strategies are something you work for.[5]

---

[5] Peter F Drucker, *Managing the Non-Profit Organisation*, Butterworth-Heinemann Ltd (Oxford, 1992), p45.

It is important for the board to devote time to determination of key results areas and key performance indicators. These can send a strong signal to the CEO, staff and stakeholders as to where the organisation's principal energies will be focused during the next few years. And, because results are how the board will measure the CEO's success in the job, it will save much debate and possible confusion later if the success factors can be clearly identified within the planning process.

Performance indicators should be linked back to the main Aims or Strategic Intents:

Organisation	Financial indicators	Non-financial indicators
Museum	■ Cash surplus of £300,000 ■ Gross and net profit margins from museum shop ■ Merchandise income per visitor	■ Exhibitions presented ■ Publications by staff ■ People accessing Outreach Programme ■ Consultancies undertaken
Retirement Village	■ Monthly and year-to-date variations ■ Ratio of key expenses to total income	■ Vacancy factors ■ Variations in personnel ■ Statistics on workplace accidents

The frequency with which these performance indicators are reported to the board is a matter of judgement, but quarterly or six-monthly reports against key performance indicators is generally preferable to annual reports, if only because an annual report is unlikely to feed back into corrective action, or be used to seize timely opportunities, when there are shortfalls or positive results.

Using consultants

Many organisations use a consultant or facilitator within their strategic planning process. This can be motivated by:

■ the lack of time the board or CEO have to devote to the planning process;

■ the need to have someone push the process forward;

■ a lack of planning expertise at board or CEO level;

■ the need for neutral facilitation of discussions;

■ the need for research skills or industry knowledge to be bought in to inform elements of the planning process (e.g. environmental analysis);

■ the suggestion or insistence of a funding body.

Apart from the careful selection of a consultant with an appropriate track record, the paramount issue is to avoid abdicating the board's (and the CEO's) responsibility at the minimum stages suggested earlier (see p121). The consultant must not write the plan – only facilitate the process. The penalty for taking the 'easy' way out and handing over the whole process, authorship included, to the consultant will be a plan that lacks credibility and ownership – pretty much a waste of time and money.

Using the plan

A good plan is a well-thumbed plan. Require the CEO to report against it on a regular basis. Re-read it before the planning retreat. And, most of all, adopt it, even if it has imperfections, rather than honing it and refining it for month after month until everyone is heartily sick of it. You can always make it better next time.

Questions the board should ask during the planning process

✔ Does the mission statement need revision?

✔ Are the plan's assumptions about the organisation and its environment complete, current, and realistic?

✔ Are any major components missing?

✔ What are the cost/benefit ratios of the organisation's programmes and services?

✔ How can we reach a wider audience?

✔ Which of the initiatives proposed in the plan are most promising?

✔ Are the priorities clearly stated and the proposals for funding them realistic?

✔ Which initiatives can and should be self-supporting?

✔ What policy should the board adopt about cultural inclusiveness on the board, in our artistic work, and in the office?

✔ What are the staff requirements for proposed new programmes and services?

✔ How will additional staff positions be funded?

✔ Is it time for a comprehensive review of the organisation's governance structure – board members' roles, board membership, organisation, and performance?

✔ How realistic are the financial projections based on recent income and expenditure trends?

✔ What should be the organisation's goal for financial reserves?

✔ Are we adequately staffed for ambitious fundraising?

✔ Are the relative fundraising roles of board, CEO and staff clear?

Summary

- Time devoted to policy formulation is time well spent – it helps the board to speak with one voice and encourages consistency in the organisation's processes.

- The preparation of a strategic plan also helps to focus the board, provides a means of measuring organisational and board performance, and provides a clear framework for the CEO's work.

- The level of board involvement in preparing the strategic plan will vary according to the professional resources of the organisation – but adoption and monitoring of the plan are key board activities.

- Discussion of vision, mission and values brings the board to the heart of why the organisation exists, and can expose differences which, left unresolved, will create friction within the organisation.

- Potential strategies, programmes and projects should be exposed to critical analysis – there is a range of possible tools to evaluate proposed strategies.

- The adoption of performance indicators should occur as an integral part of the planning process.

AN INTERVIEW WITH ROGER SINGLETON, CHIEF EXECUTIVE, BARNARDO'S

Barnardo's is the UK's largest children's charity, working with over 55,000 children, young people and their families on a continuing basis, as well as supporting many more through specific projects.

Barnardo's Vision: *Barnardo's believes that the lives of all children should be free from poverty, abuse and discrimination.*

Barnardo's Purpose: *To help the most vulnerable children and young people transform their lives and fulfil their potential.*

Roger Singleton has been Chief Executive of Barnardo's since 1984, having previously been the organisation's Deputy Director.

What are Barnardo's current priorities?
The organisation has three key objectives:

1   to achieve excellence in services to children and families – the best possible services within the resources available, bench-marked externally against other organisations' standards and achievements;
2   to pack more punch in influencing policy-makers on behalf of children and young people, campaigning and lobbying on the basis of our experience of working with families; and
3   to enable the participation of children and young people, listening to their views and acting on them.

These are the 'self-declared' objectives, the 'what we are going to do'. Then there's the 'how', where we have two challenges. First, 95 per cent of the population knows that Barnardo's work with children, but there are lingering misperceptions that we run homes or orphanages. Second, we face major challenges to generate the money we need. Currently our turnover is £150 million, of which £72 million comes from donations, legacies and fundraising – the remainder from statutory authorities in the form of fees and grants for services.

Our recently adopted five-year development plan draws attention to both the objectives above, and to the enabling conditions for these to occur. To succeed we need to maintain a strong commitment to our people, both staff and volunteers, addressing professional and personal development needs.

INTERVIEW

What environmental changes have had an effect on Barnardo's?

Since 1997 the Labour Government has taken positive steps in our field:

1   A policy commitment to eliminate child poverty over the next 20 years.
2   Prioritising the needs of younger children. There are now more opportunities for parents to access childcare so they can go to work (e.g. the Surestart initiative, in which Barnardo's is actively involved).
3   Improving the lives of young people in the public care system, although the energy invested in this seems to be on the wane.

The establishment of the Scottish Parliament and the Northen Ireland and Welsh Assemblies has also had an impact on our structural arrangements.

What are Barnardo's governance arrangements?

Barnardo's is a company limited by guarantee. The trustees comprise the board, which is responsible for our work throughout the UK. The Memorandum and Articles allow for a maxium of 30 board members, and there are currently 17. We would consider 20 to be an appropriate number. There are no external nominations, so we are free to build the board as we see fit.

We aim to have two board members from each of Scotland, Wales and Northern Ireland, the rest from England with a reasonable geographical spread (one from each of the English regions). However, when you're on the UK board there is a strong tradition that you look after the interests of Barnardo's as a whole, not your particular patch.

There is a Scottish Committee, Welsh Committee and Northern Ireland Committee; each includes the two trustees from that area, plus four others who have knowledge or influence in the area. The UK board delegates some responsibility to these committees, such as approval of the annual plan and some of the reporting requirements (inspection reports, health and safety, HR, complaints).

The Board is also supported by an Audit Committee, Investment Committee, Trading Committee, Nominations Committee, Remuneration Committee and an Adoption Committee (which considers issues arising from our status as an adoption agency).

What significant governance developments have occurred recently?
There have been changes to our governance processes and senior management structures to accommodate devolution in Scotland and Wales, and the establishment of the Northern Ireland Executive, in order to make our advocacy efforts in those areas more effective. Regionalisation has also had some effect in England, but with less far-reaching impacts.

Within the three nations and the six regions of England we are trying to bring together the different functions of Barnardo's so there's more integration. These functions include fundraising, IT, property, human resources and finance.

We have tried to make board membership a more transparent process, and now advertise to recruit trustees.

The board is less involved in managerial issues these days than it used to be. Board meetings consider financial reports, but focus on the bottom line, not on the details.

How is the board involved in planning?
At each board meeting we tackle one significant strategic issue, building up to the annual review/plan. The board also concerns itself with organisational views on key policy issues.

We hold an annual two-day residential meeting to address blue-sky issues – for example, should we continue to provide the breadth of services, or narrow the focus?

A development plan is prepared at five-yearly intervals; then annual updates or corrections are made in the light of internal and external influences.

As part of the process of implementing the current development plan we are working through issues with the assistance of six strategic planning groups, which are investigating current performance in relation to children's participation, excellent service, influencing and marketing, people, income generation and financial management. These groups report to the organisation's Strategy Board, which determines the proposals that should be put to the trustees.

What are the communications between Chair and Chief Executive?
The Chair has a formal meeting with the CEO once a month, plus
a phone update once a week. We have clearly defined roles, and
we both have a job description.

What advice would you give to a potential or new board member?
New board members should receive an induction that comprises
both information pack and personal meetings, and that is important. Additionally, my advice is:

- don't be too concerned if it takes time to familiarise yourself
  with the board and the organisation – it is an investment that
  is very necessary; and
- consider the value of a further induction after 9–12 months.
  There may be a range of topics you would want to explore
  with Chair, CEO or others once you have been through the
  initial process of settling in.

9 Marketing, advocacy and fundraising

Marketing

Most marketing staff shudder at the thought of board involvement in marketing. Everyone thinks they know how to improve the organisation's efforts to reach the marketplace. It is an area that, more than most, tempts the board member into tunnelling away at the detail, without any clear view of the strategic issues. But when this occurs, it may be the CEO and marketing staff who are to blame – because the board has not been educated in either the bigger picture issues (particularly in an industry which may not be their sphere of expertise), nor in strategic marketing approaches. Small wonder they ask about the advertising schedules or poster sites – the tangibles they can comprehend.

In many non-profits it is unusual for a marketing representative to be present at board meetings. In most for-profit organisations this would be regarded as a bizarre omission. If there is one fundamental success factor for the commercial organisation it is that sales must be achieved – and sales depend upon effective competitive positioning in the marketplace. It is all about marketing.

In successful for-profit organisations the selection and development of products and services is considered to be an integral part of marketing. In many non-profits the products or services are chosen, then 'marketing' is used to sell them. The marketing function is sometimes interpreted only as a publicity and promotion function, divorced from product/service choice or development.

This is not to say there are no differences between marketing in a for-profit and marketing in a non-profit environment. Because many non-profit services are provided below cost price or free to the customer/beneficiary, the non-profit organisation lacks the final arbiters of market demand or profitability, and this clearly has implications for marketing objectives. However, in some cases this has led to marketing being afforded a lower status than is wise, and to the absence of a strong customer focus. Whether it is the chicken or the egg, the most successful non-profit organisations are often characterised by a strong and mature marketing function, and a clear customer focus. They know how important it is. They know too that marketing is a valuable servant, not a master.

There are a number of definitions of marketing in the for-profit world, and there is one definition that seems to capture particularly well the scope of marketing in the non-profit world:

> 'Marketing is a way to harmonise the needs and wants of the outside world with the purposes and the resources and the objectives of the institution.'[1]

This recognises that the non-profit is driven by a number of factors that influence the choice of products and services, other than shareholder value. It also implies that there has to be a bringing together of the services and the customers, not through a process of compromise, but in a way that satisfies organisational and individual needs.

While the primary customers for a non-profit are the service recipients, there are other constituencies whose needs must be met. These may include:

- **Government:** in return for funding there may be clear targets or service levels which have been contractually agreed.
- **Members:** there may be a support base that is separate from (but possibly overlapping with) the service recipients.
- **Sponsors and donors:** some of whom may have laid down clear expectations of the return expected for their investment or support.
- **Partners:** the non-profit may have alliances with other organisations.
- **Volunteers.**
- **Staff.**

The primary market is the service recipients, and these may sub-divide into a number of market segments – groups or constituencies characterised by different sets of needs.

In some cases, the marketing needs of these constituencies will be confined to the area of communications. In other cases there may be implications for the priority afforded to particular services or programmes.

---

[1] Philip Kotler, quoted in Peter F Drucker, *Managing the Non-Profit Organisation*, Butterworth-Heinemann Ltd (Oxford, 1992), p63.

The marketing plan

Whether the board is involved in the development of the marketing plan will depend partly on the balance of board and staff skills. If there are dedicated marketing staff the board can take an arms-length approach, focusing only on the top-level issues and ultimately approving and adopting the plan when it is presented.

9.1 Contents of a marketing plan

Current marketing situation	data on current markets, services, marketing activities, recent results, competition
Internal analysis	strengths and weaknesses of current marketing operation (and other internal factors which affect the marketing operation)
External analysis	environmental factors and trends or changes anticipated: social and demographic changes, competition, cultural change
Objectives	both marketing (e.g. achieving specific outcomes with specific market segments, or achieving brand enhancement) and financial. Some call 'objectives' 'outcomes' or 'strategic intents' and couch the wording differently – but the function is the same: what do we want to have seen happen in three or five years' time?
Strategy	broad approach of marketing programme, including use of marketing 'tools' (*see Strategy Statement*, p142). There will also be specific strategies related to each objective
Action programmes	what will be done, when, by whom and at what cost
Budgets	resources to be devoted to implementation of the action programmes
Performance measures	how will results be monitored

In relation to marketing planning, the board should:

- require formal marketing planning, integrated with the organisation's strategic plan;
- confirm the primary marketing objectives;
- endorse the selection of key target groups (ensuring they are in line with the core business of the organisation);

- help to resolve conflicts in strategic priorities (e.g. investment in reaching one target group over another);
- ensure that the organisation's policies and priorities adopted can be realistically sustained by the organisation's marketing activity (i.e. ensure that there is not a gap between the service aspirations and the marketing resources);
- endeavour to include strategic marketing expertise amongst the board's collective strengths.

In turn the marketing representative in close liaison with the CEO has these responsibilities to the board:

- maintain a selective information flow to the board to help them become familiar with programmes or projects and key messages;
- supply regular sales or activity reports (compared with budget and agreed targets) with accompanying commentary, and occasionally copy press coverage to keep the board up to date with media coverage and issues;
- alert the board to anything that is negatively, or positively, affecting the reputation of the organisation;
- supply regular evaluations of market research results relating to programmes or projects – perhaps requesting one board meeting each year to focus on strategic marketing issues;
- educate the board on marketing concepts, e.g. the scope of marketing, positioning and branding, growth vector analysis (levels of risk in reaching new audiences/launching new products or services).

There is one area where the board should be especially analytical. When the CEO or marketing representative proposes new services or new markets, it is important for these to be rigorously evaluated. Many commercial organisations have made the mistake of over-extending their operations, either by moving too far in relation either to product or service development, or to new customer groups, or sometimes in relation to both. The 'safest' territory is to be supplying existing services to existing markets. The riskiest is new services to new markets. The growth vector diagram on the next page characterises the range of variations on this.

NEW MARKET	Market development	Market extension	Conglomerate diversification
EXPANDED MARKET	Aggressive promotion	Market segmentation Product differentiation	Vertical diversification
EXISTING MARKET	Market penetration	Product variants/ imitations	Product line extension
	PRESENT PRODUCTS	IMPROVED PRODUCTS	NEW PRODUCTS

Figure 9a Growth vector analysis

Where service or market extensions are proposed, the board should be satisfied that there are clear, costed plans to implement these. This is not to encourage conservatism, but to impose a sense of discipline in an area of development that can easily bring an organisation to grief. In the healthy organisation, this will be a fairly regular area of debate, because it will be seeking to maximise its impact through service and market development.

9.2 Marketing strategy statement

Statement of target market/s: which are the main constituencies (or primary market) we are trying to reach?

Positioning: how do we want to be perceived as an organisation – what image or brand characteristics are we trying to convey?

Product: what are we offering, and what distinguishes our 'offer' from those of other organisations?

Price: what do we charge, how do we differentiate, what is our pricing 'philosophy'?

Place or Distribution: where do we make contact with our market/s, what are the physical points of connection?

Service/style: what characterises our contact with customers/service users – speed, courtesy, efficiency, friendliness, warmth?

Promotion: how do we communicate with our customers/service users – advertising, direct mail?

Market research: what research do we undertake, how do we stay in touch with any shifts in perceptions of our organisation?

Advocacy

The board has a valuable advocacy role to play because its members will have credibility in a number of areas of the community, and may be influential in a number of sectors, where the CEO holds less sway. Moreover, the job of advocacy is so broad that a larger team effort will achieve more. Consider the constituencies listed above that the organisation needs to communicate with and influence, and add press and other media, and local and national politicians to the list. In organisations with no dedicated marketing staff, this places huge demands on the CEO, and even where there are marketing staff, the extended networks that the board can deploy will be of great benefit.

To be an effective advocate, the board member needs to be motivated. The passion and enthusiasm the CEO can express about the organisation is a great motivator, along with the encouragement of the Chair.

The board member needs to be properly informed – on programmes, issues, future plans, problem areas, and the shopping list of 101 projects and capital improvements that the organisation has in mind. The kinds of questions board members need to be able to answer with confidence are:

- What are we doing as an organisation?
- What are we planning to do?
- What key developments have happened recently?
- What is our competition?
- What are we seeking money for?
- Where do we find out more?

Avoid maverick behaviour. It is important for board members to get the message that the CEO and the Chair are the key spokespeople (unless there is a designated Press Officer). The organisation's external communications must be consistent, so board members should follow these guidelines:

1 Check your facts with the CEO.
2 Report back significant queries or coverage.
3 Report back any contacts made.
4 Be calm in times of trouble.
5 Be positive – always.

9.3 Cue cards

The General Manager of one major cultural organisation helped to ensure that the board members stayed on-song by providing each of them with an identical set of a dozen prompt cards, which were renewed on a monthly basis.

Each card had a set of facts or other information that covered key messages the organisation wanted to disseminate. One contained some recent press quotes, the next contained the programme for the next twelve months, the next contained a list of key equipment purchases the organisation was aiming for, and another contained an overview of financial results for the last five years.

The cards were small enough to carry in a pocket, and succinct enough for board members to brief themselves when opportunities arose to spread the word about the organisation's work and aspirations.

The board can be an extension of the public relations function of the organisation, if used in the right way. If there is an unforeseen crisis the board will be far more effective and easier to mobilise if they are accustomed to advocacy as a normal responsibility.

Board members marketing and advocacy responsibilities

✔ Be familiar with programmes and key messages

✔ Network on behalf of the organisation

✔ Defer to official spokespeople (CEO, Chair, Press Officer), rather than communicating independently on behalf of the organisation

✔ Delegate all marketing operational detail to staff via the CEO

✔ Be familiar with sales reports and market research results, and be alert for income downturns or shortfalls against budget – seek explanations from the CEO about the causes for these

✔ Avoid becoming over-exercised about publicity material (too often a matter of personal taste), although matters of legality, propriety and truthfulness are legitimate board concerns

✔ As your organisation has competitors, respect confidentiality with regard to marketing and promotional strategies

Fundraising

Some of the American literature on boards presses strongly for the active involvement of board members in the fundraising process. With the rallying cry 'Give, Get or Get Off', board members are exhorted to make personal donations, solicit their contacts to do so, or to leave the board. It is hard to say how far this philosophy is fulfilled in reality – certainly there is a gentler counter-cry, 'Wealth, Wisdom or Work', recognising that not all board members are rich or well-connected, but they may have other things to bring to the organisation – in the form of wisdom (expertise, knowledge) or their time and effort.

Outside the US, Government plays a more active role in providing funds to sustain activities undertaken by non-profit organisations. Partly because of this cultural difference, most boards in the UK would consider the concept of 'Give, Get or Get off' as anathema. Many board members are alienated by fundraising, and feel uncomfortable at the thought that they are expected to bring, and use, their connections (or resentful that they are devalued for not moving in the 'right' circles). Yet the board clearly does have a responsibility to ensure that the organisation is properly resourced, whether from Government or from private sector sources. Without resources, none of the programmes or activities can take place.

In a number of Western countries, individual giving is expected to increase very significantly over the next decade or so – principally because of the huge transfer of wealth to the baby-boomer generation. They are bigger spenders than their parents – and many are seeking meaning through association with religious, environmental, cultural, welfare and other good causes.

This represents a significant opportunity for all those in the non-profit sector. Success will depend upon the professionalism of the fundraising function, the investment of appropriate resources, and the capacity to build strong and enduring relationships with donors.

The board member's involvement in fundraising can occur at a number of levels.

Strategy

First, as with marketing, the board can and should require the organisation to have a fundraising strategy, however simple or sophisticated. It is important to be clear about the parameters and objectives of the organisation's fundraising activities, the strategies to be adopted, and the resources to be devoted to this aspect of the operations.

Marketing is an essential component of fundraising – some would say fundraising is a marketing activity ('selling' benefits to donors in return for their support and, more obviously, selling 'benefits' to corporate sponsors in return for their investment). The fundraising strategy, therefore, may be expected to share similarities with the marketing strategy.

9.4 Content of a fundraising strategy

The fundraising strategy should address the organisation's approach to securing resources from individual giving, donations, support from grant-making trusts or Foundations, corporate help-in-kind, corporate sponsorship and partnerships. Some would include Government support within the strategy also. The strategy might include:

Principles and values	there may some areas of fundraising, or perhaps some industry sectors, which are inappropriate for your organisation to be associated with. These should be identified and discussed at an early stage, to avoid wasted energy, or embarrassments, further down the track. They can be summarised in a statement of principles
Donor market	a map of the range of donors which may be accessible to your organisation (what type, how many, what track record for giving/sponsorship), the degree of competition by other fund seekers
Analysis of current situation	*internally:* your fundraising resources, strengths and weaknesses, the quality of your products and services and your overall organisational reputation, the level of fundraising skill, the range of contacts (including board contacts)
	externally: current and likely future competition, and your relative strength to competitors, economic growth or downturn, industry trends
Objectives	what you are aiming to achieve in relation to success in different areas of donor development, resourcing for particular developments, and financial targets
Strategies	the principal ways in which these objectives will be achieved
Action programmes	what will be done, when, by whom and at what cost
Resources	personnel, equipment, financial support to implement the fundraising strategy
Performance monitoring	how progress and results will be monitored

Before any forms of fundraising are explored, the organisation must ensure that its earned income is being maximised. The organisation that is actively pursuing its markets, and securing fee income where that is appropriate, is not only increasing the size of the cake, but also making itself more attractive to donors and sponsors. Success breeds success; hence the primacy of marketing in this chapter.

The board should ensure that *all* avenues of resourcing are considered and weighed, to identify those that are most likely to yield results, and to be cost-effective in terms of staff time invested. The sources of income may include:

- a grant from a central government department;
- a grant from a quasi-governmental agency (such as the Arts Council);
- a grant from local government;
- a contract with one of the above to deliver a specified service;
- a contract with another body (perhaps a commercial organisation or another voluntary agency) to deliver a service;
- support from individuals through membership or donations, and legacy income (eventually);
- support from individuals raised through collections, fundraising and entertainment events and activities;
- grants from foundations and other grant-making bodies;
- support from companies (in-kind, sponsorship, facilities, skills, secondments);
- support from individuals in the form of their time (as volunteers).[2]

Which of these may prove fruitful will depend on the services or product of the non-profit organisation, its track record in fundraising or 'development', and the time and resources available.

Some board members are tempted to encourage or pressure staff to pursue sponsorship at the expense of other sources of income. It seems more familiar, and they are frustrated that their organisation doesn't seem to be getting a fair slice of the pie. If only sponsorship were as easy as slicing pie!

Contacts and advocacy

A second way in which the board may play a part in fundraising is opening up contacts and networks. Every fundraiser (or 'Development Officer', as they are often called) will look to the board for this. Through the board members' business and social networks there may be knowledge or contacts that can be of help to the organisation – local firms that are in a growth period, individuals who may be interested in the organisation's work. The assertive Development Officer (or fundraising savvy CEO) will prise open the board's address books and secure a dozen names from each of them. It is a practical way in which the board can help.

When approaches are made to potential donors or sponsors that are known to a board member, a personal note appended to the formal

---

[2] List adapted from Sam Clarke, *The Complete Fundraising Handbook*, 1st edn. Directory of Social Change (London, 1992), pp25–6.

written approach from the CEO or fundraiser can be powerful. It may be a simple as 'Jane, hope you'll give this careful consideration'. It is the personal point of contact that counts.

When the organisation arranges site visits or 'cultivation' events for prospective donors, board members can swell the ranks of hosts and well-informed supporters of the organisation – especially when there are guests that are known to them.

Structures

There are differing opinions on the most appropriate Committee structures for fundraising.

A major capital appeal (a new wing of a hospital, a new church, an addition to an university campus) will certainly require a dedicated Appeal Committee chosen for its connections, willingness to work hard, and ability to personally donate to the cause.[3] However, a continuing process of fundraising for general revenue or specific projects may be handled:

- directly by the board;
- by a sub-committee established solely to oversee and assist in fundraising;
- by an independent Foundation, possibly with some main board members also comprising Foundation board members.

9.5 In-house or independent?

Advantages of a separate fundraising body

The advantages of a separate legal entity, dedicated to fundraising for the benefit of the parent body, include:

- the focus created by a 'single issue' organisation;
- the opportunity to secure the support and involvement of a dedicated group of individuals with appropriate corporate contacts and personal networks;
- the opportunity to keep capital/endowment funds separate from the parent body's general operational finances.

continued

---

[3] Marion Allford's *Charity Appeals: The Complete Guide to Success*, JM Dent & Sons Ltd (London, 1993), is an exhaustive guide to the process of planning and running a major appeal.

> **Disadvantages of a separate fundraising body**
>
> Two disadvantages of Foundation or independent status include:
>
> - the danger that the board of a separate entity could move in a different direction from the board of the parent organisation;
> - the challenge of securing coordinated effort and common purpose when the development activities are split between two organisations.
>
> In the case of one UK cultural organisation that I assisted, the assets had been vested in one body, while the operations were managed by a separate entity. Over time the boards of the two bodies diverged to the point where there were serious differences of view as to the future direction of the organisation. In this situation, the operating company found itself unable to progress, because it had no control over the asset base. Moreover, when it faced financial difficulties, it had no collateral to offer the bank to secure overdraft facilities.

Whether the fundraising sits within the main organisation or in a separate Foundation, the role of the board and the Chair is important. In the area of individual donations, it will often be personal approaches by board members that unlock the majority of individual giving. In some cases, nearly all donations come through this route.

Although time input varies, it is evident that Chairs typically give between half a day and two days per week in support of the fundraising function. The Chair's role may be described as:

- the principal door-opener to donations or sponsorship connections – that is, the Chair leads by example;
- the motivator of other board members;
- the partner of the professional member of staff with lead responsibility for the organisation's development/fundraising effort.

In my conversations with non-profit CEOs and board members, the energising of the development function was repeatedly described as coming from the Chair, whether of a separate Foundation, or of a subgroup (e.g. a Development Committee) within the main organisation. The Chair could not regard their role as purely a facilitator of meetings. It needed to be a hands-on role.

Resources

The fundraising resources of non-profit organisations vary widely. There are organisations (even quite large ones) where the board members themselves undertake most of the fundraising activity. Typically, a sub-group of the board, with corporate connections and expertise (and previous involvement in fundraising or sponsorship), will form an independent task force and make direct approaches to prospective targets, with appropriate support from the CEO.

In other organisations there will be a dedicated Development Officer, or a larger Development Department, where specific donor-segments may be targeted by different officers (e.g. 'corporate', 'major gifts', 'international').

When a non-profit has no fundraising staff but wants to embark upon the road to Development, it is not unusual for the board initially to consider the engagement of a fundraiser on a contract basis. Some board members will propose that the fundraiser could be paid on a commission basis, that is, paid only on results. There are a couple of practical problems with this. First, if an independent fundraiser is engaged by other clients on a fixed fee or time-based fee, they will naturally give much higher priority to these clients than to an organisation that is remunerating them only on success. Secondly, most fundraising professional associations oppose commission-based fundraising, and their member code of conduct precludes it – largely because it would encourage the fundraiser to prioritise those donations that will be most lucrative for them, not those that may be best for the organisation. There is no such thing as a free fundraiser.

Resource 6 (pp291–2) contains summary advice on the appointment of fundraising consultants, and refers to further guidance available from the Institute of Fundraising (formerly the Institute of Charity Fundraising Managers).

Generally, the most appropriate use of independent fundraisers is in building up and managing a major appeal. Even here, some of the leading fundraising firms seek to establish resources in-house within the non-profit organisation, so that their role comprises development of the overall strategy, building up the Development/Appeal department and then, progressively, taking a more back-seat role – available to provide advice and support. This recognises that the most powerful approaches to prospective donors are those that come from the organisation itself, not from professional fundraisers. By the same token, experienced fundraising consultants could be used to assist in establishing a permanent Development function within the non-profit organisation.

Those organisations that are experienced in fundraising know all too well that this is an area of activity which requires investment and long-term commitment. It is not a quick fix for a short-term budget problem. Effective fundraising (and sponsorship) depends upon building up relationships – a process of years not months. The board, therefore, will need to recognise this in the budgets it approves, and in the expectations it has of the staff or volunteers dedicated to this function. It will also influence the performance monitoring, in that progress towards financial success can be measured in targeted research, contacts made and negotiations begun, as well as in the handover of a cheque.

This is not to say that the board should shy away from proper concerns with cost-effectiveness. As with any other area of organisational planning, the choice of strategies and action programmes should be scrutinised to ensure these are the strongest lines to pursue, with the potential for a good return on investment.

A number of common success factors characterise the organisations with more effective fundraising track records:

- The significant role played by an active and carefully constructed board, who are willing to use their networks of contacts and, in some cases, to donate substantial sums personally.
- The essential leadership (and significant time input) needed from a committed Chair, who is also able and willing to deploy useful contacts and influence.
- The value of professional staff with previous development/fundraising experience.
- The importance of establishing clear development/fundraising objectives.
- The significance of a high quality product or services (in relation to the main/parent organisation's activities).
- The importance of understanding the motivation of individual donors, and progressively building close relationships between potential donors and the organisation.
- The importance of coordinating fundraising and development activity across all areas of the organisation.
- The supportive role which the CEO can play, in helping donors feel valued, motivating the board or Development Committee and assisting in sponsorship negotiations when appropriate.

■ A competitive attitude, recognising that fundraising and development require a will to succeed, regardless of short-term set-backs or frustrations.

Marketing and fundraising review

✔ Do board members understand the key strategic marketing issues facing the organisation?

✔ Are board members familiar with current and planned programmes and key developments?

✔ Do we have a media strategy for dealing with contentious issues, which clarifies who is responsible for media relations?

✔ Are board members contributing contacts and effecting introductions to assist with fundraising?

✔ Are board members attending donor-cultivation events?

✔ Do we have clear performance measures to assist in monitoring our progress in marketing and fundraising?

Summary

● The board should ensure there is a marketing plan, commensurate with the resources of the organisation.

● Ensuring the organisation is properly resourced is a key board responsibility.

● The board can play an especially valuable role in acting as advocates or ambassadors for the organisation.

● Up-to-date information, an understanding of key messages, and coordination all support the board's advocacy role.

● Through opening up contacts and networking the board can enhance the organisation's fundraising activities.

CASE STUDY: ENGLISH NATIONAL OPERA

Never think you need to apologise for asking someone to give to a worthy object

John D Rockefeller

When English National Opera began planning a major refurbishment of the Coliseum, the grand Edwardian theatre that has been its home for over 30 years, the trustees recognised that an injection of new energy into their ranks was necessary if the organisation was to achieve its fundraising target of £18 million. As the Chairman, John Baker, was approaching retirement they set out to find someone as his replacement who could provide vigour, focus and leadership.

Russell Willis Taylor, then Executive Director, knew exactly whom she wanted. Martin Smith was a merchant banker with a powerful track record of helping other arts organisations, including the Wigmore Hall, the South Bank Centre and the Orchestra of the Age of Enlightenment, where he had helped to raise significant sums. Taylor and Baker approached Smith and presented the opportunities that lay ahead for ENO and the role he could play in realising them. The capital project was clearly high on their agenda, and together they discussed the need for a Chairman who had the potential to raise significant funds, or the potential to make a leading gift – and preferably both. Smith agreed to join the board as Chairman, and to encourage the board to take the lead in securing the funds for the refurbishment. To reinforce this, he personally pledged to make a major gift prior to assuming his position in April 2001.

Having had preliminary discussions with key board members and potential donors, Martin Smith opened his first board meeting by acknowledging the magnitude of the task ahead. 'We need to raise £18 million,' he said. 'There is simply no way we have the authority to do this unless each of us gives, and collectively we give at least £7 million.'

He promptly set about making sure that he and the board would be properly supported, by recruiting a Campaign Director with whom he had worked at the Wigmore Hall. Emily Stubbs had previously worked for ENO and was therefore familiar with many of the trustees and other donors. She and Smith agreed which of them should approach the other trustees to discuss their contributions. As Smith's own gift had yet to be finalised, however, her first step was to take Martin Smith himself to one side and say, 'before I meet anyone else I need to know precisely how much you will give'. He said £1 million – more than he had ever given to any other cause. This set a clear precedent for his colleagues.

In the months that followed, the trustees were approached individually to discuss the campaign and the contribution they wished to make. Although initially some expressed reservations, in time they all came to share Smith's view that no board should expect a project of this scale to be achieved without the members' active participation and manifest support.

One year later, all the trustees had made a commitment, and collectively they had donated over £7.2 million. One trustee, Vernon Ellis, Chairman of management consultants Accenture, gave £5 million – one of the largest individual gifts to the arts in the UK. Another, MP Shaun Woodward, has given £1 million. Thus contributions reflected the textbook rule that 90 per cent of the funds will come from 10 per cent of the donors.

During the 1990s, competition for philanthropic support for the arts in London increased substantially, with three major arts institutions alone running appeals for between £50 million and £100 million. Without the board's public support at this level ENO's relatively small but vital campaign may not have registered on the philanthropic scale. Instead, the company has been able to sign contracts on time, as everyone concerned has been confident of success.

'We all want to be sure we're backing a winner. Why should we expect others who are not as close to the company as we are to give more?' asked Smith.

Case study prepared by Frankie Airey of Oxford Philanthropic

Case Study: What is a Fundraising Board?

For some boards fundraising for the organisation is one of their primary responsibilities, and a clearly stated expectation of all members. Others rely much more on their board to 'open up doors' for professional development officers. In many cases the expectation that the board has a specific role to play in fundraising is a recent phenomenon.

Mr Ian Donaldson, Chair of the Leukaemia Foundation of Queensland, does not see his board as a 'fundraising' board in the sense in which the term is commonly used. In fact the organisation has resisted solely having members whose strength lies in their corporate connections. It is anticipated that the newly formed national body, Leukaemia Foundation Australia, will have within its charter a remit to engage with national and international corporations, whereas its State-based members such as the Leukaemia Foundation of Queensland will continue to raise funds from State-based sources.

Ian sees the composition of the board of the Leukaemia Foundation of Queensland as a reflection of its stage of evolution, and therefore board members include representatives of the medical fraternity, nursing and other patient support service providers, branches of the foundation, corporate supporters, and families who have had a member suffer from leukaemia. Yet in their own ways, nearly every single member of the current board of the Leukaemia Foundation of Queensland plays a role in fundraising, including:

- the Chair, through 'opening doors', and as Chair of the fundraising committee;
- the Deputy Chair, through being one of the founding members of the organisation, being an advocate for the foundation in his local community (fundraising) organisation, and (at the age of 80) still travelling throughout the State to attend and address different branch functions;
- a medical officer, who brought to the attention of the committee a patient's idea of 'head shaving' to raise money for research – an idea which now raises more money each year than any other fundraising event;
- two branch representatives, both actively involved in grassroots fundraising at branch level; and
- a professional member who has hosted cocktail functions.

Furthermore, a former board member raised over AUS$1 million for the Foundation over a period of 11 years through running flea markets!

There are, then, many ways in which a board might define its role in relation to fundraising.

AN INTERVIEW WITH LYNETTE MOORE, EXECUTIVE DIRECTOR, ALZHEIMER'S ASSOCIATION VICTORIA

Dementia is set to become a *major* health issue. By 2016 it is predicted to be the greatest health burden for women – ahead of cancer, heart disease and strokes.

Lynette Moore has been Executive Director of Alzheimer's Association Victoria for five years, and during that time has also worked closely with the national organisation, Alzheimer's Australia.

What is the story of the Association?

The Association started in 1983 as an entirely volunteer-resourced body. Over time, a process of professionalisation occurred. I would characterise Alzheimer's Association Victoria now as a 'young adult' organisation. It still retains significant volunteer input – there are 60 active volunteers – but the stakes are much higher than in its early days, with a turnover of $4 million and 50 paid staff.

The Association's work divides between advocacy and policy development, raising awareness in the community, and providing counselling, support and education services.

Each State and Territory has its own Association, and there is a national body, Alzheimer's Australia. Dealings with Federal Government are now handled through that national body. In addition to running the Victorian Association, I am an active participant in Alzheimer's Australia. The Victorian Association is also contracted to provide financial services to the national body, taking advantage of the qualified staff available.

Where does the income come from?

Eighty per cent of the Association's income comes from Government (55 per cent State, 25 per cent Federal); the remaining income is secured through fundraising. Although the Association secured a six-figure donation shortly after I started as Executive Director (a coincidence!), bequests and major donations are rare. There is a lot more work to do on building up fundraising strategy. In Victoria, where there are a disproportionate number of Australia's trusts and foundations, the opportunities are greater than elsewhere. Currently, we have two full-time fundraising staff, plus part-time support for data entry.

What are the key issues currently facing the organisation?
Ensuring that the Federal and State Governments focus on research to examine prevention, cure or inhibiting the progress of the disease; and ensuring Government responds to the huge increase in numbers that are likely to have the disease in the near future, as a result of the ageing population.

What is the structure of your board?
Alzheimer's Association Victoria currently has ten board members, although the Constitution allows for up to fifteen. I report to the board and, in turn, four senior managers report to me. There are four Executive members of the board: President, Vice President, Treasurer and Secretary – effectively this group acts as a finance and audit committee. By scrutinising the finances closely, they are able to talk about financial issues at board meetings. There are no standing committees (other than this Executive group). There are, however, task forces, the most important of which is responsible for the major building redevelopment, our extended headquarters, which is currently taking place.

The board meets eleven times each year – for some there are additional subcommittee or task force responsibilities, but it is rare for board members to be called upon beyond this.

What are the main issues the board is dealing with?
The greatest issues facing the board relate to securing resources – but the practicalities of addressing this tend to fall to the staff. With the projected growth in dementia, resource issues are only going to increase.

There is also a task force addressing documentation of board policies, and clarifying the role of the board. The board members do have a duty statement, but it needs reviewing. Formalising some of the board's processes and policies needs to be dealt with.

Before I arrived, there had already been a shift towards a more strategic focus by the board. The board is noticeably more concerned with legal and fiduciary responsibilities than it was a few years ago. There is an increasing scrutiny of insurance, health and safety and financial matters.

What is the board's involvement in strategic planning?

Planning is a joint effort between staff and board. The previous plan was initiated with the board identifying broad strategies through a workshop process, then passing it on to the staff to progress the detail. This didn't result in a high sense of ownership by staff, so the most recent planning process started with a staff workshop, attended by some board members, with the results being taken up to the full board subsequently. After the board had reviewed the staff's planning work, the process was passed back to the staff for completion. The strategic plan is now reviewed on an annual basis, with six-monthly progress reports.

How would you like to see the board develop?

Ideally, I would like to see the board as fundraising champions for the organisation. The current composition of the board brings high quality professional experience, but not necessarily the connections (or experience) that will deliver fundraising results. Beyond this, I see the board as challenging the organisation's thinking, questioning its role, pushing the Association to think big and look five to ten years down the track.

I wonder sometimes whether I have engaged the board sufficiently as Executive Director – the downside of discouraging board involvement in operational matters is the risk of distancing them from the organisation as a whole.

How do you see the link between Executive Director and Chair?

I look to the Chair to provide support, a sounding board for ideas, and feedback. It's important also to have the opportunity to raise sensitive issues in private with the Chair before they are raised in the more public arena of a board meeting. In turn, I see it as my responsibility to keep the Chair fully aware of issues that may be coming up. I regard the relationship between myself and the board as harmonious – partly because of good communication, partly because I am given clear direction.

What would be your advice to a new board member?

Make sure you really have the commitment – both emotional and practical. It takes time to do the board's job properly.

PART 3

BOARD PROCESSES

10 Effective board meetings

Nothing is more frustrating than spending a year on a board and, at the end of it, sitting down and racking one's brains to think whether one has had any effect whatsoever

Sir John Harvey Jones

Why have meetings?

Meetings can make or break a board. Attendance at a series of undirected or ill-prepared meetings can sap the energy and enthusiasm of the most positive-spirited board member or CEO. Equally, in my experience, attendance at a series of purposeful and well-organised meetings can build the organisation's sense of direction, and motivate the board members and staff involved.

The formal business of the board is predominantly conducted through meetings. The organisation's constitution or articles will specify a minimum number of times that the board must meet during a year because, for the most part, it is only in group sessions that group decisions can be made appropriately – even if there are provisions for emergency action by the Chair, or decisions made by group e-mail or circularised note. The principles for effective meetings contained in this chapter are related to full meetings of the board, but are generally applicable to smaller sub-committee meetings too.

The constitution lays down specific requirements with regard to calling board meetings, the minimum frequency of board or management committee meetings per year, and the recording of minutes.

The normal purposes of a non-profit organisation's board meetings are:
1 to receive information;
2 for the CEO to consult the board on specific issues;
3 to formulate policy;
4 to make decisions which are beyond the remit of the CEO;
5 to monitor progress.

Planning the meeting

The ingredients for an effective meeting include:

- an agenda;
- preparation by Chair and CEO;
- appropriate papers supplied, and read, in advance;
- a suitable physical environment;
- competent chairing;
- cooperative board members;
- useful minutes;
- de-briefing;
- appropriate frequency and duration;
- a manageable size of board.

The agenda is a tool for managing the meeting. It needs to be prepared and circulated at least a week ahead of the meeting, along with any papers that have been prepared. There are a number of ways in which the agenda can be optimised:

1 Structure it to give priority to key issues, rather than adopting a standard format from one meeting to the next. This carries the danger of routine items always being dealt with early and strategic or developmental issues being dealt with later when energy levels are low, or being deferred for lack of time.

2 Similarly, divide the agenda clearly between policy development and strategic issues, and monitoring/reporting routines. This helps to ensure that appropriate time is devoted to bigger picture issues rather than falling into the temptation of attending to the detail which sits within board members' comfort zones.

3 Adopt the convention of identifying those items on the agenda which are for information only, those which are for discussion, and those which require a decision and subsequent action. This helps to clarify the status of each item, and alerts the board member to concentrate on the decision-making items.

4 Against specific items on the agenda, identify whether anyone is making a report (and who), and if there are any relevant background briefing papers appended or to follow.

5 Remind everyone when and where the meeting is.

Board papers and preparation

Regardless of the person who first drafts the agenda, it should be agreed between the Chair and the CEO, even if it is, strictly, a board prerogative.

At the time of drafting there should be some consideration of the relevant importance of individual items, especially where there are policy implications, to assist the Chair in managing the meeting appropriately. Papers for circulation should be ready for circulation with the agenda – but if any are not, or if the Chair feels some additional material is needed to inform or guide the board, it is better to circulate them closer to the time of the meeting than to table them at the meeting. If reports are tabled at the meeting, or just delivered verbally, this will usually result in the board sitting passively while staff provide them with information that they could and should have been given prior to the meeting.

It should be assumed that any papers that have been supplied a few days in advance have been read. If in doubt, a show of hands will indicate whether or not a majority have read the papers – if they have, the Chair can proceed accordingly. If a minority of board members have read the papers then a verbal report may be necessary to initiate discussion, if the item needs to be resolved at the present meeting. The reasons why the papers had not been read should be explored, perhaps later in the meeting, to ascertain whether there were avoidable factors at work.

The room should be reasonably comfortable, and free of distractions, with non-alcoholic refreshments available.

The Chair needs to provide appropriate leadership for the meeting. The role of the Chair is considered in a later chapter.

Minutes of the previous meeting should not await circulation with the next meeting's agenda, but should have been distributed within a few days of the last meeting – so that they act as a reminder of any actions which the board or CEO have agreed to undertake. The style of the minutes and the process for preparing them are a matter of judgement. Generally, minutes should not be prepared as a comprehensive record of a meeting for the benefit of absentees, but as a succinct reminder for those who were present. Decisions need to be clearly recorded, along with proposing, seconding and voting details on the occasions when formal votes take place. The draft minutes should go to the Chair for checking before they are distributed. However, they can only be approved at the next meeting.

When complex or sensitive matters are under consideration there is a case for holding a de-briefing session between the Chair and CEO a few days after the meeting. Chairs of relevant sub-committees, if there are any, could also be involved in this. The purpose is to ensure that everyone is quite clear on the actions that need to take place before the next meeting. This has the merit of discouraging detailed consideration of implementation issues within the board meeting, but the disadvantage of taking up yet more time.

How do we rate our board meetings?

Criteria	Always	Usually	Rarely	Never
Is there a high level of attendance?				
Do we have the right mix of skills and experience?				
Is the agenda well prepared?				
Are we clear on the decisions we are required to take?				
Are supporting papers distributed in advance?				
Do board members do their homework?				
Do we have a good balance between routine monitoring and more strategic, long-range issues?				
Does the Chair manage the meeting effectively?				
Do the meetings run to time?				
Is the atmosphere constructive?				
Does everyone contribute?				
Are decisions taken with proper evidence and well-structured debate?				
Do decisions receive the support of the whole board?				
Do we review our meeting processes periodically?				

Timing and frequency

While the constitution will lay down a minimum number of board meetings in the year, there is no point meeting so frequently that there is little for the board to discuss or decide, nor so infrequently that you continually fail to address all the agenda items. Meetings should be scheduled on a day and at a time that is convenient for most of the board members. They should be timed so that all business can be completed before members are obliged to leave because of other commitments or sheer exhaustion, otherwise, there is a danger that important decisions are devolved to a small caucus of members. Whatever timing is chosen for meetings, towards the end of the calendar or fiscal year, the meetings for the whole of the next year should be scheduled, to give busy board members plenty of notice.

Large boards may be necessary in some organisations, but there is an inverse relationship between size and manageability – larger boards tend to enjoy less critical or in-depth debate, require a high degree of formality in their proceedings, and give the individual less opportunity to contribute.

Periodically, the board should consider:

- whether the frequency, timing and duration of meetings are still appropriate;
- the style and detail of minutes, and arrangements for their preparation;
- the papers which board members wish to receive, their structure and level of detail; brevity is a virtue – and board members will often need signposts to the most important issues or options.

I always try to bear in mind the need to avoid burdening the CEO and staff with inessential paperwork, and the need for the CEO to spend the great majority of their time getting the organisation's business done, not keeping the board happy. In fact, getting the organisation's business done should be the primary stimulus of board satisfaction.

To maintain a sense of purpose and focus for each board meeting, it can help to map out some of the key meetings for the year. For example, the timing of when next year's budget has to be adopted is predictable; in turn, that dictates the timing for when the first draft of next year's budget should be seen by the board, which will need to be accompanied by an outline of the programmes and services which the budget reflects. Equally, if the board undertakes to approve an annual update of the organisation's Strategic Plan, or to start the planning process afresh, there may be a specific point in the year (ahead of the budget confirming process), which will be a logical time for this to occur. This raises the prospect of a 'cycle of meetings', where key decision-making and planning processes are scheduled well in advance, and which highlights those meetings where it may be possible or timely to devote more attention to policy development or other matters.

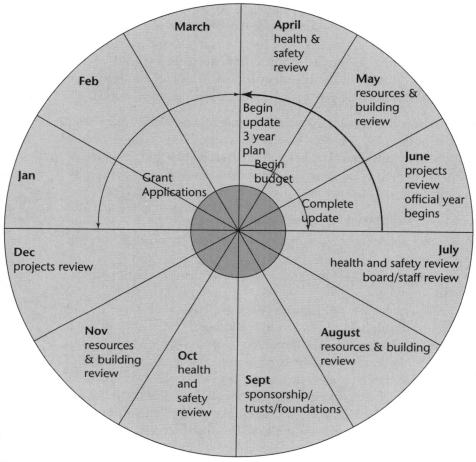

Figure 10a The cycle of meetings

The board member's contribution

Every board member can make a difference to the quality of the meeting. Consider what you can do for your Chair to help the meeting to be as effective as possible. This will include:

- attending and participating in the meeting, and arriving on time;
- agreeing to accept special assignments between meetings – so that substantive issues can be progressed without clogging up the meetings themselves;
- being willing to accept leadership roles, whether as an Officer of the board, or Chair of a sub-committee or task force – the whole weight of leadership cannot be carried by the Chair alone;

- developing a thorough knowledge of the organisation and the sector within which it operates – through background reading, asking questions of the CEO, and of other board members;
- reading carefully the board papers which you are sent in advance, and trying to resolve points of clarification before the meeting, where possible;
- listening carefully to what others are saying;
- being willing to question and challenge;
- being supportive of others' contributions;
- retaining your sense of humour – sometimes the issues under consideration are literally life and death matters, especially with non-profits operating in the health, emergency services or care for the elderly sectors, but most of the time the consequences of the board's decisions will not be as profound. This is worth remembering when the temperature is rising in a board debate;
- not interrupting or losing your temper (or tapping your pencil, or doodling conspicuously, or turning your back on the speaker, or slumping in your chair, or talking *sotto voce* to your neighbour . . . but see Box 10.1 on the following page);
- remaining loyal to decisions of the board – even where you may not have agreed with the decision. There needs to be a sense of collective responsibility for the board team to maintain mutual respect, and to continue working together positively;
- maintaining confidentiality with regard to board deliberations. The board as a whole may determine that summary minutes are circulated to non-board members, or that specific issues are communicated to staff or stakeholders – but it is not for the individual board member to do this;
- supporting the CEO, and not criticising him or her in front of staff;
- understanding the concept of fiduciary care, and being guided by it;
- avoiding conflicts of interest, and declaring them where they are unavoidable;
- suggesting future board members who may strengthen the organisation.

Other aspects of the individual board member's meeting behaviour will be covered in a role description and a code of conduct, which help to articulate the board members' mutual obligations and expectations. The role description might specify what proportion of the meetings you are expected to attend – or that you will voluntarily step down if you are unable to attend for a lengthy period.

10.1 Twenty ways to disrupt a meetings

The aim of this book is to make a positive contribution to the worth of not-for-profit boards. However, for the bloody-minded, here are some infallible tips for putting a spanner in the works of any board meeting. These are my favourites – you may have your own:

1 Arrive late
2 Interrupt
3 Talk too much
4 Be called away
5 Hold side discussions with your neighbours
6 Introduce red herrings
7 Stay silent
8 Fly off on tangents
9 Be too formal
10 Use aggressive body language (folded arms, back turned to the speaker)
11 Be rude
12 Yawn
13 Read other papers
14 Don't listen
15 Be pointlessly provocative
16 Pursue hidden agendas
17 Be emotional
18 Show disrespect
19 Use jargon
20 Be unprepared

Of course, if you observe any other board member deploying one or more of these techniques, a gentle tap on the shins may be called for.

Neither timidity nor aggression makes for good board debate. The middle way, assertive behaviour, is more effective and helps to build a functioning and enjoyable team.

Keep your contributions short: your point is more likely to be understood and to have impact if you keep it reasonably short.

Avoid interrupting others to make your contribution, and do not let others interrupt you: when more people follow the hint above, the whole business of interrupting is less of an issue.

Timing your contributions: if you want to influence a meeting, it is not just what you say that counts, but also when you say it. If you fail to raise a point at the *relevant* time, then its impact is diminished. If the board are on the verge of making a decision when you suddenly come up with your doubts or disagreements for the first time, then other people will be irritated ('Why didn't you say that earlier?').

Changing your mind: it can be assertive to do this, especially in the light of new information or better ideas coming up in the meeting.

Falling in with the majority: if you give yourself the right to make various contributions to a meeting, then you also have the responsibility to control your contributions so they help the meeting to progress. Because of this, it will sometimes be assertive to fall in with the majority.

Helping the Chair: sometimes the meeting's effectiveness would be improved if you were to influence the *behaviour* of other members, for example by:

- asking a member who has made a long 'speech' to summarise the main points;
- inviting a quiet member to contribute when you see he is trying (unsuccessfully) to get into the discussion;
- asking a member who is continually disagreeing what suggestion she has that she would like to see taken up by the meeting;
- asking the Chair for a summary, when you feel the meeting is getting bogged down;
- asking a colleague, whose non-verbal behaviour seems to indicate agreement or disagreement, to make their views known.

These are examples of influencing people's behaviour *for the better* – to be more helpful to the meeting. It is an area that is traditionally seen as the Chair's preserve. But if the Chair is not handling this side of things very well, you should try and help the meeting along. It is also crucial that you do not make too many contributions in this area; otherwise you will be seen as trying to take over the meeting. Once this happens, the quality of the content of your contributions will be overlooked and the 'suspected' motive behind your making them becomes the dominant issue to which others react.

A board member's checklist for the meeting

Before the Meeting

✔ Be sure you are clear on the decisions needed.
✔ Prepare more. Do your homework.
✔ Form a tentative judgement on all issues.
✔ Be aware of the particular customs, rules and etiquette for the meeting.

At the Meeting

✔ Approach the meeting and your board colleagues with a positive attitude.
✔ Arrive early.
✔ Separate facts from beliefs, look out for emotional build-ups, clarify agreement and disagreement, make people feel important, protect the integrity of the group and the individual members.
✔ As a participant, contribute early, clearly and often – but thoughtfully.
✔ Divide big problems into sub-problems, and address them separately whenever possible.
✔ Separate the problems discussed from the people discussing them.
✔ Make your own points clearly and concisely. Don't get lost in philosophy.
✔ Don't waste your bullets on issues not important to you. Know when to quit.
✔ Look for every opportunity to show courtesy and respect. Listen attentively and demonstrate your attention to others.
✔ Be there in mind as well as body – give one hundred per cent of yourself.

After the Meeting

✔ Follow up assignments quickly.

Board retreats or away days?

From time to time it is necessary for board members to gather to undertake a more thorough-going review and more detailed forward planning than is possible in the usual board meeting. A board retreat may be called to devote focused time to the planning process, to inform and educate the board on significant topical issues, to evaluative the board's own progress and contribution to the organisation, or to build the relationship between board members and between the board and CEO. Retreats can achieve all these things, but it is important to be clear on the objectives and to keep them at a realistic level.

It helps for the retreat to occupy at least a full day, and to incorporate informal sessions as well as structured working sessions – an overnight stay, or at least an evening meal, can help to achieve this. This is not only to prevent important issues being rushed, but to take advantage of the opportunity to build trust and understanding between board members – team 'capital' that can serve the organisation well in future board meetings.

It is valuable to have an independent facilitator to plan and run the retreat, for neutrality and for their facilitation expertise, but also because key players, such as the Chair and CEO, may not have the time to devote to detailed preparation.

In addition to meeting with the Chair and CEO to become familiar with the key issues to cover during the retreat, the facilitator might circulate a brief, confidential questionnaire to participants, to learn more about their aspirations and expectations for the retreat, and to be aware of any other issues that are priorities for board members. From this, and background documentation, the facilitator can map out a proposed schedule for the retreat, although this will not be applied as formally or inflexibly as an agenda.

One critical factor for a successful retreat is a high level of attendance. If key individuals are missing, there is a high risk that debate and decisions arrived at during the retreat will lack credibility when they are translated into subsequent formal board processes. The retreat is an opportunity for the whole decision-making team to share the same information at the same time.

The presence of staff at board retreats (and indeed at board meetings) is a question that exercises boards' minds from time to time. The retreat structure can allow for the board to have its own *in camera time* if necessary, as part of the process, but can also allow for staff with specialist knowledge or expertise to join the proceedings for part of the time. Normally, the CEO would be present for most or all of the retreat. In smaller organisations, and organisations which place a high value on consensual decision-making, it is not unusual for all staff to be present for most or all of the retreat. There are, however, two dangers in not having any time allocated for the separate board discussion: first, that board concerns about sensitive issues related to personnel may be suppressed; and second, that there will be tendency to pass on the actions and work that flow from the retreat to the staff, who are conveniently on-hand to receive it, rather than focusing on actions that the board should be taking themselves.

10.2 Planning a successful board retreat

- Develop appropriate goals for the retreat.
- Agree an attendance list (some personnel may be invited for part of the retreat only).
- Confirm the timing and location.
- Select a facilitator, if necessary, and any guest speakers who may contribute specialist input.
- Potentially, circulate a confidential questionnaire to participants to identify key issues.
- Commission any discussion documents to be circulated in advance.
- Prepare a detailed schedule for the retreat.
- Allow adequate time for summary and action planning towards the end of the retreat.
- Organise room layout, break rooms, refreshments, meals.
- Provide leadership for the follow-up from the retreat.

There are a few subsidiary issues which are likely to need resolving:

- Are board members paying for themselves, or is the organisation paying for them?
- Are partners/spouses to be invited?
- Apart from the CEO, are any other staff to attend?

Summary

- Purposeful meetings are important for morale as well as efficiency.
- Meetings should be actively planned by the Chair and CEO.
- Individual board members' behaviour can strongly influence the quality of the meeting.
- Independently facilitated board retreats can be valuable both for planning and for team building.
- Periodically, the board should review the frequency of its meetings, the nature of information supplied, and other meeting elements.

11 Committee structures

Form a team, not a committee

Mark McCormack

The principal reason for an organisation to establish or maintain sub-committees is to relieve pressure on the main board meetings. Where an issue requires regular close monitoring, or a new development demands detailed planning, it may be considered a poor use of board time to attend to this in the main meetings. But the board is under no obligation to establish sub-committees, and should consider carefully before they are initiated.

The establishment of a sub-committee creates an opportunity for the Chair to harness the energies of current board members by giving them specific areas of responsibility. It enables detailed board work to be undertaken by a small group, operating with less formality. It provides a mechanism to engage staff members who do not customarily attend board meetings, and to bring in outside advisers who may be considered future potential board members, subject to the organisation's normal election or co-option procedures. Finally, it enables leadership to be developed within the board, spreading responsibility for convening and chairing meetings.

None of these benefits provides a good enough reason to set up sub-committees unless there is a compelling need, because sub-committees present some significant disadvantages too:

- They are time-consuming, both for board and staff.
- They can usurp the authority of the main board, because of the natural tendency to adopt their reports uncritically (fellow board members have given up their time to work on this issue – we wouldn't want to give them too hard a time when they report back to the main board).
- Their terms of reference and level of decision-making authority may not be clearly defined, resulting in time wasting or confusion.
- They may lead to the development of two-tier board membership, with those not on sub-committees feeling alienated from the 'real' business.

- They may gain a life of their own – beyond the task that was set for them.

11.1 Too many committees

One of the conclusions of my first board retreat was that the range of issues to be tackled over the next year or so could not be achieved by the main board alone. Discussion followed on what sub-committees might be formed to share the load, and relieve pressure on the main board meeting. Within an hour, eight sub-committees had been established – ranging from finance, employment and premises to marketing and programme development.

In the following months it became very clear that the amount of staff and board time required to service and attend these sub-committees outweighed their practical value. The number of sub-committees was reduced to four, one of which was charged with disbanding once it had completed its time-limited task.

These are not uncommon problems. It is wise for sub-committees to be given a time-limited task where possible, and to have their terms of reference or brief, and their reporting process to the main board, set out clearly.

In larger organisations, there is likely to be a need for continuing or 'standing' sub-committees, for example covering finance or employment. In smaller organisations, it may be possible for all the board's business to be transacted at main meetings, with occasional working groups or task forces to deal with specific issues as they arise. See Box 11.2 on the following page.

11.2 A menu of sub-committees

Some types of sub-committee which may be considered include:

Sub-committee	Parameters
Finance	To oversee the organisation's finances, examine proposed budget, review monthly or quarterly management accounts, consider the authorities given to staff to incur expenditure. In a small non-profit these tasks might be undertaken by a Treasurer.
Audit	Periodically to review the organisation's financial procedures and legal compliance – ensure there are proper controls in place to minimise risk exposure. Most common in commercial organisations, but relevant for non-profits also. See p96 for further comment.
Investment	To oversee the control of the organisation's investments. In some organisations this might be an additional responsibility of the finance sub-committee.
Governance	To maintain the health and effectiveness of the board (see *Assessing and Improving the Board*, p247), including board recruitment, induction and evaluation; sometimes concerned also with planning an annual board retreat, and alerting board members to training opportunities.
Nominating	A sub-sector of the 'governance' committee's remit, focusing on recruitment and induction of new board members.
Programme	To oversee the organisation's service range and quality, and review proposed programmes and projects; monitoring programme evaluations; prepare policy recommendations regarding future programme directions. Those boards which believe policy-setting is their key purpose are unlikely to delegate this to a sub-committee.
Marketing	Oversight of marketing, press and public relations activities. Given that advocacy is an important board contribution, this may also encompass coordination of the board's advocacy activities.
Fundraising or 'development'	To oversee the sponsorship and fundraising activities of the organisation, contribute contacts and effect introductions for staff charged with fundraising or development, assist in preparing fundraising policies and strategies. Some experienced Development Officers do not welcome the delegation to a sub-committee, preferring to stress that the full board has responsibility for ensuring the organisation is properly resourced.
Personnel or employment	The development of employment policies, and potentially court-of-appeal within disciplinary or grievance procedure.

Particular industry sectors will give rise to other specialist sub-committees also – collections management for museums, curriculum development for education, case review for welfare organisations, and so on. For example, I know of one Christian welfare organisation concerned with helping the needy that has four sub-committees: Finance, Audit and Compliance, Pastoral Care and Properties Development.

In the case of these and the preceding list of sub-committees, there is a balance to be struck between monitoring and providing advice to the staff concerned. To avoid friction it will be important for both staff and board to have the same understanding of why the sub-committee is there. In organisations that have specialist staff covering the sub-committees' skills areas, the board members will normally find themselves in a more strategic monitoring role. Where there are no specialist staff, the board may find itself rolling up sleeves to take a more hands-on role.

Some organisations opt for an Executive Committee, or a Finance and General Purposes Committee, which combines the remits of several of those listed above, including perhaps finance and employment. This is more common where there is both a large organisation and a large board (it is fairly common in the US, where boards tend to be much larger than in the UK). However, the problem of creating an inner sanctum of 'senior' board members is almost unavoidable once an Executive Committee has been established, and this is likely to have an effect on the enthusiasm of the other board members. If such a Committee is felt to be necessary, it would be wise to preclude it from having decision-making power, except in federally structured organisations where the full board might meet only once or twice a year.

Recruitment and briefing

Recruitment of sub-committee members is a Chair's task. The selection will depend upon skills, willingness and time available. If the need for the sub-committee existence has been clearly thought through, then this is a group with a serious job in hand. The quality of the group's work has consequences for the organisation, and therefore the member-ship of the team matters. The temptation is to appoint the first three or four who put their hands up. But the Chair should consider whether they are the best group for the job, and may bear in mind other tasks which one or more of these individuals may be fulfilling during the next few months, including on other task forces or working groups.

The smaller the sub-committee the better. Although a sub-committee or task force should have the skills necessary to get the job done, it is counter-productive to create large groups. This absorbs more board member time and energy, and will tend to diminish the level of engagement of the individual chosen. Two or three people, supplemented by appropriate staff, will often be enough.

Having chosen the membership of the sub-committee, the terms of reference should be clearly articulated. Each sub-committee should receive explicit instructions from the full board, in writing. This acts as a kind of contract for committees, spelling out the committee's task in clear terms. It should specify a time-line, establishing a date and a form for the committee's reports to the board as a whole, and a final completion date. The remit should limit the lifespan of a committee: when the specified task is completed, the committee should disband.

The terms of reference are not carved in stone: the board can review and revise them based on changing circumstances and new findings from the committee itself. Should the board wish the committee to continue its work after the original completion date has passed, then a new remit should be drafted, and a new set of terms drawn up by the board.

The Chair of the sub-committee, whether chosen by the board or by the sub-committee members themselves, should be given the power necessary to provide effective leadership. This includes the power to convene meetings, require attendance, draft agendas and make reasonable calls on staff time. However, it is often possible for sub-committees to operate with a greater level of informality than the main board, and this may be the most efficient way of operating – avoiding time devoted to committee procedure and detailed minute-taking. It may be agreed that there will not be formal 'agendas', and that the minutes will be limited to a brief action list between meetings, and set of recommendations taken back to the main board at the end of the sub-committees deliberations.

Sub-committee findings should be brought back to the boardroom table, and discussed by the board at large. Assuming the sub-committee is meeting several times, the board might also be given brief progress updates to maintain good communication flow.

11.3 Sub-committee safety rules

- Keep sub-committees to a minimum: be sure that those you have and those you are considering are needed, and that there are not alternative and possibly more efficient ways of tackling the issue at stake.
- Provide clear and specific terms of reference, in writing.
- Keep sub-committees as small as possible, consistent with the need to contain the appropriate skills.
- Use them as a basis for identifying new talent and developing board leadership.
- Give their Chairs the authority to convene meetings, and to draw on reasonable resources to get the job done.
- Impose time limits where possible. Be rigorous in examining proposals to establish standing committees.
- Avoid too much staff time servicing sub-committees. As far as possible, make them self-service bodies.
- Review your sub-committees annually – make sure you still need them.

Summary

- Sub-committees can be useful for attending to tasks in greater detail than is practical in full board meetings.
- Sub-committees create an opportunity to develop leadership within the board, and introduce new potential board members to the organisation.
- Clear terms of reference and authorities are necessary for the sub-committee to operate effectively.
- Distinguish between standing sub-committees, which may serve a long-term purpose, and temporary task forces, which can be disbanded when the job in hand is complete.

INTERVIEW WITH ANNE MOUNTFIELD, CHAIR, TOWER HAMLETS' OLD PEOPLE'S WELFARE TRUST

Anne Mountfield is a member of two boards, for the Tower Hamlets' Old People's Welfare Trust and for the Age Exchange Theatre Trust.

Tower Hamlets' Old People's Welfare Trust, also known as Friends and Neighbours, was established (under a different name) in 1947, and provides services to support the personal and social needs of older people in the area. Age Exchange was founded in 1982 by Pam Schweitzer, and uses theatre and other creative arts, in a number of contexts, to dramatise, display and record the reminiscences of older people, often changing how older people are viewed and the way they view themselves.

Let's talk about Tower Hamlets' Old People's Welfare Trust first. Tell me about the organisation's work.

The Trust has been organising regular home visits and support by carers since the 1940s, originally as the Stepney Old People's Welfare Trust. It also organises outings and events, and maintains liaison with statutory and medical agencies. Last year a total of 283 older people received visits from the staff. We provide a 'good neighbour' service, helping with form filling, taking someone to a hospital appointment, and occasionally helping with practical tasks at home. We also sometimes provide first-level advice on welfare issues. In summer we organise a number of outings, taking between five and ten people, depending on how many wheelchair-users are in the group. We also make our mini-bus available to the local Community Transport group for other visits and shopping expeditions throughout the year.

What is the staffing?

It is a very small organisation, with one Care Supervisor and at present just four paid visiting carers. There is also a Volunteer Organiser – volunteers have played an important part in the past in helping with home visits, driving and administration. There are currently 12 part-time volunteers. We have recently recruited a Director, who has experience of working in Tower Hamlets, one of the poorest boroughs in the UK. This is part of a process of professionalisation for the organisation. Prior to the Director's appointment I was asked to act for a short period as an Executive

Trustee and become actively involved in day-to-day operations – there was a need to reassess our structure and activities, and systems were not up to speed. My main achievements were to propose and raise three-year funding for the new post of Director and later, working with him, for the post of Volunteer Organiser.

What are the main challenges or developments facing the Trust currently?

We need to recruit more volunteers of different ethnicities, such as Bangladeshi and Somali – because the composition of our community has changed significantly over the years. In a sense, we have remained too white an organisation for the multicultural community we now find ourselves serving. This is part of the focus for the Volunteer Organiser, who has been in post for under a year.

We also need to formalise some of our personnel and administration arrangements, and we need to make our fundraising more focused on long-term sustainability. Although we provide a much-valued service, the organisational structure and support has not been as it good as it could be. As a matter of priority, the new Director has been addressing some of these areas, and considering salary arrangements, staff training and fundraising. In fact, as a result of these efforts we have recently confirmed a substantial donation to the organisation over the next five years.

Strategically we do need to do some refocusing. Today more basic care is available in the community, while the frailest house-bound elderly people often move into sheltered accommodation. At the same time, the proportion of people over the age of 65 is rising, and loneliness or isolation from the rest of the community remains a problem. Our services need to adapt to reflect these changes. For example, we plan to adopt the name by which we are known locally: 'Friends and Neighbours', to reflect both our ethos and the distaste our service users have for being regarded as in need of 'welfare'. We have recently conducted, with help from Guildhall University, a survey to inform us about which of our services are most valued. We are also trying to identify which of the unmet needs of older people in the borough we are best placed to provide.

What are the organisation's income sources?

Our turnover has been less than £150,000 per year up to now, though that is likely to change. In 2002 we received about

£50,000 in unrestricted donations, and a grant of nearly £21,000 from the London Borough of Tower Hamlets.

Fundraising is becoming a bigger issue for us, especially now that the new Primary Health Trusts control a large proportion of statutory funding for older people. We've been dependent on a large number of relatively small donations. We need to source more secure, longer-term income to provide the services needed.

What is the nature of the board?
We're currently a trust, and there are just six trustees. We are not incorporated, but are now looking at the process of becoming a limited company. Given the changes we're going through, and the increased awareness of risk in the care sector, this is probably going to be necessary. We also need to have trustees who are users of the services, and people from different ethnicities to reflect the community we work within. One of my first tasks as the newly appointed Chair has been to draw up a trustee recruitment policy and strategy.

Let's talk about the other organisation you're involved in, Age Exchange Theatre Trust. How long have you been involved?
I've been on the board for three years, compared with nearly eight at Tower Hamlets.

And what is the nature of their work?
Age Exchange is a very unusual organisation. For 20 years they have been using theatre and other arts-based skills to work with older people, unlocking their reminiscences and putting these to wider community use through a range of artistic, educational and welfare activities. The original function of the Trust was to present the reminiscences of elderly people as a social resource, using performance, photographic and memorabilia collections and oral history. Age Exchange has now developed a range of programmes that create links between generations, cultures and communities. In particular, its use of reminiscence as a positive intervention in dementia care is widely acknowledged and valued. There is a book of this project, *Reminiscing with People with Dementia*, which has been translated and published in several countries. There's a lot more going on too, with museums, housing associations and other organisations.

Age Exchange is based at the 'Reminiscence Centre' in Blackheath, in south east London, which attracts around 20,000 local visitors each year and also many from further afield who come for training courses, remedial sessions for dementia sufferers and their carers and special events. The Centre incorporates a small hands-on museum of everyday objects from early decades of the last century, a community cafe and an exhibition space.

What about the finances?
We have a turnover of around £300,000. Over half of this is in the form of donations and grants, from London boroughs, government departments, the Lottery and from a range of grant-making trusts and foundations. The remainder comes from earned income in the form of fees and sales.

We have had financial difficulties in recent years. Partly as a result of some shaky administration a few years ago we incurred a deficit of over £70,000, which we are now proud to have eliminated, though with some sacrifices along the way. We have a good degree of security through owning valuable property, but of course this doesn't relieve the cash-flow problems created by a deficit. However, we have established a useful group of 'Friends' and I'm delighted that we recently received a donation of £25,000 for five years and some major grants. Provided we observe the more stringent financial systems we now have in place, this should enable us to keep in modest surplus over the next few years.

In general, the income patterns of Age Exchange are more volatile than those for the other organisation I'm involved in. It's in the nature of a project-based organisation, which has to earn or fundraise a lot of its income each year. It also has the greater potential for generating more of its own income, from training, conferences and publications.

What are the staffing arrangements?
Well, it has been run by its Founder-Director for a long time. But after 20 years she would now much prefer to concentrate on artistic direction, not administration, so this is an important period of change. We now need to get to grips with a number of issues. The senior staff currently work as a cooperative management team, reporting to an Executive Chair. This is working fairly

well in the short term with the current personalities, but we are not convinced it will remain practical in the longer term once there are any changes in the team or the dynamics. We have set up a few working parties to focus on specific aspects of development, and this seems to have been welcomed by the staff. However, we prefer to keep long term, formally constituted sub-committees to a minimum.

What is the nature of the board?

We have a large group of trustees – currently 19 of them. Then there is a Council of Management (we are a limited company), which operates as the board, and meets four times a year. The board has a Finance and Human Resources Committee, which meets more regularly, and there is a working group on education issues.

We need to look at the composition of the board. It has now become more focused than in the past. And, like all others, our board is probably going to need to be even more actively engaged in the future.

12 The role of the Chair

It is only when you become aware of the range, scope and incredible responsibility of the job, that you realise there is an almost limitless opportunity to be ineffective, unless you are totally clear about how you are going to set about it

Sir John Harvey Jones

The Chair acts as a figurehead for the organisation, and leader of the board. In both functions the Chair has a strong influence on operational style, and a fair amount of flexibility as to how the role will be interpreted. The Chair also largely determines the culture of the board.

The Chair's degree of intervention can range from a passive and minimalist role – turning up for meetings and 'chairing' them – to a frequent, even daily presence in the organisation. Chairs can range from hands-off supporters of the CEO to far more executive styles of involvement, including maintaining an office in the organisation's building and spending several days a week there. There is considerable variation in the interpretation of how the role should be fulfilled and, perhaps more than any other role in the organisation (with the possible exception of CEO), the Chair has freedom to determine what approach they want to adopt for the job. This choice will be influenced by:

- the style and capabilities of the CEO;
- the capabilities and degree of engagement of the other board members;
- the areas of competence, and previous experience, of the Chair;
- board traditions;
- problems the Chair thinks need to be fixed.

Where there are others who can share in the leadership of the organisation, the Chair is going to achieve the greatest impact by harnessing their energies rather than trying to do everything solo. This applies as much to the willingness of other board members to share the load and accept special responsibilities, as to the nature of the CEO's front-line leadership.

The Chair's leadership style

Where there are strong personalities around the table, perhaps including board members who are high achievers in their respective fields of work, the Chair may be most effective playing a more neutral and even-handed role, focusing especially on process. A strong lead from the Chair may backfire in these cases. Of course, this depends upon personality – some people only have the capability to lead from the front.

Where there is evidently a leadership vacuum, i.e. a lack of strong direction from the CEO, the Chair will be most effective providing the lead – energising the organisation. In some cases this may be resented by the CEO, but an organisation without direction is too high a price to pay for short-term conflict avoidance.

On appointment as Chair, proclaim the new regime. For the sake of clarity, and in order to consolidate your leadership position, you will benefit from explaining how you intend to interpret and realise your role. If a change of approach is intended, this gives others the opportunity to consider how this affects their contribution to the board, and the sort of preparation and commitment that will be expected of them. How this is done is entirely dependent upon the circumstances – the previous Chair may be sitting at the table, or may have been ousted in a palace coup. The idea is not to arrive swinging a sledgehammer, but to use the change of Chair as an opportunity to effect changes in style or process which may be timely.

12.1 A tale of two Chairs

Paul was one of the most charming men I have met. Ex-Navy, and manager of a medium-scale retail operation in the centre of town, he was always exceptionally well turned-out. As one of the sons of the city, he had good contact networks, although they were largely with those who had been more influential in the city's life ten or twenty years earlier than they were now. He was a first-rate speaker, often invited to deliver after-dinner speeches.

Board meetings were friendly and fairly informal. They also lasted far too long. By nine o'clock those with children or other commitments were drifting away, and the business of the agenda was often uncompleted. Because Paul had an aversion to even a hint of conflict or friction, issues were sometimes not pushed as far as they needed to be for the sake of the organisation. Over time meetings that had been anticipated with pleasure became a source of irritation – there seemed to be no purpose to them.

Pressures within Paul's retail business led to him needing to step down from the Chair. He was succeeded by Bill, a younger and more dynamic businessman, leading an engineering firm which was going through a period of significant expansion. The day after Bill was appointed he came to see me (as General Manager of the organisation) and proceeded to lay down the law as to how board meetings were to be organised in the future, especially regarding:

- agenda drafting;
- preparation of briefing papers for the board;
- time-limited board meetings;
- promptness of preparing the minutes, and their approval and circulation.

The tone of board meetings changed markedly. They lasted between an hour and a half and two hours. They were far better served. They were brisk, but all members were encouraged to have their say. And, regardless of the problems and issues at stake (and there were plenty), each meeting was followed by a glass of wine, courtesy of the Chair, before board members drifted off to their homes.

One organisation; two completely different approaches to getting through the board's business.

Relationship with the CEO

In commercial organisations the Chair is the top job. In non-profit organisations the Chair's authority is more complex and subtle, involving partnership with the CEO on most key decisions.

The degree to which the Chair or the CEO provides leadership in specific areas will vary in each organisation. For example, in some organisations it will be rare for the Chair to act as spokesperson, except in times of ceremonial significance or in times of crisis. In others, it may be quite usual for the Chair to front the organisation in discussions with stakeholders, or even with the media. There is no hard and fast rule as to when the Chair should be the spokesperson. But it is important for the Chair and CEO to discuss and agree between them their respective leadership and figurehead roles, to ensure the organisation provides a united and coordinated front, and to avoid potential friction.

More broadly, as Chair you will need to agree with the CEO how you are going to work together. This will include:

1 agreeing the key things we need to achieve in the next year;
2 confirming the expectations each has of the other;
3 confirming how the board will interact with and assist the organisation and the CEO:
   ■ what support and advice does the CEO want?
   ■ what are the protocols for board-staff communications?
4 confirming how the CEO will report to the board, and how the CEO's performance will be reviewed;
5 discussing how board meetings will be organised and serviced:
   ■ how are we going to prepare board agendas?
   ■ what are the key areas the board needs to focus upon?
   ■ what papers will be prepared for board meetings, and in what format?
   ■ who will minute the meetings, and in what level of detail?
6 clarifying the role the CEO has in making the board effective, including recruitment of future board members;
7 clarifying what information you want, and do not want, as Chair;
8 confirming who will be the principal external spokesperson for the organisation.

Establishing these parameters will not necessarily be accomplished in a single meeting, but may be addressed through a series of discussions between Chair and CEO. It is for the Chair to take the lead in this – you act on behalf of the board as the employer of the CEO, even if, for practical purposes, you must operate as a partnership.

Some Chairs are on the phone daily to the CEO. Others build the relationship around a weekly meeting. Whatever frequency or communication process is determined, both the Chair and CEO should feel it is appropriate and workable. And for the sake of avoiding organisational drift, it is wiser to formalise and regularise the arrangement than to communicate only when there are problems to solve (there are, of course, *always* problems to solve!). Just as the board should divide its time between monitoring and housekeeping duties, and policy development and strategy, so meetings between the Chair and CEO will achieve most for the organisation if they address longer-range agenda-setting as well as dealing with short-term issues or constraints.

If the relationship between the Chair and CEO is unfailing sweetness and light, there is probably something wrong. Two capable individuals, both caring about the health and aspirations of the organisation, are very likely to have differences. Where there is not the relative simplicity of bottom-line financial results to establish priorities and the organization faces many choices as to how to allocate resources, it would be surprising if Chair and CEO always agreed. The secret of success is in openness and communication.

Many CEOs look to the Chair for mentoring, for a sounding board. The CEO's job can be lonely, and it may be inappropriate for them to develop an inner-circle relationship with one or more of their senior managers – if they have any.

Wherever possible the Chair and CEO should have a common understanding on key issues when going into board meetings. If this is not the case, the board will become confused. But where it is not possible to achieve a common view, the Chair's role is to Chair – that is, to facilitate discussion amongst board members in order for the board as a whole to reach a view or a decision.

Running the meetings

The chapter devoted to Effective Board Meetings (Chapter 10), identified a number of process and organisational matters that directly involve the Chair – from agenda-setting through to approval of the minutes and any follow-up required. Implicit behind all of these suggested actions was an assumption that the meeting must be purposeful. Through discussion with the CEO, the Chair should approach the meeting knowing the key issues to be covered, and where decisions are needed. If the agenda and supporting papers have been considered in advance, the Chair should feel well briefed. This is not to say that there will be no difficult or contentious matters to deal with – but that the Chair will be aware of the issues and be more capable of focusing on productive process to deal with them.

This concentration on process is a key skill for the Chair. In the meeting itself, the Chair's role should be to steer the board through the agenda, encouraging the less assertive board members and, where necessary, drawing a line under lengthy, irrelevant or personalised contributions.

12.2 Chairing the meeting

Consider all the business and only the business: stick to the agenda, and encourage all others in the meeting to do the same. If new issues arise, they will often be best dealt with by deferring to a future meeting, or by establishing a small working group to consider the issue between meetings.

Know what you are trying to achieve: remind yourself of the key matters that need to be resolved; try to make the time allocation and priorities of the meeting reflect this.

Introduce items effectively: whether it is Chair, CEO, or someone else, each agenda item should be briefly but clearly introduced, to set the scene and refocus the board members' attention, including clarifying whether the item is for information or decision.

Keep it moving – don't let it stray: it is easy to get bogged down in detail – aim for completion on each item, without making board members feel steam-rollered into submission.

Process not content: the Chair will have an opinion as much as any other board member (perhaps more so), but the Chair's job is to be neutral, even self-effacing, in the interests of ensuring that the board as a whole has had its say and given a good airing to those issues which need it. Focus on the process of the meeting. Use reiteration and summary to check on what has been said, and what you believe has been agreed. Where decisions are needed, follow a logical and consistent process for arriving at the decision.

Protect the weak, control the strong: some board members who have useful contributions to make can be hampered by timidity – draw them out, ask for their opinion when they haven't spoken for a while. And some board members may be tempted to talk too much – help them to help themselves by choosing your moment to conclude their contribution and move to another board member, or to a conclusion.

Watch the audience: good chairing requires a sensitivity to the mood of the board members. Be aware of body language indicating rejection, dissent or boredom. Discourage side discussions and whispering caucuses. Don't be afraid of cracking a joke when it's needed to break the tension (but choose your jokes carefully!).

Get results: no-one wants their time wasted – work to ensure that the meeting has moved the organisation forward, not only in terms of decisions taken, but also including time devoted to longer-range planning and policy discussion.

Taking decisions

'In every success story you find someone has made a courageous decision.'

(Peter Drucker)

Most of the time, boards make decisions without a vote. But there are occasions when an issue is so significant or contentious that it requires a vote. When decisions are being taken, it helps to:

- clarify what is being decided;
- spend time generating and exploring alternative courses of action – a common weakness of decision-making is to assume there are two alternatives – there are often more;
- consider the strengths and weaknesses of the alternatives;
- ensure that any necessary factual data, or expert advice, has been sourced;
- make the decision;
- ensure those implementing the decision are clear on what they have to do;
- follow up.

The quality of the decision-making matters. Decisions that have major financial or strategic consequences should not be rushed. The board must be confident it has taken well-informed decisions, and has considered the implications of alternative courses of action. If a decision is put to a vote, the results will need to be minuted, including recording any dissenting views.

The Chair needs to ensure that decisions are reached. There are good quality decisions and poor quality decisions. Good decisions are based on a coherent, logical process, and are well informed. The greater the consequences, financially or otherwise, the more important it is for the board to base its decision on high quality information and advice. This does not guarantee that the right decision will have been taken (in retrospect), but it is the best we can do. It is a basis for the board to work together cooperatively, and it provides some real protection if things don't turn out as expected. It is in the nature and quality of its decision-making that the board's standards of care and diligence will most clearly be judged.

12.3 Replacing a fleet of aircraft

Small aircraft are an essential component of the organisation's service. With an ageing fleet it was apparent that if we were to continue our operations and expand our service then an upgrade of the aviation fleet was essential. But what would be the most appropriate aircraft to purchase? Getting the process right was clearly a priority for a $28 million purchasing decision, and a commitment to capital equipment that would be intended to last for the next 15 years.

To start the decision-making process, we mapped out the services the organisation aimed to provide in the future, during a strategic planning workshop. Once the service requirements were clarified, minimum aircraft capability requirements were identified and evaluation criteria were set.

Different aircraft options were then examined and graded against the evaluation criteria. This was done through a small think tank, which was a subset of our strategic planning process. The aim was to draw out all the issues related to aircraft replacement. Staff and board members known to have differing views were included as part of the process.

Viable options were identified as an outcome of this evaluation process and Senior Management/CEO then prepared a paper covering all aspects of the issue, including detailed reports on financial requirements. The outcomes of the strategic planning process were used as a basis for this paper. This paper was submitted to the board and included a Senior Management/CEO recommendation.

The initial recommendations of management were rejected. A number of issues were raised by board members, which needed further examination by the CEO/Senior Management. These largely related to safety issues, which required more feedback from fieldworkers who would depend on the aircraft. The board was particularly sensitive to these as the purchase involved switching from twin-engined to single-engined aircraft.

A second paper was prepared and Senior Management made a further series of recommendations. There continued to be some very divergent views on the programme. Three methods were used to deal with the issues that were raised.

The first was for Senior Management to give very detailed responses to each issue raised by the board. The second was to use independent experts outside the organisation to cover some of the more sensitive issues. For example, to cover the issue of safety an expert from a large international aviation organisation was engaged. The third was that the Chair invoked formal meeting rules to ensure all board members had the opportunity to speak and put their case forward. This avoided individual arguments around the table and gave all parties the chance to have their say. The Chair was very conscious of wanting to avoid a board split on the issue.

After the board resolved the issue, implementation was left in the hands of Management. A board sub-committee was established to deal with the funding issues created as a result of the decision. These included foreign currency and borrowing considerations.

Specific contracts arising from the decision were presented to the board through the CEO, and the board was kept informed of the progress of the project through the monthly CEO report.

The project has only recently been completed, and early indications are that the needs are being met. However, it is too soon to make a full evaluation of the success of the decisions made.

A number of specific lessons for the organisation came out of this process.

- Major decisions of an organisation need input from all levels. If possible Senior Management should have the support of staff when taking major issues forward.
- Detailed documentation is required to support Management recommendations.
- Management should always make recommendations when putting papers forward.
- Enlist the use of outside experts on sensitive issues with divided views.
- Where possible, use independent external studies to validate the case.
- Ensure strict meeting procedures are followed when difficult/emotional issues discussed.
- The Chair should keep as much emotion as possible out of the board discussions.

The Chair's role in good decision-making is:

1 to filter issues so that only those requiring a board decision come before the board – there are many operational issues which remain within the province of the CEO;
2 to structure the agenda so that significant issues requiring decisions are allotted adequate time;

3 to ensure that the staff have provided the best information available, and that papers provided to assist in reaching a decision are structured clearly, including, for example, a presentation of options, an evaluation of options and a recommendation;

4 to ensure that significant or complex decisions are preceded by agreement on how the decision is going to be reached – to confirm the process before getting into the detailed debate;

5 to facilitate open and efficient discussion at the board meeting (and therefore to resist the temptation of authoritarianism, which can only hinder good decision-making), and to stimulate discussion where a major decision seems to be going through without proper consideration;

6 to handle differences rather than suppressing them;

7 to move to the point of taking the decision.

'Whatever you do, don't camp at the fork in the road. Decide. It's far better to make a wrong decision than to not make one at all.'

Jim Rohn

A decision only exists where there is more than one possible course of action. Often the decision is presented as 'do this or do that', a choice between just two courses. And often this polarisation neither reflects the true range of options available, nor encourages good quality decision-making. The board can add value to the process by encouraging the generation of a range of alternatives or options – but early enough in the process for these options to be evaluated.

There is a range of tools for evaluating alternative courses of action. A piece of paper with a line down the middle (pros one side, cons the other) is a starting point. Other techniques include:

■ a resources/impact matrix (a grid which facilitates positioning of different actions or strategies according to their likely impact and the level of resources needed to implement them);

■ risk analysis;

■ decision trees (a visualisation of the flow-on effects of alternative courses of action in relation to their consequences, their probability or other criteria);

■ cost-benefit analysis;

■ critical path analysis.

(Some of these techniques were introduced earlier in Chapter 8, *Policy and Planning Toolkit*.)

Decision-making is influenced as much by the dynamics of the group as by calibre of the briefing papers or sharpness of the analytical tools. Well-organised and effectively chaired meetings encourage positive group dynamics. A logical process also helps.

Decision process

✔ Why is a decision needed – what is at stake?
✔ What are the issues we are trying to decide on – are there several issues, can we disentangle them?
✔ Do we have the information we need?
✔ Can we generate a range of alternative solutions or options – have we considered all the possibilities?
✔ How will we evaluate each option?
✔ How will the decision be taken?
✔ Who will be involved in implementing it – who will be affected by it?
✔ How and when will we review progress?

Finally, where formal voting is required the parliamentary-minded will be aware that there are set procedures for considering a decision. The most widely adopted are *Robert's Rules of Order*, which provide for a structured and logical approach. See Resource 11 for a fuller version of *Roberts Rules of Order*. To summarise:

- One of the members will **move** that a decision be made (this is proposing that the board go on record in favour of a certain definite action).
- Another member of the group will **second** the motion, which means 'support' for the action proposed. (The second is necessary to be certain that the issue is of interest to more than one person.)
- Once the motion has been made and seconded there is **discussion**, **clarification**, and **debate**.
- When the subject has been covered fully, there is the **vote**.
- Prior to both discussion and vote, the person in the chair should restate the motion to be certain everyone knows what is being discussed and decided.[1]

---

[1] Brian O'Connell, *The Board Member's Book: Making a Difference in Voluntary Organisations*, The Foundation Center (New York, 1985), p106.

Between board meetings

The chair has a number of tasks and responsibilities besides the business of running meetings. He or she must:

- develop agendas for each meeting and ensure supporting papers are prepared;
- monitor the work of any sub-committees;
- motivate individual board members – with tasks and praise;
- induct new board members, and meet with potential board members;
- provide leadership for the planning process;
- review the board's progress;
- confirm the annual decision-making cycle;
- provide advice and support for the CEO;
- front the organisation as agreed with the CEO, and be a principal advocate for its mission;
- create clear expectations for the board;
- create clear expectations for the CEO;
- do whatever else is necessary and prudent to ensure the organisation performs.

12.4 Chair's role description

- Oversee board meetings.
- Work with the CEO in preparing agenda for board meetings.
- Serve as an ex-officio member of other board committees.
- Work in partnership with the CEO to make sure board resolutions are carried out.
- Take decisions between meetings where necessary, and within parameters agreed by the board.
- Call special meetings if necessary.
- Confirm appointment of Committee Chairs and recommend board members to serve on Committees.
- Coordinate the CEO's performance evaluation.
- Oversee searches for a new CEO.
- Work with the nominating Committee to recruit new board members.
- Coordinate periodic board assessment with the CEO.
- Act as an alternative spokesperson for the organisation.
- Periodically consult with board members on their roles and help them assess their performance.

A more detailed Chair's role description will be found at Resource 5 (pp284–90).

Building the board

The board is the Chair's team, and team building is an art. It commences with selecting the right team members, not only for their skills but also their willingness to become part of the team. It requires effective induction – and a sensitivity to the different stages which characterise the formation, flourishing and ultimately dissolution of a team.

Much team building occurs through action, that is, through the board members undertaking tasks together, beyond the formal business of attending meetings. The Chair's allocation of specific tasks to board members may be regarded in one sense as imposing a burden – taking up a board member's time – but it is also helping to unlock the board's potential and integrate the individuals, and increase their sense of purpose and commitment. Through action, the board members also gain a deeper knowledge of the organisation – and create opportunities for the Chair (and CEO) to praise them.

Sometimes the most effective motivation is just to say 'thank you'.

The meetings also contribute to team building. If the Chair steers the meetings away from personal comment or criticism, stays focused on the organisation's purposes, and maintains good humour, the board members may look forward to meetings and enjoy each other's contributions.

Periodically, the Chair may meet individual board members to review their progress and motivation, to thank them for the efforts they have made, and to consider both whether they wish to continue in the future, and what specific areas they would most like to become involved in. These informal appraisals with board members may also provide an opportunity to weed out under-performing board members who are frequently absent from meetings, or who seem unable or unwilling to make an active contribution to the board's business. There may be very good reasons why they are not realising their potential – but for the sake of the team as a whole it is unwise to allow passengers on board, unless there are compelling political reasons to do so.

Handling conflict

Conflict is a natural part of organisational life. Sooner or later, most boards will encounter it. Conflict arises from differences of outlook between people. Some boards adopt an ostrich-like approach to conflict – burying their heads in the sand and hoping it will just go away.

Board members each have their own view of the world. The effective board relies on trust, honesty and respect between members. Problems begin to escalate towards conflict when the people concerned stop listening to each other, and then lose trust and respect. All parties can rapidly and easily descend into a cycle of accusation and blame.

In organisations, conflict most often arises because of:

- differences of perception, opinion or beliefs about power and authority – who's in control;
- differences regarding the vision, aims and priorities of the organisation;
- poor or inadequate procedures and systems so that people feel badly managed or unclear about what is going on;
- inadequate resources to do the work, so that people feel pressurised and undervalued.

Or it arises because of unresolved conflicts that simmer on from the past, hidden agendas, or because of clashes of personality.

Box 12.5 provides an example of conflict where the board, and in particular the Chair, of a non-profit organisation had to provide strong leadership to resolve tensions.

12.5 Roots and branches: handling a conflict

The structure of many non-profits includes representation from a wide membership or branch structure. These structures can be unique to the organisation – but the inherent tensions between centre and branches (or between one branch and another) are common to many. An organisation can go through a period of many years enjoying total harmony between the constituent elements, but the energy of the organisation can be sapped rapidly if factionalism emerges.

Because non-profits are so value-driven, factional dissent can lead to passionate differences, when individuals or groups not only want their voice to be heard, but want to see change take place on policy issues dear to their heart. Such passions are heightened when the organisation is operating within the health sector and is delivering services to those affected by life-threatening illnesses with the emotions that are naturally aroused.

The Chair of one major non-profit in the health sector talked of his role in such a situation. A board member representing and sympathetic to the concerns within one particular branch of the organisation, aligned himself with an issue that the Chair and other board members believed was not appropriate to the direction of the organisation as a whole.

The Chair's initial thought was to find that particular board member a fulfilling role on the board – to divert his energy into another key issue and function. When this didn't work, the Chair took it upon himself to 'counsel' the member out of the organisation, by informing the member, first privately and then publicly at a board meeting, that his actions were against the interests of the organisation as a whole. A resignation followed.

The situation did not end there as the disquiet and concern of the branch in question still had to be resolved. It was the duty of the board to understand why this situation had become acrimonious. This part of the process was acted upon in partnership with the CEO, and involved implementing better lines of communication with the branches of the organisation, including the creation of a post of Branch Coordinator, and ensuring better mechanisms for resolving future concerns at an early stage.

If conflict arises between board members the Chair should reassure all concerned that their voices will be heard and that a reasonable solution will be sought.

- Each person should be heard and allowed to explain their side of the matter.
- Discussion should focus on specific facts, events and incidents rather than on speculation and hearsay.
- Avoid attributing personal motives, or making personal attacks on the other parties.
- The process should seek to identify common ground and common interests.
- Encourage all parties to search for a solution that is in the interests of the organisation.

Summary

- The Chair is the leader of the board 'team' and largely establishes the board's 'corporate culture'.
- The relationship between Chair and CEO is probably the most important linkage in the organisation – it is essential that they clarify their responsibilities and their mutual obligations, and work out protocols for dealing with specific issues.
- The Chair is responsible for running effective meetings, and securing decisions from the board.
- Between meetings, the Chair can continue to help the CEO drive the organisation forward, and ensure board members are fulfilling their agreed tasks.

13 The board and the chief executive

The relationship between a non-profit's board and its chief staff officer is so important that it can make or break an organisation. A good working alliance can be a prime factor in success. Conversely, strong unresolved differences are probably the greatest single reason for mediocre or unsatisfactory performance

Knauft, Berger and Gray

The key constituencies that make up the organisational structure of many non-profits include volunteers, staff, executive staff and board members. The relationship between each of these will determine the overall health and spirit of the organisation, but it is the relationship between the CEO and the board which has the greatest influence on organisational success, and this in turn is largely determined by the nature of the partnership between the CEO and the Chair.

The relationship between board and CEO is a negotiation. Successful negotiators do not enter the conference chamber without considering the other party's needs and perceptions, as well as their own. The board that is concerned to develop an effective relationship with the CEO needs to start with a consideration of the CEO's own role and perspective.

The CEO's work in context

As non-profit industry sectors have increasingly professionalised, the demands upon the CEO have increased in breadth and sophistication. It is arguable that the quality of leadership which is required in a substantial commercial organisation is required in a markedly smaller non-profit, because of the complexity of the environment within which the non-profit leader operates:

> 'We work within an unbelievably complex web. I worked for a retail organisation with 1,000 staff. It was very simple. At the Royal Flying Doctor Service I have 100 staff, and it's extremely complicated.'[1]

---

[1] Interview with Bruce Maguire, CEO, Royal Flying Doctor Service, Queensland.

The effective non-profit CEO will be concerned with most or all of the following issues:

1 Positioning the organisation, setting its direction, and developing a strategy to achieve the greatest long-term effectiveness, including choosing the 'right' community needs to address.
2 Measuring effectiveness, especially the tangible long-term benefits to the community of the organisation's activities.
3 Forming alliances and coalitions with other organisations and constituencies in the public, private and non-profit sectors, and managing the resulting shared responsibilities.
4 Providing active community leadership in building consensus, addressing social problems, and promoting philanthropy and volunteerism.
5 Hiring, developing and motivating effective leaders, managers and professional staff.
6 Raising the programme quality or improving the level of leadership, management and community impact of programmes.
7 Designing or ensuring the proper internal infrastructure – that is, effective organisations and processes, including the proper use of information technology – to ensure the cost effectiveness of operations.
8 Increasing the funds available for annual operations, or managing these assets while still maintaining a high level of service.
9 Maintaining excellent relations with important outside constituencies – including relations with potential donors, the media, local government and so on – to ensure visibility and a favourable climate of public opinion.
10 Adapting to frequent changes in the tax law, community needs and expectations, and other social, political and economic factors.
11 Playing a role in the development of an appropriate board and, with the Chair, employing board members effectively to achieve the organisation's mission.

In the case of many cultural organisations, the CEO will also be the Artistic Director – and judged first by their ability to deliver high quality work on-stage or in the gallery, and then by the preceding list of other leadership responsibilities. Small wonder that many cultural organisations opt for a double-headed executive – typically Artistic Director and General Manager – in order to cope with this diverse portfolio.

Clearly, the non-profit leader must be able to:

- reconcile the conflicting demands of clients, public and private sector partners, donors, volunteers and others, and align their energies in pursuit of socially, culturally or educationally useful services;
- inspire trust, confidence and optimism among those who care about an issue or cause and are willing to volunteer time or money to help address it;
- ensure that the organisation is financially sound, ethically above reproach and fully accountable to the community it serves;
- position the organisation for the future in the face of the severe challenges of limited resources and frequent changes in the external environment, and accomplish this through flexibility, innovative strategies and rapid adaptation to threats and opportunities; and
- help develop leaders on the board, in other parts of the organisation, among the volunteers, and in the community to carry on the work of the organisation.[2]

Another way of identifying the range of demands on the CEO is to consider the number of constituencies with whom the CEO must connect and communicate effectively on behalf of the organisation.

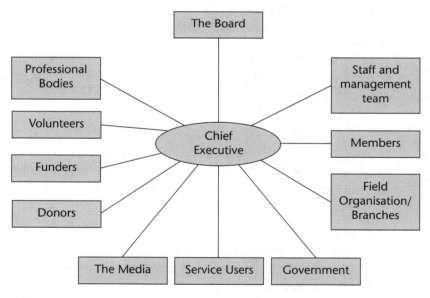

Figure 13a

---

[2] Adapted from B Nanus and S M Dobbs, *Leaders Who Make a Difference*, Jossey-Bass (San Francisco, 1999) pp15–16.

This is not to suggest the board is more or less important than other stakeholders. Collectively the board remains the CEO's employer – but the board should be sensitive to the need for the CEO to keep a number of other constituencies onside too, through investment of time and energy. If the board-CEO relationship is characterised by frequent and onerous reporting requirements, the CEO will be diverted from building these other crucial relationships.

What every CEO wants

The quality of CEO-leaders of non-profits differs as widely as any group of individuals may. In varying degrees they have ability, intellect, charisma and intuitive political nous – or not. Some have risen through the ranks; others have been selected from another institution's rising managers. Whatever their calibre or capacity, the CEO looks to the board for a few key helpful behaviours, including certainty, respect, support and competence.

Certainty means that when a board makes a decision it will stick to it. Few things are more unnerving for a CEO than when a board has made a decision and there is uncertainty as to whether or not it can be relied upon. This sometimes occurs when a board member has missed a meeting or a new board member has been appointed. On these occasions, it is imperative that the other members bring their colleague into line, gently but firmly, and say that the matter has previously been discussed and resolved

Respect is a two-way street. When a CEO hears that he or she, or the organisation, is being criticised by a board member, or that political games are being played within the sponsoring body, it becomes very difficult for a CEO to maintain the respect for the board that is vital for the effective functioning of the organisation.

Support is essential, and it is nothing more than a recognition that both the board and executive are on the same side, serving the customers/clients. If the CEO is not confident that his or her decisions will have the support of the board, then inevitably the CEO will pull back into the zone where he or she does feel such confidence. Ambivalence, or perceived ambivalence, in a board's support for the CEO will reduce the ability of the organisation to respond to change.

Competence means not only in the particular expertise that the board members bring to the board, but also the professionalism in their conduct as board members.[3]

In short, within the context of an increasingly sophisticated operating environment, in fields of non-profit work which become more technically and logistically demanding, the CEO looks to the board to raise its game, support the CEO's position, and develop a more professional approach to its organisational contribution.

Of course, it takes two to tango. For a successful relationship to develop the CEO also needs to respect the board's perceptions. Board members sometimes feel excluded and disempowered. They may feel it is a struggle to secure the information they need, or that a dominant CEO expects them only to ratify or rubber-stamp the CEO's decisions or faits accomplis. These feelings will reduce their sense of commitment and enthusiasm – and encourage the board to under-perform.

If some board members do not appreciate the pressure on the CEO of even a modest-scale non-profit, many CEOs equally regard the board as a monkey on their back, and probably one that doesn't even know how to pass around the tin when the barrel organ is playing. This perception may be a result of the board defaulting to its comfort zone of monitoring and controlling (so much easier than actually *doing* something) in the absence of leadership from the Chair; or it may be a self-fulfilling prophecy on the part of the CEO: if the board is treated as a burden and not serviced or informed effectively, its members are likely to become that much less cooperative.

It does not make encouraging reading to learn that in a recent survey of over 100 non-profit organisations, while 20 per cent of CEOs felt their boards were not fulfilling their responsibilities, no less than 50 per cent of boards felt that the CEOs were not supporting the board.[4]

---

[3] The four elements of certainty, respect, support and competence are highlighted by Jim Longley, FAICD, CEO, in 'Anglican Retirement Villages', in *The Not-for-Profit Director*, ed. Fran Morris, AICD (Sydney, 1999), pp74–5.

[4] Damien J Smith, Steve Bowman and Sean C Millard, *The Not for Profit Board and Management Guide*, Enterprise Care Consulting Group Pty Ltd (Melbourne, 1999).

13.1 What board members want from the CEO

- Commitment to organisational mission and policies.
- Sensitivity to the community.
- Responsible performance of fundamental administrative tasks.
- A structure that promotes a productive working atmosphere – effective staff relations.
- Clear communication on financial and administrative matters.
- Effective representation of the organisation, enhancing its public image.
- Prompt responses to reasonable requests for information.
- Honesty.
- Respect.

Reflecting the unusual power-paradigm of a professional CEO reporting to a volunteer board, the board member is motivated most highly when he or she enjoys leadership from the Chair and is respected and supported by the CEO, and when the board collectively is provided with timely and adequate information to fulfil its obligations and add real value to the non-profit's business. In turn, the CEO is most motivated when the board seeks to help the CEO achieve and succeed, reinforces the status of the CEO and respects the CEO's own leadership role.

Responsibilities and mutual obligations

> 'Both the board and the executive will be helped in their relationship with one another if each of them understands the need for the other to be capable and powerful.'
>
> Cyril Houle

The board that regards itself as steward of the non-profit's assets and values will tend to regard the CEO (more or less) as a temporary servant-officer. The board that regards itself as representing external constituencies of interest will, similarly, consider the CEO as there to implement the will of the membership or constituencies as articulated through the decisions of the board. The board that regards itself as a contributor to the overall management function is more likely to regard the CEO as a partner in fulfilling the management needs of the organisation.

For the non-profit which is neither so small as not to employ professional staff nor so large as to employ hundreds, the relationship between board and CEO should be characterised by the best principles of teamwork – mutual respect, an understanding of each individual's own contribution, an awareness and reasonable degree of tolerance of each other's weaknesses or constraints and, overall, a sense of common purpose. In law, the board carries ultimate accountability and authority (within limits determined partly by the membership or key stakeholders). In practice, however, both board and staff know that it is the CEO who carries the can, and wields much of the power and authority on a day-to-day and week-by-week basis.

Shared responsibility calls for a relationship characterised by a fair degree of subtlety, a relationship that cannot easily be reduced to a list of 'your job' and 'our job'. In fact, any attempt to draw up such a list breaks down under the weight of qualifying statements. While it is certainly true that the CEO (and staff) are paid to get on with the daily job of policy implementation, in many non-profits the board members will find themselves rolling up their sleeves to help in a variety of ways. Even in formal meetings the board has certain executive duties it cannot abrogate – from the appointment of the CEO to the approval of major purchases or developments.

This does not lead us to the conclusion that there is no difference between the board's job and the CEO's. But the difference can be more fully understood by considering the attributes of these two distinct organisms:[5] See table on the following page.

An awareness of these differences can be the basis of a more mature mutual understanding – on the board's part, that the CEO needs room to manoeuvre, has a right to establish his or her own style of leadership on the organisation, occupies a lonely and challenging position, and will normally be highly dedicated to the success of the non-profit. On the CEO's part, that the board is a necessarily complex animal, that individual board members may bring a high degree of expertise and level of care to the organisation, and that harnessing the energy of the board requires close partnership with the Chair, and attention to the motivations and perceptions of individual board members as well as to the group as a whole.

---

[5] This comparison owes much to Cyril Houle's comments in his *Governing Boards*, Jossey-Bass/National Center for Non-profit Boards (San Francisco, 1997), pp87–8.

Parallel processes

	Board		**CEO**
Corporate	decisions are based on group discussion, and are subject to the nature and quality of information provided by the CEO and staff; debate does not always lead to clear decision or consensus	**Individual**	single authority, with decisions taken on the basis of the individual's leadershipstyle; considerable autonomy, and capacity to shape the organization
Continuous	members may come and go, but the concept of the board is of a continuous entity. This should encourage long-term perspective	**Temporary**	from a year to twenty years, but the CEO is time-limited; and this encourages a need to secure short-term results, as well as consider long-term development
Part-time	the board member's primary focus, and livelihood, normally lies elsewhere	**Full-time**	personal/professional success inextricably linked with the fortunes of the organisation
Voluntary	many board members are not experts in the organisation's field of work, most are unpaid, and all are making a voluntary personal commitment. They may bring valuable professional, commercial or community assets	**Professional**	increasingly, the CEO brings substantial relevant experience (it was not always so). This work is their primary professional focus, and in many cases represents a major commitment
Representative	whether or not the board member is formally nominated by an external constituency, there is often a sense of stewardship on behalf of a broader community or communities	**Distinctive**	while good leadership requires an awareness and sensitivity to the needs of different constituencies, the CEO will often endeavour to build an organisation which reflects individual concerns and strengths

There are a number of basic ingredients for success in the board/CEO relationship:

1 **Clarity of board function:** the board must have a common understanding of its own role in the organisation.

2 **Clarity of CEO role and responsibilities:** both board and CEO need to be clear on the purpose of the CEO's position, based on discussion and reflected in an up-to-date job description.

3 **A mutually agreed strategic plan** or at least a set of agreed key objectives for the organisation.

4 **Regular communication and coordination** between Chair and CEO – somewhere between daily and weekly according to the current demands.

5 **A recognition of the difference frameworks** within which board and CEO operate (the characteristics described above).

6 **Appropriate observance of protocol** in board members' dealings with staff (other than the CEO).

7 **Fulfilment of the mutual obligations** that bind the CEO and board in common cause.

13.2 Mutual obligations

The board's obligations to the CEO include:

- remuneration benefits, and a working atmosphere that make the CEO's position attractive to the best possible candidates;
- a clear job description and performance goals;
- regular formal performance reviews;
- constructive informal feedback on job performance;
- rewards for tasks well done;
- respect for the CEO's authority over staff;
- prompt and thoughtful response to request for guidance or assistance.

The CEO's obligations to the board include:

- commitment to the organisation's mission and sensitivity to the communities it serves;
- responsible performance of fundamental organisational and administrative tasks;
- an administrative structure and decision-making mechanism that promote a productive working atmosphere and effective staff relations;
- thorough and timely communication with the board on financial and administrative matters;
- effective representation of the organisation in the community and commitment to enhancing its public image;
- prompt and thoughtful response to board members' requests for information.

Generally, information requests from the board should be confined to those which arise during board meetings, are channelled through the Chair between meetings, or which are specifically relevant to the work of a sub-committee or task force.

13.3 Passing the buck

It was a stimulating and productive retreat, building bridges between board members, and between the board and executive staff. All went smoothly until the last half-hour, when one of the more experienced board members, a capable lawyer, turned to her yellow legal notepad, and read out a list of several dozen items for action which she had noted during the course of the weekend. Upon concluding the list she tore the pages from her notepad, and handed them to me, the CEO, with a smile: 'There you are. You can get started on those on Monday.'

And I had thought it was a *board* retreat!

The Chair-CEO partnership

The CEO wants support and advice. The Chair wants no surprises. The CEO wants the space to get on with the job. The Chair wants to be associated with a successful organisation.

At its best the Chair-CEO partnership will be mutually respectful and productive. They do not have to be the best of friends – in fact, this would create more problems than it would solve – but if their relationship is confined only to the business of running the board meetings, with little other contact, the organisation will be deprived of an important component of the overall leadership mix.

Privately, the Chair and CEO should talk through their needs and aspirations to clarify their expectations of each other, and to ensure there are no (avoidable) areas of overlap or potential conflict.

While the Chair will naturally want the CEO to meet as fully as possible the range of responsibilities outlined earlier in this chapter, the CEO may reasonably look to the Chair to accept the board as his or her team and manage them accordingly, providing board leadership, organisation and motivation.

13.4 How the CEO can help the board to help the CEO

There are some simple, practical steps the CEO can take to help the board, and in so doing, help themselves.

Show consideration and respect towards board members:

- be aware of their needs;
- be fair and objective.

Encourage the board to be involved:

- help them to achieve consensus;
- view them as a team.

Raise the board's awareness of industry change and developments:

- inform them of the changing environment;
- engage them in developing new solutions to the organisation's problems;
- encourage discussion of the organisation's purpose and vision.

Promote board accomplishments and productivity:

- use their time considerately;
- offer praise and thanks for individual efforts.

Service the board meetings effectively:

- ensure board members receive their papers in advance;
- assist the Chair in allocating clear assignments to board members;
- help the Chair to run the meetings well;
- ensure good minutes are kept, and distributed promptly as a reminder of actions agreed.

Provide helpful information to the board:

- ensure papers are succinct, clear and timely;
- selectively, pass on relevant industry information.

Regarding that last item, an article in the non-profit e-newsletter, Board Café, recorded the likes and dislikes of over 50 board members in a straw-poll:

'Board members feel disrespected when board packets are late or sloppy, and feel railroaded when background information isn't included for an upcoming decision . . . a thoughtful packet [of board papers] not only provides the board with the information it needs for the meeting, but increases board confidence in the staff and in the board-staff relationship.'[6]

---

6 www.boardcafe.org. Accessed 28/1/01.

Monitoring the CEO's work

Some CEOs I have talked to feel that they do not receive enough feedback. Given the complex dimensions of the job, and their unique position between staff and board, working in a 'vacuum' is an obvious danger. As with any appraisal process it is in the organisation's interest to establish regular communications. Feedback can take the form of praise and encouragement for work well done, which encourages and motivates the CEO, or it can take the form of picking up on problems or issues before they have escalated. The simple fact of communication between board and CEO can also educate both – in the case of a 'problem', for example, there may be resource or priority issues which need to be addressed for the CEO to operate effectively.

Monitoring the CEO's work can occur at different levels:

1 Informal feedback by the Chair, or by other board members – most common when the organisation is in its early stages, and the delineation between board and CEO is more blurred than in larger or more mature organisations.
2 More formal periodic assessment of the CEO – perhaps on an annual, structured basis.
3 Annual review by a board committee – this may involve an assessment of the CEO's performance, tied in with an assessment of organisational progress.

Informal feedback should happen as a matter of course – although it is mainly praise rather than criticism which should be communicated in this way. If there were regular or serious criticism, it should not be handled informally, or confined to a dialogue between the Chair and CEO. There is too great a danger of breaching principles of natural justice, or breaching the organisation's own disciplinary process by doing this.

The main focus of CEO assessment or monitoring should be results. How far has the organisation fulfilled the objectives laid out in the Strategic Plan? How does our performance rate compared with the targets and performance measures we adopted? Assuming the strategic plan has been produced in a close-knit joint exercise between the board and the CEO, amongst others, it effectively becomes a 'contract' between them, and the basis on which the CEO's work can be monitored. Of course, there may be reasons beyond the CEO's control why things are not going according to plan – but even that may suggest that CEO action should have occurred at an earlier stage than the appraisal or assessment.

There are a number of factors which may corrupt the assessment process:

- The halo effect – becoming preoccupied with an outstanding positive quality, or a recent success or achievement.
- Personality-rating – focusing too much on the kind of person the CEO is, rather than on their performance.
- Subjectivity – board members displacing appraisal against agreed criteria or the strategic plan with appraisal based on personal likes and dislikes.
- Leniency – a tendency to avoid confrontation, a reluctance to make an unfavourable assessment.
- Severity – when things have not gone well in the past, a tendency to allow that to influence the current assessment.
- Dramatic incident – judgement on the basis of a single event or area of work, but ignoring overall performance.[7]

Avoiding these problems requires a clear process, similar to the appraisal structure described in Chapter 7, *People Matter*. The assessment should:

- be timetabled in advance, so that both the board (or Chair) and the CEO can prepare for it; and it should be regular, whether twice-yearly, annual or biennial;
- be clearly articulated, so that the board and CEO are clear how the assessment will be conducted;
- be divided into consideration of different aspects of the CEO's areas of responsibility or, if the assessment is to be strictly confined to performance against the strategic plan, divided into consideration of different elements of that plan;
- include an element of self-assessment by the CEO – apart from encouraging a healthy self-awareness, the CEO's own candour will make it easier for the board and CEO to discuss problem areas;
- include a review of the CEO's job description, in order to assess it against key areas of responsibility to ensure it is still accurate, and to amend it if necessary;
- include an assessment of the board's own contribution to organisational success, and to the CEO's ability to succeed;
- include a quantified assessment in relation to different areas of performance.

---

[7] See William R Conrad and Hank Rubin, 'Performance Appraisal of the Staff Chief Executive', quoted in John W Nason, *Board Assessment of The Chief Executive: A Responsibility Essential to Good Governance*, National Center for Nonprofit Boards (Washington DC, 1990), pp6–7.

There may be value in engaging an external consultant to advise on the assessment process, or facilitate it, especially where there are difficult issues to address, or where there is dissatisfaction with the CEO's performance. However, this step depends in part on the degree of management expertise that exists on the board.

A more detailed outline of a CEO assessment process is included at Resource 9 (pp299–300).

Summary

- Organisational health and success relies on a strong relationship between the board and the CEO, and the partnership between the Chair and CEO is the most important element in this.
- The board is one of a series of stakeholders that the CEO must serve effectively.
- The CEO needs consistency and support from the board; in turn the board looks for honesty and openness from the CEO.
- Role clarity, an agreed strategic plan, regular communication and mutual respect are the foundations of a productive board-CEO relationship.

AN INTERVIEW WITH JANE HOLDEN, EXECUTIVE DIRECTOR, ROYAL NEW ZEALAND FOUNDATION FOR THE BLIND

The Royal New Zealand Foundation for the Blind has been in operation for around 120 years, and is the only provider of support services for blind people in New Zealand. It is a statutory body, governed under the Royal Foundation for the Blind Act of 1963. Its services include rehabilitation, library support and guide dogs, amongst others.

Jane Holden has been Executive Director for three years. Jane also sits on two commercial boards and is the Chair of the Health Research Council of New Zealand.

INTERVIEW

How your board has changed in recent years?
There have not been changes in terms of numbers or composition over recent years. However, there has been a change of focus. We now have a much clearer understanding of the distinct roles of management and governance. This has clarified the roles of board members and staff, and has reduced instances of conflict and misunderstanding.

A significant future change lies in a whole raft of governance reforms proposed, including changes to the structure of the board. This should come into effect by the end of the year, and is driven by the principal of self-determination. To date, members of the board have either been appointed by the Minister or elected by region, and are accountable to the Crown. We are moving to a structure where board membership will drop from fourteen to nine and all of the members will be elected nationally by the membership, and will be accountable to the membership. To reflect this shift we are also changing our name from the Royal NZ Foundation for the Blind to the Royal NZ Foundation of the Blind.

This change has been the undercurrent of my three years with the organisation. The decisions have been finalised and we are now waiting for the changes to the Act to be read before Parliament and then to be ratified by referendum by the membership. This marks the end result of a hard-fought battle – one driven by philosophy and goodwill for the future of the organisation and the membership. We have had to convince people that there are no hidden agendas in these changes, and we have succeeded.

What significant issues or problems has the board faced in the past?
There is quite a big issue for charitable organisations where members are also recipients of the services of that organisation. There are issues of separation of personal issues and wants of board members from what is good for the whole organisation and the whole of the membership.

With regard to the board's own composition there is the issue of getting the right kind of competencies on the board, particularly in the finance area.

There has also been the challenge for this organisation of being seen to be working for blind people but not being accountable to them, which is why we are undertaking the reforms I have described.

What sort of demands are made upon your board members?
We meet seven or eight times per year. We used to meet more often – once a month – but have managed to reduce the number since we worked through the changes regarding role clarity. We send out papers one week before the meeting in readable format for all the members. It is a prerequisite that board members have IT skills, so we will train them up, and even buy them a computer if necessary.

We spend our time looking at policy and resource allocation and have spent a lot of time on the changes. People work on regional sub-committees as well. The amount of work really depends on the person and how involved they want to be. The regional committees meet four times a year and there are also board sub-committees.

Members cannot miss more than three meetings in a row, and they are expected to follow the board member position description.

How is the board involved in planning?
The strategic plan belongs to the board. It is the document they govern from and it is usually a three-yearly plan. 'Seed' or discussion papers are prepared by the Executive Director and go out for consultation to the membership. The board gets feedback and then makes a decision on behalf of all members.

And how would you describe the board's role in fundraising?
Our board is not as you might expect – a fundraising or profile-raising board. Sometimes a board member will speak at a function for fundraising but that's about it. It's not like an American board. Our fundraising is professional and staff-driven. The board will give directions as to the kinds of areas we can and cannot fundraise in. They set fundraising guidelines and policy.

How do you see the role of the Chair?
We have just had a change of chair. We have a traditional functional role for the Chair, but the position varies with the style of the person in that position. Our previous Chair was very consultative and played a facilitation role on the board, while our new Chair is a more proactive leader, presenting issues to the board and driving them forward. I personally prefer the latter style because it creates momentum.

A good Chair needs to be in touch with the organisation and on top of current issues. They need to make sure that everyone is well briefed and that discussions are well informed. They need to lead the agenda but not dominate it. They need to keep it balanced. And they need to be enthusiastic, of course.

How would you describe the relationship between board and Executive Director?

I would describe our relationship as strong. The primary board-CEO relationship is between the Chair and myself.

The board is not afraid of asking questions and monitoring my performance. The board also gets to meet divisional managers, so that is not always the Executive Director's views the board gets to hear. The board provides leadership on matters of policy and things that will affect the membership and community. It is my job to implement these policies and stick to the business plan.

This is the only service in the country for the blind, so service decisions have a big effect. The challenge is for board members to look at the big picture, and for the agenda not to be captured by just a few loud voices.

What strategic choices and challenges are facing the board now and over the next couple of years?

I think once the current changes have gone through the greatest challenge for the board and the organisation will be to ask: If we can't grow resources, what services are we willing to let go? How do we prioritise our service provision?

What advice would you give to a potential new board member?

In my view, there is not that much difference between being on a for-profit or not-for-profit board. Consultation might need to be a bit stronger because of stakeholders but there is no difference in accountabilities. However, people approach being on a not-for-profit board with a softer touch. They do not prepare themselves very well. Many not-for-profits are now being run like for-profits and need to be taken just as seriously. I have found that there is a lack of preparation and a lack of reading. There needs to be due diligence. I have rarely been asked for the financial statements before someone accepts a position on the board. So:

■ undertake some orientation, and seek out some Director training;

■ understand the financials of the organisation;

■ understand the board position description and the responsibilities of a board member;

■ understand that time commitments can be very variable.

It is a collective accountability and if a decision is made then board members need to stand by that decision together.

AN INTERVIEW WITH JONATHAN MOSEN, CHAIRMAN, ROYAL NEW ZEALAND FOUNDATION FOR THE BLIND

Jonathan Mosen has been Chairman since mid-2002.

What prompted you to join the board of the Foundation?

I am a blind person myself and have been a consumer of the Foundation's services all my life. I have also been strongly involved in the consumer movement and have held the position of Chair of the Association of Blind Citizens, an advocacy organisation which has lobbied the Foundation for better services. I formerly held a position as a senior staff member with the Foundation, a position I decided to leave when the relationship between the advocacy organisation and the Foundation became strained. Subsequently, I was invited to join the Foundation's board and was elected Chair in May 2002.

Jane Holden, Executive Director, has talked of some of the board changes there have been, and others that are planned for the Foundation. What is your perspective on these changes?

The Foundation was formed and is governed by a parliamentary Act. It is an old organisation and difficult to change. There has been a programme of governance reforms in progress, and a referendum of the membership in which 80 per cent supported the changes. The main thrust of the changes will be that board members will be elected by blind people and be accountable to blind people.

The reform process has been painful. The advocacy organisation I was involved with has been one of the key driving forces for this change. We believe 'nothing for us without us'. Things became so difficult to negotiate that the board at the time was asked to step back and a governance task force was set up to review and recommend changes. The ultimate result is a negotiated compromise between the Association and the Foundation, and the resulting changes have been loudly endorsed. We are moving to a board of nine elected members and two positions that can be filled if there is a skill that is lacking on the board. The point of the change is that self-determination is at the centre.

What are the other key issues the board has addressed recently?
Like any board we grapple with the question of where the boundary lines are between governance and management. We have commissioned corporate governance workshops for the Foundation's board. I am not a purist about the separation of the roles. I think that ultimately the board takes the rap, so the outcomes need to be ones that we want.

We are hampered by the fact that we do not receive enough funding to provide the services we need to. We always struggle with the finances. The organisation is 112 years old and is virtually a monopoly. There are a few other services for the blind around, but we run the majority of them. This makes decisions very emotional for all involved. Even though we are virtually a government instrument, government funding only provides 25 per cent of our income – the rest comes through fundraising.

How do you see the role of the Chair?
I think the there are three key roles for the Chair:

1 To act as a sounding board for the CEO and to monitor their performance on behalf of the board.
2 To facilitate the board's processes so that everyone feels that their input is being heard and valued. That means taking the time to make decisions in a quality way.
3 To be a spokesperson for the organisation when needed.

I am hoping that my role can be as a facilitator of communication between the various stakeholders in the sector, so that trust can be built up. Because of my role as a consumer advocate I have a lot of popular support. I am hoping to be a trusted voice for and to the community. I am also hoping that this new board will have better and more frequent dialogue with consumers and be able to explain its position better. Under the new system blind people will be the stakeholders and the Foundation will be accountable to those they serve. There will be a high level of trusteeship expected of board members.

How would you characterise the relationship between Chair and Executive Director?

I think a good working relationship is vital for the organisation to run well. My relationship with Jane [Holden] has evolved over the years. I have the greatest admiration for her. I have found her to be professional and excellent at her job. We have worked with and against each other in many roles over the years and now we are working together on governance reform and a new vision for the organisation. I think she really appreciates the feedback I can give her from the membership.

What expectations do you have of the individual board member?

People must not miss more than three meetings without good cause, but in my experience it has never been a problem. Board members are very dedicated. We meet every two to three months. We have trimmed back the number of committees and try to make sure that committee meetings coincide with the main meetings and can be added onto the beginning or the end. Those people who have been elected to the board by an advisory committee will often have to meet and report back to that committee, so their time commitments can be a bit higher. Being on our board is completely voluntary so people have to be dedicated to the cause.

What do you see as the board's role in strategic planning?

The board needs to own the strategic plan. Every meeting we take time out to look at strategic issues. The CEO reports in detail on various strategic issues and the board considers them at meetings. In our next planning process we need to ask – why is the organisation here? What do we do well? What can others do?

The CEO does the legwork of a strategic plan but the board approves it. All managers need to justify activity against the strategic plan.

I am hoping that the Foundation and other service providers can put together an overall blind people services strategic plan, and then all of our individual organisations will develop our strategic plans under that one. This will hopefully maximise efficiencies and prevent duplication of services.

What role does the board play in fundraising?

The organisation raises around $12 million a year. All the fundraising is done by the professional fundraising staff, and the board makes policy around how to fundraise. With our organisation there is always tension between using sad images to collect more money and protecting the dignity of blind people. The board has to manage this tension.

What advice would you give to a new board member?

This has been a good board to be on. It does not matter if a board member is blind or not – what matters is who they are accountable to. The changes will make it better. I would say to a new board member, make it your business to know what blind people are thinking and feeling about an issue, and take that to the board meeting.

14 Recruiting the CEO

The single most important task that a board undertakes is the choice of the chief executive

Graham Berry and Paul Pia[1]

Whichever view one takes of the proper role and functions of a board, the appointment of a CEO is a key board decision, and one which is likely to occur so rarely that the board member will have little or no opportunity to practise getting it right.

The principles for recruiting a CEO are no different from those for recruiting any other member of staff. The complications are that the organisational stakes are higher than for other posts, and that the board are part-time and drawn from a variety of backgrounds, possibly excluding the industry sector for which this key appointment is being made. Board members have fewer points of reference than they would in recruiting within their own professional or commercial environment – all the more reason to be thorough, systematic and proactive!

A thorough and systematic approach includes developing a clear job description, covering:

- who the CEO reports to (the board);
- who reports to the CEO;
- a statement of main purpose of the job;
- key responsibilities and key results areas;
- principal relationships and stakeholders;
- authorities (limitations to the CEO's independent decision-making role);
- candidate specification (skills, knowledge, experience required by the successful candidate – taking care to focus only on what is essential. It is all too easy to insert spurious requirements, such as 'ten years' experience'. Why not nine?).

Much of this will be drawn up with reference to the organisation's current strategic plan or the articulated policies and objectives of the organisation.

---

[1] Graham Berry and Paul Pia (eds), *Care, Diligence and Skill*, Scottish Arts Council (Edinburgh, 1995), p28.

Although every organisation will define the CEO's job description to suit its specific purposes, it may be helpful to bench-test the current job description against the generic example given in Box 14.1 to see if there are any obvious areas that need working on.

14.1 Sample CEO job description

The CEO reports to the Board of Directors, and is responsible for the organisation's consistent achievement of its mission and financial objectives.

In programme development and administration, the CEO will:

1 ensure that the organisation has a long-range strategy which achieves its mission, and towards which it makes consistent and timely progress;
2 provide leadership in developing programme, organisational and financial plans with the Board of Directors and staff, and carry out plans and policies authorised by the board;
3 promote active and broad participation by volunteers in all areas of the organisation's work;
4 maintain official records and documents, and ensure compliance with national and local regulations;
5 maintain a working knowledge of significant developments and trends in the field.

In communications, the CEO will:

1 see that the board is kept fully informed on the condition of the organisation and all important factors influencing it;
2 publicise the activities of the organisation, its programmes and goals;
3 establish sound working relationships and cooperative arrangements with community groups and organisations;
4 represent the programmes and point of view of the organisation to agencies, organisations and the general public.

In relations with staff, the CEO will:

1 be responsible for the recruitment, employment and dismissal of all personnel, both paid staff and volunteers;
2 ensure that job descriptions are developed, that regular performance evaluations are held, and that sound human resource practices are in place;
3 see that an effective management team, with appropriate provision for succession, is in place;
4 encourage staff and volunteer development and education, and assist programme staff in relating their specialised work to the total programme of the organisation;

continued

5 maintain a climate which attracts, keeps and motivates a diverse staff of top quality people.

In budget and finance, the CEO will:

1 be responsible for developing and maintaining sound financial practices;
2 work with the staff, Finance Committee and the board in preparing a budget, seeing that the organisation operates within budget guidelines;
3 ensure that adequate funds are available to permit the organisation to carry out its work;
4 jointly, with the president and secretary of the board of directors, conduct the official correspondence of the organisation, and jointly, with designated officers, execute legal documents.

If the current CEO is leaving in reasonably happy circumstances, it would be productive for the board or selection panel to have a debriefing session with him or her, to reflect on what has worked well: whether there are elements of the job, or the relationship with the board, that need to be reconsidered, and what the highest priorities should be for a new CEO. This may help to shape the job description, refine the candidate specification or even influence the wording of any advertising that is taking place.

A systematic approach also calls for the establishment of a search and selection panel with agreed terms of reference and a schedule for the recruitment process, along with clarification of whether the appointment will need to be ratified by the full board.

Key steps for a search and selection process

✔ Definition of the job description and candidate specification.
✔ Review of pay and terms.
✔ Determination of recruitment budget.
✔ Determination of whether a recruitment/Executive Search agency is to be used.
✔ Agreement on advertising schedule.
✔ Agreement on any further promotion or search activities.
✔ Confirmation that the overall procedure conforms to the letter and spirit of the organisation's equal opportunity policies and procedures.

✔ Copy for advertisement.
✔ Information pack for candidates, including
  – organisational data;
  – board details;
  – application process [and form, if one is to be used];
  – equal opportunities monitoring form [if one is to be used].
✔ Short-listing process.
✔ Interview plan.
✔ Other selection tests.
✔ Take-up and documentation of references.
✔ Offer and negotiation with the preferred candidate.
✔ Communication with unsuccessful candidates.
✔ Structured induction process for the successful candidate.

The terms of reference of a selection panel need to make clear whether the board expects the panel to report back at the shortlisting stage, or to report back at the end of the process with a recommendation. It would be unwise for the selection panel to be given the delegated authority to confirm the new CEO appointment before the rest of the board have had the opportunity to discuss any recommendation from the selection panel.

Further details on the search and selection process are included at Resource 8 (pp295–8).

Summary

- The appointment of the CEO is probably the single most important decision the board takes.
- The board should adopt a thorough, structured approach to the recruitment and evaluation of the potential CEO.
- In addition to external and internal advertising, consider an active search process to maximise the pool of suitable candidates.
- A clear interview plan will help in the selection process, but beware of over-dependence on the interview – other forms of evidence should also inform the selection process.
- An appropriate induction should follow the appointment, with key board officers maintaining close contact with the new CEO during his or her initial period with the organisation, or elevation from a less demanding position.

15 Monitoring our progress

The most important factor in achieving non-profit success is the desire to improve and the willingness to make an ongoing commitment to excellence

Paul Light

One of the distinguishing characteristics of the non-profit sector is the absence of a fully competitive market environment – Government subsidy and private donations often result in the client-customer not meeting the full cost of service delivery. The 'uneconomic' nature of the activity usually limits or precludes the presence of competitor organisations – a situation only experienced by monopolies in the commercial world, where market entry barriers inhibit competition.

If the services your organisation is providing are not as good as they should be, often the client cannot vote with their feet or their wallet. In this context, the board has a responsibility to make an additional effort to listen, and to work to improve standards and maintain relevance in the light of client, and volunteer, feedback. The same effort would be driven in a commercial environment by the fear of loss of market share or being forced out of business. There is no such compelling driver in the non-profit sector.

The healthy non-profit organisation is concerned with effectiveness. The organisation was founded to achieve social, cultural, welfare or religious objectives. The board needs to know how far these objectives are being achieved, and whether there are better ways of achieving them.

Effectiveness is not the only thing the board will wish to monitor. Legal compliance, performance against budget, delivery against the organisation's strategic plan or policies, also demand attention. Periodically, specific strands of work or individual programmes and projects will benefit from evaluation, to assess their impact and to identify improvements or efficiencies. And, as described in Chapter 16, *Assessing and Improving the Board*, the board should also evaluate its own workings and composition, to see how it can enhance its contribution to the life of the organisation.

15.1 Why bother monitoring?

The potential benefits of monitoring and evaluation include:

- learning from experience;
- identifying how far success is being achieved – what impact the organisation's work is having;
- linking individual performance and organisational performance, through appraisal processes;
- recognising achievement and creating opportunities for individual recognition;
- averting major problems by identifying them at an early stage, and taking corrective action;
- identifying opportunities to increase efficiency or effectiveness;
- providing data which will assist in reporting to stakeholders;
- ensuring the organisation is complying with legal requirements.

Monitoring and evaluation is easier said than done. Many organisations baulk at the time and cost implications of it, and there is clearly a balance to be struck. Disproportionate investment in evaluation processes would itself be an inefficient use of resources. But this is a matter of judgement. Some aspects of the organisation's work may be amenable to routine monitoring; others may require more thorough-going analysis, including the engagement of external consultants.

In this section, we consider what needs monitoring, and suggest some tools that may assist the board. Monitoring the organisation's financial performance is dealt with in Chapter 6, *Cheques and Balances*. Monitoring legal compliance is covered in Chapter 5, *Keeping to the Straight and Narrow*. Here we are principally concerned with monitoring the organisation's impact and efficiency.

Efficiency, effectiveness and economy

The three 'E's of 'efficiency', 'effectiveness' and 'economy' have been broadly adopted as a basis for organisational monitoring, at least by Government. **Efficiency** is concerned with the relationship between inputs and outputs – what level of investment of resources does the organisation make to achieve specific results. Put in other terms, efficiency addresses unit cost. For example, how much staff time and financial commitment are we making to serve a specific constituency or individual?

The organisation may be concerned to compare the efficiency, or unit cost, of one of its programmes or projects with another. Or, it may be concerned to compare unit costs of its programmes with those of other individual organisations, through a benchmarking process, or with accepted industry standards.

The Achilles' heel of efficiency in a non-profit context is that it fails to respect quality or depth of experience. The fact that the organisation has chosen to invest substantially to meet the needs of one constituency, when it could have reached a lot more people, does not establish that the organisation is poorly managed or governed. If this were the only basis of assessment, the needs of those most profoundly disadvantaged would be permanently excluded from the radar of non-profit organisations. Equally, the artistic endeavours of theatres and galleries would be wholly focused on pot-boilers.

By itself, efficiency is an inadequate basis for gauging the organisation's progress. But ignoring efficiency entirely would be equally unwise. Used judiciously, measures of efficiency can help the board and external stakeholders to identify systemic improvements.

Effectiveness is concerned with how far the outputs generated by the organisation achieve intended objectives. This is critical to the evaluation of non-profit organisations. They are there for a purpose. The degree to which the organisation achieves that purpose is a core issue for the board. This is considered further under 'outputs and outcomes' below.

Finally, **economy** is concerned with the degree to which input costs can be minimised, and the relationship between actual and anticipated costs.

Outputs and outcomes

Unless the organisation has an understanding of where it is heading, there is no basis for assessing progress – effectively there is nothing to monitor. So, a prerequisite for purposeful monitoring is the existence of a clearly articulated mission and strategies, or policies. Of course, the absence of such a sense of direction might be the trigger for a more fundamental evaluation of the organisation – but there are few non-profits today that have not been required to embrace strategic planning by one or more of their stakeholders.

There is a natural tendency to monitor what is easy to monitor. Outputs are more easily measured than outcomes. Outputs describe the amount of work the organisation does – number of clients served, hot meals delivered, children educated. Outcomes describe the effect the organisation's work has had – better community health, improved quality of education, richer cultural experiences. It is far easier to measure the work than its result – generally far cheaper too. However, there are compelling reasons for the board to focus on monitoring outcomes. Outcomes relate directly to the organisation's mission, and a focus on them keeps the board, and the organisation, oriented towards the market you are trying to serve, because you will be regularly considering what effect your work has had on your clients and customers.

Perhaps some types of non-profit activity are also easier to measure and monitor than others. For example, it is easier to measure exam results at a school than the 'educational progression' that the pupils have experienced – which may include socialisation and communication skills, amongst other factors.[1] It is easier to measure audience attendances at a theatre than the quality of the work on stage. Beyond this it might be argued that certain sub-sectors of the non-profit field are more susceptible to monitoring than others – organisational results in medical research, health and welfare services might be considered more 'measurable' than those in the cultural, religious or educational fields. But every organisation has the opportunity to address the question 'have we been making a difference?'

Whatever the level of challenge presented by evaluation, the board has to start somewhere.

Two questions can initiate the process: What are we trying to measure, and how are we going to measure it?

What are we going to measure?

Broadly, the board will be concerned with measuring:

1 the results of specific programmes, projects, or strands of work;
2 the implementation of strategies identified in the organisation's plan;
3 overall organisational performance.

---

[1] For this, amongst other reasons, many have been opposed to the concept of educational 'league tables'. Not only are they an out-of-context assessment of schools' performances, they may be measuring the wrong things.

Regarding *programme outputs and outcomes*, the board might want to know:

Outputs
■ How many people were reached?
■ How many were reached within the key target group?
■ What inputs or resources were devoted to the programme, and how do the costs and benefits compare with other programmes we implement, and with programmes undertaken by other organisations?
■ What is the staff assessment of the impact of this programme/ project?
■ What is the volunteers' assessment of this programme/project?

Outcomes
■ What is the client or customer's assessment of the programme – in terms of personal impact, quality of the work, access to the services?
■ What difference in behaviour or environment has the programme made?

In the case of those questions which can elicit a quantifiable response (how many, what inputs used) the board will wish to compare the actual result with the anticipated result. Did we reach more or less people than we anticipated when this programme was adopted? Did the project cost more or less than we expected it to?

Regarding *the implementation of strategies* contained in the organisation's plan, ideally the board will have agreed milestones and performance indicators at the time the strategic plan was prepared. In other words, the basis of measuring progress and success will have been agreed between the CEO and board at the point where the strategies were approved. The milestones will represent key stages in the implementation of the strategies, and the performance indicators will focus on outputs or outcomes resulting from those strategies.

Beyond monitoring the implementation of individual strategies, the board may be concerned with the implementation of policy objectives. This involves taking a step further back, and raising the question of whether the organisation has the right strategies in place, rather than taking them as a 'given'.

Reviewing *overall organisational performance* is likely to be a less frequent activity. However, prior to embarking on the development of a strategic plan, or at a time of significant environmental change, or perhaps when a new CEO has taken up the post, there will be value in taking stock of the organisation's progress at a broader level.

How are we going to measure it?

As far as possible, monitoring processes should be integrated into the organisation's work. Routine gathering of quantifiable data related to projects and programmes will minimise the cost implications of monitoring and evaluation. The best use of time will be achieved if the basis of evaluation and the monitoring necessary to serve this has been agreed at the inception of the programme, or at the start of implementing a particular phase of the programme.

Where it is a programme or project that has been brought to the board for approval, the board should also be approving the basis on which success will be judged. In the case of programmes and projects that do not require board approval, the board should be satisfied that it is part of management procedure to confirm evaluation methods at the time programmes are initiated. In this way, irrelevant and costly data capture can be avoided – the investment in evaluation can be balanced with organisational resources. Client, staff and volunteer feedback or comment forms, for example, could be integrated into the programme's daily processes. Staff or volunteer group discussion of aspects of the programme could be scheduled well in advance.

Routine data capture has its limits. Some issues cannot be addressed through simple questionnaires or quantitative recording, but require qualitative information based on interviews or, for example, client group discussions. A client or customer feedback form may record on a scale of 1-10 the degree of satisfaction with an element of the programme – but management and board will be hungry for more information. Why did he or she give that score? What would have made a difference? How does it compare with other services? It is difficult to secure this level of understanding of the client's, or volunteer's, perspective from a form. Personal interview or facilitated debate may be needed to explore issues in sufficient depth to reveal information that can positively influence the organisation's future actions.

This presents a dilemma. Objectivity and confidentiality require that someone not directly involved in that programme's delivery undertake any interviews – possibly another member of staff, possibly an independent market researcher. Budget constraints, however, militate against this. Every penny is needed for the programmes and projects. Market research and evaluation processes seem to be a luxury. They can be time-consuming and expensive. But the alternative is an organisation that risks losing touch with its constituency, and settling for service standards that are not as high as they could or should be.

For the sake of the clients, and for the long-term health of the organisation, the board should be working to ensure that 'listening mechanisms' are in place and form an integral element within the cycle of planning, monitoring and evaluation. Together with the CEO, the board will determine what level of resources is merited, and what economies effected in the monitoring processes.

Performance indicators

Performance indicators are a commonly adopted, and often stakeholder required, tool for tracking progress. Developed during the planning process, performance indicators can compare performance during this period with a previous period; actual performance against a pre-determined target level of performance; or performance against an industry norm.

The board should be wary of adopting more than a modest number of indicators, at least at the strategic level – a larger number will be appropriate at other, operational levels in the organisation. The board should seek to select indicators that relate to the key objectives and strategic intentions of the organisation. What are the three or four key things we are trying to achieve? What would be the best indicators (perhaps one or two per objective) that would help us track our progress in these areas? A few examples of indicators were provided on p233. Some more are shown in the table opposite.

Taking the technique of using performance measures a step further, Richard Chait and his colleagues developed the simple and attractive concept of the Dashboard.[2] A vehicle dashboard presents the driver with a few key indictors – speed, fuel level, engine temperature, warning lights. Because the driver cannot afford to stare long and hard at the indicators, they are presented in a simple visual format that can be absorbed at a glance. Translating that into non-profit parlance, the board does not have time to examine every facet of the organisation, and needs to be presented with information in an accessible format.

---

[2] Richard P Chait, Thomas P Holland and Barbara E Taylor, *Improving the Performance of Governing Boards*, American Council on Education (Phoenix, AZ, 1996), p104.

Sample performance indicators

Organisation	Financial Indicators	Non-financial Indicators
Amateur Rugby Association	■ sales volume from merchandising ■ attendance levels and ticket yield ■ sponsorship as a percentage of turnover	■ number of affiliated clubs ■ number of injuries ■ retention level of recreational players ■ number of accredited officials (referees, linesmen)
Theatre Company	■ percentage seating capacity achieved for productions ■ level of reserves ■ subscriber renewal rates	■ number of works by new playwrights ■ number of national tours ■ safety outcomes in production department
University	■ tuition fees as a percentage of total income ■ teaching/tuition costs as a percentage of total expenditure ■ cost of tuition per student per programme	■ student satisfaction with course structure ■ student acceptances as a percentage of applicants ■ number of new subjects offered ■ student completions as a percentage of enrolments

Non-profit dashboard indicators can be developed by:

■ agreeing between board and executive staff what are the critical success factors or key results areas;

■ identifying indicators – qualitative and quantitative data – that convey progress in these areas;

■ establishing standards that define the level of performance expected or required (on the basis of industry norms, or previous organisational performance, for example);

■ development of a prototype dashboard that presents the indicators effectively.

The resulting dashboard may be used for routine monitoring, perhaps every quarter or half-year; but may also be used to trigger an alert if an area is performing at unacceptable levels – that is, the CEO would be obliged to bring this to the board's attention.

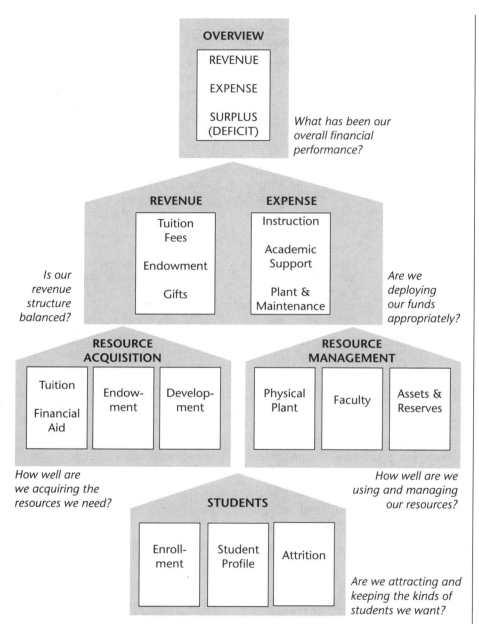

Figure 15a Select gauges from the dashboard of 'Redbrick University'³
Redbrick University Report Structure

Chait *et al. Improving the Performance of Governing Boards*, Exhibit 4.2, p105.
Reproduced by permission of the American Council on Education

---

³ Chait *et al.*, p105.

Drilling down below this overview, Chait and his colleagues illustrate how each element of the dashboard can lead to a simple visualisation of more detailed data. For example, in relation to tuition and fee income in Figure 15a above, the university's board receives an indicator of income comparisons for the preceding four years, benchmarked against an industry standard. In one chart, the board can secure an understanding of progress in both absolute and industry-relative terms:[4]

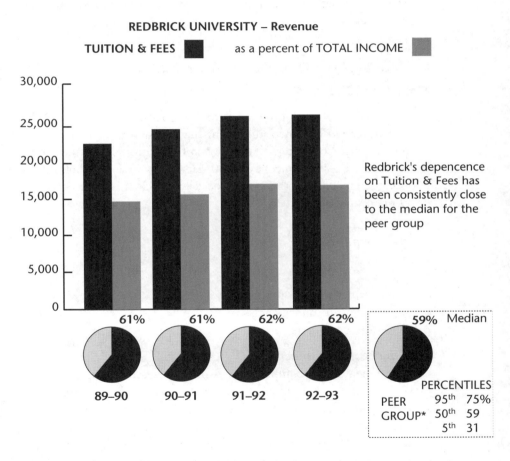

Figure 15b Redbrick University – revenue

* Peer Group = 140 private four-year colleges with tuitions over $10,000 from national survey reported in:
Taylor, Meyerson and Massey, *Strategic Indicators for Higher Education: Improving Performance*, Princeton, NJ: Peterson's Guides, 1993.

Chait *et al. Improving the Performance of Governing Boards*, Exhibit 4.2, p108.
Reproduced by permission of the American Council on Education

___

[4] Chait *et al.*, p108.

The entire process of selecting and refining indicators for the dashboard, and testing out the best way of presenting them to make the board's task easier, will generate dividends. The board and CEO will be spending time thinking about what they should be concerned with, helping the board to concentrate on a strategic rather than operational focus. They are limiting the information presented to that which is most pertinent. They are defining where monitoring resources should be devoted. And they are learning more about the organisation and the industry sector.

Reviewing organisational performance

When the time comes to undertake a more broad-ranging review of the organisation's performance, the board may need a range of inputs to supplement the knowledge that has been built through routine monitoring processes. The concept of '360-degree evaluation' is helpful. In 360-degree evaluation[5] the board seeks feedback from the organisation's main stakeholders, i.e.

- staff
- board members
- volunteers
- donors
- sponsors and business partners
- government funding agencies
- clients and customers.

Staff and board members

Staff and board can complete an Annual Assessment or a 'climate survey' to learn more about their perspective of the organisation's strengths and weaknesses. These responses may be given directly to the board's Chair and can be submitted anonymously if necessary. A summary of the staff and board's feedback would be shared with the CEO. Board members, or a small committee of the board, should meet with staff to respond to concerns and recommendations.

Sponsors and government funding agencies

Board members can conduct a series of telephone interviews with foundation and government programme officers. For example, they can ask

---

[5] BOARD CAFÉ: *The Newsletter Exclusively for Members of Nonprofit Boards of Directors*, e-mail newsletter published monthly by CompassPoint Nonprofit Services, San Francisco. E-mail: boardcafe@compasspoint.org; website: www.compasspoint.org/ index.html.

for comments on the quality of written proposals, quantity and quality of interaction with the non-profit organisation, the organisation's reputation in the community, and suggested areas for improvement or change. Funders will almost always welcome such calls from board members and be impressed that the organisation's volunteer leadership is committed to securing feedback.

Donors and volunteers

Staff or board members can conduct telephone interviews with major donors and key volunteers, asking for feedback on how well the organisation involves and informs them. Donors and volunteers should also be asked to share their perceptions about the organisation's effectiveness.

Clients and customers

Consider holding one or two focus groups with clients and patrons, facilitated by an experienced focus group facilitator, during which clients can give feedback on current services and unmet needs. A more extensive client survey can involve a written questionnaire, a telephone survey, or in-person interviews. An extensive survey may be undertaken as part of a strategic planning process, or such customer/user-service information may be collected routinely through follow-up contact.

Beyond the use of its own and staff resources, the board may contract a consultant to conduct a management audit of the organisation. Professional evaluators would assess the service programmes and projects both to find ways that they can be improved and to identify the outcomes of the organisation's services and the impact on clients and the community. In some cases, a marketing audit, technical or IT audit, or other specific evaluations may call for the services of external specialists.

Benchmarking

Finally, reference has been made to comparing the organisation's performance with industry norms or the performance of other individual organisations. Benchmarking is a tool that focuses the organisation on learning from best practice in other organisations, or transferring best practice in one part of an organisation to another. Commercial organisations have used benchmarking to identify ways in which their processes can be made more efficient, or quality standards improved, by analysing the processes and costs of their competitors or, where this is impractical, examining organisations which have parallel processes in other industry sectors.

15.2 Benchmarking by steps

Planning

1 Identify product, service, or process to be benchmarked.
2 Identify comparative organisations
3 Determine data collection method and collect data.

Analysis

1 Determine current performance 'gaps'.
2 Project future performance levels.

Integration

1 Communicate benchmark findings and gain acceptance.
2 Establish improvement levels.

Action

1 Develop action plans.
2 Implement specific actions and monitor progress.
3 Recalibrate benchmarks.

Benchmarking is not for the faint-hearted. It takes commitment and follow-through. It also requires the organisation to have a clear understanding of its own processes. There can be a natural resistance to this at staff level – when organisational processes have been developed and established over years, it is not surprising that the implication that others' processes may be more efficient may be resented or disbelieved. But benchmarking is a natural step beyond the development of performance indicators and 'dashboards'. The organisation that has accepted the value of improvement in standards and efficiency, will not hold back from using additional tools and techniques to achieve such improvements.

15.3 Learning from within

An example of an organisation using internal benchmarking is afforded by CARE USA's analysis of best practice within the organisation, initiated to combat the perception by some staff that every aspect of CARE's diverse project portfolio was so unique that comparisons didn't make sense.

Headquarters-based technical groups organised workshops with project managers and jointly identified the keys to best practices. They then had project managers evaluate their own projects and develop self-improvement plans. They organised 'lessons learned' and 'lessons applied' seminars.

For example, the analysis of water projects began with the creation of performance indicators that would describe a successful outcome. Since the water projects aim to create a sustainable water supply that supports better health, the indicators focused on longer-term maintenance of the systems, along with local health conditions, captured (for example) by the incidence of diarrhoea. Staff gathered information on these indicators, as well as on project costs, for 31 systems with similar characteristics. From this information, those with both high efficiency and high impact emerged as best-practice systems. With a relatively large database and considerable variation in performance, CARE could conduct an internal benchmarking process that allowed it to learn from, and benefit, its own projects.

The analysis helped CARE pinpoint the attributes that led to the successful outcomes in the 15 most effective and efficient projects. For example, high-impact projects included both sanitation and water supply, involved the community heavily in identifying the need for improved systems, delivered health education along with infrastructure, and included community contributions to the construction and maintenance costs as well as the actual construction and maintenance effort. These findings enabled CARE to develop design criteria for future water projects, significantly increasing the chances of sustained impact. They also provided data to justify project funding. At a later stage, this process was combined with regional meetings, where a new water-sector coordinator worked with the water project managers to get a joint definition of best-practice criteria.[6]

Reproduced by kind permission of John Wiley & Sons Inc.

Monitoring and evaluation can be regarded as an optional extra. Non-profits tend to be motivated by doing rather than by analysing and reflecting. But if the mission is paramount, then efficiency and effectiveness must be given organisational priority. The fact that this will be perceived to be at the expense of service delivery suggests that there will have to be pressure from the top – from both the CEO and board – to initiate and maintain learning processes that enhance the organisation's work and impact.

In most organisations, if the board do not require the development and implementation of purposeful monitoring and evaluation procedures, they will simply not happen.

---

[6] Christine W Letts, William P Ryan and Allen Grossman, *High Performance Nonprofit Organizations: Managing Upstream for Greater Impact*, John Wiley & Sons, Inc. (New York, 1999), pp91–2.

Summary

- Monitoring and evaluation are essential to maintain effectiveness, especially in an environment where commercial market forces do not prevail.
- Both outputs (work) and outcomes (results and effects) need to be measured.
- Routine data capture will minimise costs and effort, but some feedback will need to be secured through independent means.
- Key performance indicators keep the board focused on the most important success factors.
- Periodically, a more thorough '360-degree evaluation' of the organisation will identify areas for improvement.
- Benchmarking comparisons with other organisations, or other sections of your own organisation, can highlight best practice, encourage learning and maintain an impetus towards continuous improvement.

AN INTERVIEW WITH DAVID CROMBIE, CHAIR, QUEENSLAND RUGBY UNION

In addition to chairing Queensland Rugby Union, David Crombie is also the Chairman of Meat & Livestock Australia and the Rural Leadership Foundation. Meat & Livestock Australia is engaged in market development, research and other interventions which strengthen the competitiveness of Australia's livestock industries, in both domestic and export markets. The Australian Rural Leadership Foundation manages programmes for selected rural and regional leaders to develop personal growth skills, knowledge and supporting networks. David is also on the boards of two for-profit organisations: one, a listed property developer, the other an unlisted materials supply logistics and handling company.

In Australia there are over 100,000 amateur rugby players – 30,000 of them in Queensland. There are also professional teams competing at the regional, national and international levels, including the Bank of Queensland REDS.

INTERVIEW

242

David, in the mid-1990s the game of rugby professionalised in Australia. How did this affect demands on the board of Queensland Rugby Union?

Since the advent of professionalism in rugby in 1995, the Queensland Rugby Union (QRU) has undergone a major transformation, with the overlay of commercial and business imperatives on top of a 114-year amateur tradition. Prior to 1995, the QRU had the reputation of being 'highly professional' within an amateur environment. The move to professionalism has created some tension. On the one hand, the QRU is operating a professional rugby team that must be competitive in what is arguably one of the most intensive competitions in the world, the Super 12. At the same time, the QRU must address the needs of community rugby and create pathway opportunities for players to progress to the level of their choice and competence within a largely volunteer administrative environment.

The QRU cannot simply be a business where profit is the only criteria for measuring success. Sound business management is required to ensure that the REDS and our other representative teams are competitive, and that there is a seamless connection down through the grades and age groups to allow for player transition.

The major assets of the QRU are its contracted players, who also have demands at the national and local club level. The seasonal programme is conducted in accordance with national and international programmes and sponsorship requirements and, as a result, the income stream of the QRU is not within our total control. The flow on from this is a restricted opportunity to utilise our major fixed asset – the Ballymore Stadium.

What impact has this had at board level?

Historically, amateur rugby governance has been through volunteer Boards or Boards of Directors or Councils. Typically resources were limited, which encouraged ingenuity and a 'can do' mentality based on volunteer support.

With the advent of professionalism, the requirement for formalised governance procedures increased, and turnover increased with media ownership, sponsorship, player contracts and additional professional staffing and events management.

The rate of change with the introduction of increased professionalism in rugby management has not been reflected at the constitutional level in many cases, where board members are elected by Councils and are generally unpaid volunteers. While this arrangement can still deliver good outcomes, it is significantly different to for-profit organisations, where board members are generally elected by the shareholders at large, based upon a blend of skills and experience.

You are actively involved in both the non-profit and the for-profit worlds. How does board membership of one differ from the other?
The fiduciary duties for directors are the same. Directors in both circumstances have a responsibility to the company and its shareholders. Depending upon their constitutions, non-profit boards can more closely resemble local government councils, where there are sectoral influences and an expectation of ready access to board members and influence on board debate.

For-profit companies have a clear focus on enhancing shareholder value. Non-profit companies frequently have an additional role in community service and support. In rugby, this is working with the rugby community in the creation of competitions and in the provision of support to ensure that there is an opportunity for growth, and also the provision of pathways so that individuals can advance and play to the level of their choice and ability.

The skills mix and the community understanding of a non-profit rugby board is therefore quite demanding, and in many ways different to the skills required on a for-profit board – where outcomes can be more directly measured in terms of the growth in shareholder value.

What about the recruitment and remuneration of board members?
In both profit and non-profit organisations it is critical that directors have a clear understanding of the principles of Company Law and the duties of directors.

QRU board recruitment is based on a constitution that contains many of the procedures of the pre-professional era. The election of board members is through a Council, which has voting entitlements related to the various constituencies. Many non-profit organisations have similar constitutions, which need to be constantly reviewed in light of the changing nature of the organisational activities.

The skills base of a non-profit organisation can be broader and can be very demanding. Non-profit board members are frequently volunteers with extensive experience in the particular activity (rugby) and with varying levels of passion. Non-profit board members frequently devote enormous amounts of time and often overlap management functions. The fact that they are volunteers can lead to a reduced sense of obligation or contract with the company. There is a sense of individualism on the basis that '*I am giving my time, I will therefore act how I please*'. I believe that board remuneration, no matter how small, can assist in inducing a sense of obligation and improved cohesion.

In common with other countries, Australia seems to be more litigious these days. How does the board deal with this?
In rugby there are player risks (injuries) and risks associated with event management (crowd control, for example).

There exists in rugby a thorough risk assessment process, which identifies the circumstances where injuries are most likely to occur. This information is then used in the drafting of competition rules to minimise the potential for such occurrences. Our risk management also embraces a process for training and accrediting match officials who are empowered to make safety-based decisions. Regardless of all of this, rugby is a contact sport and there are risks that cannot be totally eliminated.

Event management is another area of risk and we have a number of management processes in place, such as not allowing people onto the field of play at the end of the game, and ensuring that crowds maintain an appropriate distance from the playing field in the course of a game.

How does the board approach major decisions?
From a strategic planning process. The board has developed a strategic plan, which has engaged all of its major constituents and the staff. This plan outlines the direction for the organisation and identifies particular strategies and key performance indicators and milestones to measure progress. All of the budgeting processes are linked to the strategic plan, as are the job descriptions and performance measures for senior staff.

Board meetings are clearly defined in two sections. There are issues for decision by the board, and these relate to policy, and there are information papers. Issues for policy decision are frequently raised, initially as discussion papers, and are then developed into a business plan with a recommendation for board decision. A board decision with significant financial ramifications would normally pass by the Audit and Finance Committee on the way to the boardroom. Once a business decision is made, the review process would follow two channels:

- monitoring the execution of the project in terms of financial management and financial reports and milestones achieved; and
- evaluation of the outcomes of the programme to determine the effectiveness in reaching the desired objectives.

What do you see as the essential tasks of the Chair?
- Appoint the right CEO.
- Provide leadership, clarity and consistency.
- Connect with individual board members regularly.
- Establish a clear working relationship with the CEO.
- Challenge the CEO when necessary.

What are your expectations of other board members?
- To be informed.
- To ask questions.
- To read board papers in advance.
- To attend board meetings.
- To be fully ready for the issues under debate.
- To participate in discussions.
- To act at all times in the best interests of the company and its members.
- To accept cabinet responsibility when decisions have been made.

16 Assessing and improving the board

A good board is a victory, not a gift

Cyril Houle

Basis of assessment

As the board has final responsibility for the organisation's performance, evaluation of the board is inextricably bound up with evaluation of organisational performance. If the organisation is under-performing over time, it is partly an indication that the board has not corrected process or management weaknesses. Equally, if the organisation is performing well it is likely that the board is on the job and is contributing to that success – although it is always possible for a board to bask idly in the reflected glory of a hard-working and productive CEO, for a while.

The first steps in evaluating board effectiveness and providing directions for improving the board, therefore, are regular reviews of the CEO's performance and regular monitoring of the implementation of the strategic plan. Issues will arise from these appraisal and monitoring processes that highlight areas for the board to address in its own working and composition.

Using the strategic plan

Unless the board has adopted a strategic plan (or has a clear articulation of policies, as in John Carver's approach[1]) and established means of reviewing the CEO's work, the board's self-evaluation will take place in a vacuum. And in monitoring the plan and appraising the CEO's work the board should be asking, amongst other things:

■ what does this mean for us as a board? How does our behaviour need to change, if at all, for the organisation's or CEO's performance to improve in this area?

---

[1] See Chapter 8, *Policy and Planning Toolkit.*

- where performance has met expectations, in what way did the board contribute to this? Are there things we have been doing as a board that we should be recognising as productive and effective, and building on in the future?

During the strategic planning process much of the time will be devoted to defining strategies that, ultimately, will be fulfilled by the CEO, staff and volunteers. But the board may also set objectives or targets for itself. This serves both to send a strong signal to the CEO and staff that the board takes its contribution to the organisation seriously, and to cultivate a mind-set that is directed to continuous board improvement. Clearly, if the board does adopt targets for its performance or development, these will form an important element in the self-assessment process.

In addition to measuring organisational performance and the board's contribution to this, the board's self-assessment may include:

- an individual questionnaire, to be completed by board members, soliciting views on aspects of current board performance;
- a discussion based on an analysis of the questionnaire, and considering specific ways in which board processes, composition or structures could be improved;
- a session set aside within an annual retreat to consider board processes – this may be particularly appropriate if the retreat includes a session on evaluating progress against the plan;
- benchmarking against boards of other organisations – reviewing their processes and achievements to identify areas where your board could raise its game.

Any self-assessment should be kept simple. The more subtle and complex the procedure, the less stomach the board will have for it, and the more likely it is to remain in the realm of theory rather than practice.

Self-assessment questionnaire

A questionnaire will have greatest value if it is carefully customised for the organisation and the board's present situation, and creates an opportunity for board members to comment on ways in which improvement could occur. There may be areas of change or development which have been a particular preoccupation of the board and which need to be reflected in the questionnaire and any subsequent discussion.

In completing the questionnaire each area of a board's activity is subject to the individual board member's assessment of the board's performance, and of their own personal performance. The questionnaire may give the board the opportunity to comment on board performance in relation to:

- mission, policy and planning;
- organisational and industry knowledge;
- relationship with the CEO;
- marketing and fundraising;
- financial and risk management;
- board composition and processes.

A detailed sample questionnaire is included at Resource 10 (p301).

Depending upon existing intra-board relationships, it may be practical for the questionnaire to be administered by a current board member. Alternatively, the board may want to use an independent facilitator to increase the confidentiality of the responses, and to facilitate debate based on a summary of the completed questionnaires. This will be particularly appropriate if the board is using a facilitator to assist with a forthcoming retreat, within which board self-assessment is taking place. However, the board that has reached a degree of openness and trust which makes external facilitation unnecessary is the most likely to approach self-assessment with resolve, and implement the decisions taken. And that board will save itself facilitator fees.

16.1 Board competencies

Richard Chait and his colleagues correlated the competencies of boards with the effectiveness of the non-profit organisations they manage, across six dimensions:[2]

1 Contextual Dimension
The board understands and takes into account the values and beliefs of the organisation it governs. The board:

- adapts to the distinctive characteristics and culture of the institution's environment;
- relies on the institution's mission, values and tradition as a guide for decisions;
- acts so as to exemplify and reinforce the organisation's values.

---

[2] Adapted from Richard P Chait, Thomas P Holland and Barbara E Taylor, *Improving the Performance of Governing Boards*, American Council on Education (Phoenix, AZ, 1996), pp7–8.

2 Educational Dimension
The board ensures that board members are well informed about the organisation, the profession and the board's role, responsibilities and performance.

3 Interpersonal Dimension
The board nurtures the development of members as a group and fosters a sense of cohesiveness.

4 Analytical Dimension
The board recognises complexities and subtleties of issues and accepts ambiguity and uncertainty as healthy preconditions for critical discussion.

5 Political Dimension
The board accepts as a primary responsibility the need to develop and maintain healthy relationships among major constituencies.

6 Strategic Dimension
The board helps the institution envision a direction and shape a strategy.

Chait concludes that organisations which have boards that exhibited all six competencies perform significantly better than those lacking one or more of these competencies.

Reproduced by permission of the American Council on Education

A continuous process

The Chair and board members do not have to wait for an annual evaluation to address improvements. The process starts with earlier considerations of team-building and process management, including:

- recruitment and induction of board members;
- articulation of a clear role description and standards expected of the board members;
- articulation of the Chair's role and the relationship between the board and CEO;
- adoption of a code of conduct and conflict of interest policy for board members;
- planning and running effective board meetings.

Opportunities for improvement

Board Process	Commentary
Recruitment and induction of board members	The professionalism of the initial dialogue with potential board members, through to the clarity and thoroughness of the induction process for those who ultimately join the board, will have a significant impact on how quickly new board members become productive members of the team. And the quicker this occurs, the more energised the board as a whole will be. New blood is itself a practical way of 'improving the board'.
Articulation of a clear role description and standards expected of the board members	Everyone in an organisation wants to know what is expected of them, and board members are no different. An indicative role description is included in Resource 5 (p284), but specific standards of attendance, contribution and behaviour will enhance this and give a stronger sense of the board's values, and the linkage with the organisation's values which are a key motivator in all non-profits.
Articulation of the Chair's role and the relationship between board and CEO	In addition to understanding the individual board member's role and expectations, effective boards depend on knowing their collective place in the scheme of things. So, clear delineation of the leadership role of the Chair and of the interrelationship, communications protocols and respective roles of the CEO and board help to complete the board's ability to measure their own effectiveness.
Adoption of a code documents of conduct and conflict of interest policy for board members	For all the same reasons as above, and because these will avert friction or provide the board with tools to handle friction in a coherent and constructive way.
Planning and running effective board meetings	Through well-run meetings board members learn more about the organisation, improve their debating and decision-making skills, enhance their motivation and, hopefully, enjoy their regular contact with the organisation and each other.

The Chair's role as team leader will also be influential in keeping board members focused on targets and on ways in which their contribution can be enhanced. Both task-setting and individual board member appraisal will encourage the board to be performance-oriented, to think regularly about increasing the board's capacity to add value to the organisation.

Board improvement is likely to be an incremental rather than revolutionary process. Concentrate on what can realistically be achieved in the short- and medium-term, then move on to another range of improvements. This is not about making sticks to beat your backs with, nor about tilting at some impossible ideal of board-craft – it is about staying alert to the opportunities for the time invested to be more effective and enjoyable.

Board evaluation and improvement

Some supplementary questions for board evaluation and improvement:

- ✔ How are board members carrying out their responsibilities?
- ✔ What areas need improvement?
- ✔ What can be done to effect improvements?
- ✔ Are the governing and policy documents up to date?
- ✔ Are there a sufficient number of board meetings to take care of the organisation's business?
- ✔ Is the current committee structure adequate to handle the work of the board efficiently?
- ✔ Are board meetings conducted effectively?
- ✔ Do meeting agendas cover policy issues rather than administration?
- ✔ How can the value of the meetings be enhanced?
- ✔ Is there sufficient opportunity for the board to hear about minority opinions before recommendations are presented to committees or the board as a whole for consideration?
- ✔ Is the majority of the board involved in making the board's decisions?
- ✔ Is the board supporting and evaluating the Chief Executive?

A governance committee

One tool for institutionalising board improvement is the governance committee. A governance committee can examine how the board is functioning, how board members communicate, and whether the board is fulfilling its responsibilities and living up to the objectives and aspirations set for itself and the organisation. While all board members should understand the organisation's mission and goals, the governance committee must consider them with an eye on the board's responsibility to guide the organisation, and what is required of the board to best accomplish that. The governance committee must be able to articulate the board's vision and find the individuals who can execute it.

Specific committee responsibilities could include:

1 Find, keep, and/or get rid of board members

- Develop board member job descriptions. To recruit a balanced and well-equipped board, create a board profile of what skills and expertise you need.
- Identify potential board members and maintain information about each candidate. Cultivate and recruit new members from beyond your traditional circles.
- With the board Chair, help evaluate board members' individual commitment, support and participation in governance duties.
- Observe and evaluate potential leaders within the board. Evaluate board members' eligibility for re-election.

Some organisations entrust these responsibilities to a Recruitment or Nominating Committee.

2 Educate board members

- Make a priority of orienting new board members. Ensure that they have adequate materials and understanding of their roles and responsibilities.
- Involve board members in 'continuing education' throughout their board service. The governance committee can ensure that board members are updated (about new programmes, legislative action, etc.) and continue to grow their skills as board members. This process also establishes a climate of belonging for board volunteers.
- Establish an effective communications network to keep board members appraised of activities through newsletters, board and committee minutes, media reports, phone calls, thank you notes, etc.

3 Evaluate the board's performance

- Annually conduct a self-assessment of the board and report back to the board with recommendations.
- Discuss with the chief executive staff, and perhaps other staff, about their views of the board's performance and ways to strengthen the board in both its governing and supporting role.

The spirit of the governance committee is to ensure that the board is doing its job and doing it well and, if it is not, to come up with ways to remedy that.

Summary

- A healthy and effective board is part of a successful organisation.
- If the organisation is not performing well, it is ultimately the board's responsibility to remedy this.
- Self-assessment, group discussion, an annual retreat and benchmarking may all be used to evaluate board performance.
- Board improvement is an incremental process, rather than a one-off action, and needs to be institutionalised to secure long-term benefits.
- For some organisations a governance committee will offer a useful mechanism for maintaining a diligent watch on the board's effectiveness.

17 The future of governance

Some simple principles of good governance have been emphasised in the preceding chapters of this book. The way in which these may be manifested will vary from one organisation to the next, according to their scale, resources and the nature of their work. But the basic principles of good governance remain consistent:

1 Commitment to organisational performance as well as to compliance.
2 Structured and rational approaches to decision-making.
3 Careful selection of the CEO.
4 Strategic thinking and openness to the demands of a changing environment.
5 Prediction and mitigation of risk in your operations.
6 Proper attention to the board's own health – through its recruitment, induction, meeting procedures and leadership.

If the key focus of the board can be distilled to these few elementary items, implementation of the board's work is not so simple. There are both internal and external pressures that complicate the board's task.

Internally, there are a series of stresses that affect many non-profits. They include overlapping tensions:

■ between 'amateur' board members and professional staff;
■ between the voluntary organisation and the trend to professional management;
■ between representation of member interests and the need for strategic management;
■ between democratic values and efficient decision-making;
■ between the search for competence and the need to facilitate individual and community engagement.

In the small non-profits that make up the great majority of the 'sector', board members often find themselves in a position where the lack of resources or skills at staff level requires the board to play a very active role, to give up volunteer time which goes well beyond the understanding of board membership. And in large non-profits, some of which resemble commercial organisations in all but dividend-distribution, the consequences of the board's decisions place a heavy burden on its members, individually and collectively.

As Government seeks to secure best value for the taxpayer, public interest is increasingly articulated through funding agreements or other contractual arrangements, which hold the non-profit organisation accountable for specific, quantifiable outputs. The burden of obligation grows. Doing good is not as simple as it used to be.

It is doubtful whether governments have considered fully the consequences of this apparently irreversible move to contract culture. Both the commercial and non-profit sectors have taken up the delivery of services that may not have been provided previously, or that governments themselves may formerly have delivered. For non-profits the legal, philosophical and organisational consequences are profound. A reduction in independence, much heightened expectations of quality and reliability, and the need for professionalism throughout the organisation, are just some of the necessary changes that follow.

In some cases, non-profits are being 'created' as a consequence of government policy – employment and training organisations, for example, established as vehicles to fulfil specific policy demands. They are not, in the traditional sense, a product of voluntarism or community aspirations – instead they represent a convenient legal vehicle to do a job that government prefers to be done at arms-length.

Externally, therefore, there are also a number of pressures placing strain on non-profits and the current model of governance:

- heightened expectations by stakeholders, funders and the general public;
- heightened environmental complexity;
- increased risk levels, and an increasingly litigious society;
- double income families being time-poor, threatening the supply of volunteers (including board and management committee members).

These external and internal trends oblige us to ask, is the current situation sustainable? Can we continue to rely on volunteer boards governing the work of increasingly professional organisations?

Very few people I consulted while preparing this book felt that board members of non-profits should be paid, although a few felt that payment would establish a clearer sense of contract: an obligation to meet standards of attendance and preparation. A small proportion of non-profits already pay their board members, whether for this reason or for others. Amongst larger organisations this may become the norm during the next decade.

A further question relates to whether the current legal framework is adequate to meet today's needs? Most non-profits in the UK that have paid staff are limited companies and registered charities. These legal entities, and the board arrangements that accompany them, are inherited from a time when the non-profit world was a less complex place.

In the UK and elsewhere, the Government has recently been turning its attention to the legal and regulatory environment for non-profit organisations. A recent proposal has emerged to create a new legal form, the 'public interest company' (PIC):

'As the lines among voluntary, public and private sectors become ever more blurred, the legal forms available have been increasingly stretched. Some say they have been stretched to breaking point and we now need a new basis for organisations which deliver public benefit with private sector structures or financing … a PIC could have charitable tax advantages but with much more freedom about the way it finances investment than existing forms.'[1]

In Australia, the Victorian Government has established an Inquiry into Corporate Governance in the public sector, including partnership arrangements with the non-profit sector. The Australian Commonwealth Government has also recently completed an 'Inquiry into the definition of charities and related organisations', which has recommended removal of dependence on English charity law (dating from 1601) and its preamble defining 'charitable purposes', and the introduction of a new definition. The question of whether there should be a regulatory body in Australia for the non-profit sector, similar to England's Charity Commission, is also raised.

How this debate will translate into legislation is difficult to predict. However, one prediction I will make is this: whatever legal form or framework emerges in the UK or other countries, there will continue to be a need to balance and support the Executive role in the organisation. On behalf of the members, the public and funding stakeholders, the need for effective boards will remain. As Churchill said of democracy, 'It is the worst possible system, except for all the others.'

---

[1] Roger Cowe, 'Private money, public gain', *Guardian*, Wednesday 20 March 2002, p13.

PART 4

RESOURCES

Resource **1** Five models of governance

Non-profit boards tend to follow one of five different approaches to governance. Each approach emphasises different dimensions of the roles and responsibilities of the board and each arises out of a different relationship between board members and staff members. These, in turn, reflect differences in the size, purpose and history of the organisation. I call these approaches the Advisory Board Model, the Patron Model, the Cooperative Model, the Management Team Model and the Policy Board Model.

Advisory board model

This model emphasises the helping and supportive role of the board and frequently occurs where the CEO is the founder of the organisation. The board's role is primarily that of helper/adviser to the CEO. Board members are recruited for three main reasons: they are trusted as advisers by the CEO; they have a professional skill that the organisation needs but does not want to pay for; and/or they are likely to be helpful in establishing the credibility of the organisation for fundraising and public relations purposes.

Individual board members may be quite active in performing these functions and consequently feel that they are making a valuable contribution to the organisation. Board meetings tend to be informal and task-focussed, with the agenda developed by the CEO.

The Advisory Board Model can work well for a short time in many organisations, but it exposes the board members to significant liability in that it fails to provide the accountability mechanisms that are required of boards of directors. By law, the board has the obligation to manage the affairs of the organisation and can be held accountable for certain actions of employees and committees. It must therefore maintain a superior position to the CEO. Although the board is permitted to delegate many of its responsibilities to staff or committees, it cannot make itself subordinate to them.

Patron model

Similar to the Advisory Board Model, the board of directors in the Patron Model has even less influence over the organisation than an advisory board. Composed of wealthy and influential individuals with a commitment to the mission of the organisation, the Patron board serves primarily as a figurehead for fundraising purposes. Such boards meet infrequently, as their real work is done outside board meetings. Writing cheques and getting their friends to write cheques is their contribution to the organisation.

Many organisations maintain a Patron board in addition to their governing boards. For capital campaigns, and to establish the credibility of newly formed organisations, Patron boards can be especially helpful. They cannot be relied upon, however, for governance tasks such as vision development, organisational planning, or programme monitoring.

Cooperative model

For a number of different reasons, some organisations try to avoid hierarchical structures. The decision-making structure in such organisations is typically labelled 'peer management' or 'collective management'. In this model, all responsibility is shared and there is no Chief Executive Officer. Decision-making is normally by consensus and no individual has power over another. If the law did not require it, they would not have a board of directors at all. In order to be incorporated, however, there must be a board of directors and officers. The organisation therefore strives to fit the board of directors into its organisational philosophy by creating a single managing/governing body composed of official board members, staff members, volunteers and, sometimes, clients.

Seen by its advocates as the most democratic style of management, it is also, perhaps, the most difficult of all models to maintain, requiring, among other things, a shared sense of purpose, an exceptional level of commitment by all group members, a willingness to accept personal responsibility for the work of others, and an ability to compromise. When working well, the organisation benefits from the direct involvement of front-line workers in decision-making and the synergy and camaraderie created by the interaction of board and staff.

I have noted two areas of concern with this governance model. The first is that although the ability to compromise is an essential element in the successful functioning of this model, cooperatives often arise out of a strong ideological or philosophical commitment that can be inimical to compromise. The second concern is the difficulty of implementing effective accountability structures. At the time of implementing this model, there may be a high motivation level in the organisation that obviates the need for accountability mechanisms. But, as personnel changes take place, the sense of personal commitment to the group as a whole may be lost. In the collective model, there is no effective way to ensure that accountability for individual actions is maintained.

Management team model

For many years, most non-profit organisations have been run by boards that operate according to the model of a Management Team, organising their committees and activities along functional lines. In larger organisations, the structure of the board and its committees usually mirrors the structure of the organisation's administration. Just as there are staff responsible for human resources, fundraising, finance, planning and programmes, the board creates committees with responsibility for these areas.

Where there are no paid staff, the board's committee structure becomes the organisation's administrative structure and the board members are also the managers and deliverers of programmes and services. Individually or in committees, board members take on all governance, management and operational tasks including strategic planning, bookkeeping, fundraising, newsletters, and programme planning and implementation.

The widespread adoption of the Management Team model arises out of its correspondence with modern ideas about team management and democratic structures in the workplace. It also fits well with the widely held view of non-profits as volunteer-driven, or at least non-professional organisations. This model fits well with the experience of many people as volunteers in community groups like service clubs, school groups, scouts and guides, and hobby groups. It also mirrors the processes involved in the creation of a new organisation or service. It is no wonder then, that most prescriptive books and articles written between 1970 and 1990 (and many written more recently) define this model as the ideal.

Boards that operate under the Management Team Model are characterised by a high degree of involvement in the operational and administrative activities of the organisation. In organisations with professional management this normally takes the form of highly directive supervision of the CEO and staff at all levels of the organisation. Structurally, there may be many committees and sub-committees. Decision-making extends to fine details about programmes, services and administrative practices. When working well, two criteria tend to be used in the selection of board members: their knowledge and experience in a specific field, such as business or accounting; or that they are members of a special interest group or sector that the board considers to be stakeholders.

While this model works well for all-volunteer organisations, it has proven to be less suited to organisations that already have professional management and full-time employees. Indeed, the deficiencies of this model have led to the current thinking in the field which differentiates 'governance' (the practices of boards of directors) from 'management' (the practices of employees) and the deluge of research, articles and manuals on this topic.

The most important shortcoming of this model is that, all too frequently, it degenerates into what I call the Micro-management Team Model, in which board members refuse to delegate authority, believing that their role requires them to make all operational decisions, leaving only the implementation to paid staff. The result is invariably a lack of consistency in decisions, dissatisfied board members, resentful staff and a dangerous lack of attention to planning and accountability matters.

Policy board model

As noted above, the need to differentiate the board's role from the manager's role arose from the failure of many organisations to maintain proper accountability at the highest levels and the dissatisfaction of many board members over the their inability to meet the expectations of their role. They began to ask why, when they were such competent and accomplished individuals, they felt so ineffective and frustrated as board members. This led to an examination of the role of the board, the relationship between the board and the CEO, and the relationship between the board and the community.

The originator and most influential proponent of the Policy Board Model is John Carver, whose book, *Boards that Make a Difference*, has had a great effect on thousands of non-profit organisations. All Policy Board Models share the view that the job of the board is to establish the

guiding principles and policies for the organisation; to delegate responsibility and authority to those who are responsible for enacting the
principles and policies; to monitor compliance with those guiding principles and policies; and to ensure that staff and board alike, are held
accountable for their performance.

Boards operating under the Policy Board Model are characterised by a
high level of trust and confidence in the CEO. There are relatively few
standing committees, resulting in more meetings of the full board.
Board development is given a high priority in order to ensure that new
members are able to function effectively, and recruitment is an ongoing
process. Members are recruited for their demonstrated commitment to
the values and mission of the organisation.

Where the governance models diverge is the way these jobs are done
and the extent to which strategic planning and fundraising are seen as
board jobs.

Which model is the right one?

There are a number of reasons for considering a change in your governance model. For example, when:

- board members are dissatisfied with their roles or the way the board
  operates;
- your organisation is experiencing problems that can be traced back
  to inadequacies in board structure or process;
- your organisation is entering a new phase in its life-cycle;
- the CEO has left or is leaving;
- there has been a major turnover of board members;
- there is a crisis of confidence in the board or the CEO.

The descriptions above of the various governance models, will give you
an idea of the strengths and weaknesses of each model, but the difficulty
in making the transition cannot be overstated. Changing models is like
changing lifestyles. You must abandon well-established ideas and
patterns of behaviour, replacing them with new ideas, roles and activities that will seem confusing and unfamiliar. This type of change takes
a considerable amount of time, energy and other resources to accomplish. The answers to the following questions will help you to
determine how badly you need to change your governance model, and
whether your board and organisation have the necessary commitment
and resources to do it successfully. Take your time with each question,
ensuring that each board member answers each question.

- Do we have a clear understanding and agreement on the purpose of our organisation? Is it written down?
- What are the basic values that guide our organisation and our board? Are they written down?
- How do we know whether the good our organisation does is worth what it costs to operate it?
- What financial resources do we have and can we reasonably count on for the next few years?
- To what extent are board members expected to contribute money and labour to fundraising efforts?
- Do we believe that the organisation should be run as a cooperative or collective – with staff participating along with board members in the governing of the organisation?
- How much time is each board member willing to give to the organisation in the next year (or until the end of their term)?
- How much trust does the board have in the ability of the CEO to ensure that the organisation operates in an effective and ethical manner?
- What are our expectations about attendance at board and committee meetings?
- What is the attendance record of each board member?
- How do we hold board members accountable?
- What is the record of each board member and committee with respect to meetings and results?
- How useful has each committee proven to be?
- To what extent do committees duplicate staff jobs? How satisfied are our members with the current board performance?
- Who thinks we should change our governance model?
- How much time and money are we willing to devote to increasing our own knowledge and skills to improve our performance as board members?
- How does our board deal with differences of opinion?
- How do members deal with decisions when we disagree?
- To what extent is it necessary for us (as board members) to be involved in the delivery of programmes and services, marketing, public speaking, etc.?
- Who attends our Annual General Meeting? Why do they come?
- As board members, to whom do we wish to be accountable?
- How effective is our current recruitment method in getting excellent board members?

Take some time to consider these questions. The answers will tell you the degree of difficulty you will have in changing to a new governance model and where the problems lie. For additional information, and for training and consulting services related to governance models, contact: Nathan Garber & Associates, e-mail: nathan@GarberConsulting.com.

© 1997. Reproduced by kind permission of Nathan Garber

Resource **2** Sample conflict of interest policy and declaration

Declaration

The standard of behaviour at the Anywhere Community Association is that all staff, volunteers and board members scrupulously avoid conflicts of interest between the interests of the Anywhere Community Association on the one hand, and personal, professional and business interests on the other. This includes avoiding potential and actual conflicts of interest, as well as perceptions of conflicts of interest.

I understand that the purposes of this policy are to protect the integrity of the Anywhere Community Association's decision-making process, to enable our constituencies to have confidence in our integrity, and to protect the integrity and reputations of volunteers, staff and board members. Upon or before election, hiring or appointment, I will make a full, written disclosure of interests, relationships and holdings that could potentially result in a conflict of interest. This written disclosure will be kept on file and I will update it as appropriate.

In the course of meetings or activities, I will disclose any interests in a transaction or decision where I (including in my business or other non-profit affiliations), my family and/or my significant other, employer, or close associates will receive a benefit or gain. After disclosure, I understand that I will be asked to leave the room for the discussion and will not be permitted to vote on the question.

I understand that this policy is meant to supplement good judgement, and I will respect its spirit as well as its wording.

Signed: ———————————————— Date: ————————————

Board member's annual statement concerning possible conflicts of interest

The undersigned person acknowledges receipt of a copy of the corporate 'Resolution Concerning Conflict of Interest' dated _____/_____/_____.
By my signature affixed below I acknowledge my agreement with the spirit and intent of this resolution and, I agree to report to the Chair of the Board/Management Committee any possible conflicts (other than those stated below) that may develop before completion of the next annual statement.

I _____ am not aware of any conflict of interest

I_____ have a conflict of interest or potential conflict of interest in the following area(s)

_____

_____

_____

_____

Signed: _____

Date: _____

Type or Print Name: _____

Resource **3** Risk management and insurance

Based on material prepared by Myles McGregor-Lowndes

Insurance checklist

- ✔ Public Liability
- ✔ Building and Contents
- ✔ Professional indemnity
- ✔ Workers' compensation
- ✔ Policy extensions
- ✔ Directors' and Officers' Liability
- ✔ Defamation
- ✔ Loss of documents
- ✔ Dishonesty of employees
- ✔ Breach of copyrights
- ✔ Employment practices liability
- ✔ Legal representation cost
- ✔ Outdoor events – pluvious insurance
- ✔ Special events
- ✔ Overseas travel

Business insurances:

- ✔ Fire and special perils cover
- ✔ Money
- ✔ Theft and burglary insurance
- ✔ Fidelity guarantee insurance
- ✔ Glass
- ✔ Motor vehicle insurance
- ✔ Lease agreements
- ✔ Business interruption

Accident Cover: coverage can include:

✔ death
✔ permanent disability
✔ serious/partial disability
✔ loss of income
✔ home assistance
✔ student tutoring assistance
✔ parents' inconvenience allowance
✔ non-National Health expenses (e.g. dental)
✔ accident cover for voluntary workers

Physical assets

The non-profit organisation's assets register will act as a good guide to identifying the physical assets that may require insurance cover. A non-profit organisation may have to maintain an assets register as part of its statutory obligations and, if not, it is still good management practice. Some types of property may not be found in the register, such as leased goods, a car park or stock, foodstuffs and small value items.

There are some common issues that should be considered with all physical asset insurance policies.

- Consider whether insurance should be based on reinstatement value – that is, the cost of rebuilding the property to substantially the same condition as it was when new – or just indemnity. Indemnity will replace only the value of the used asset at the time of loss.
- Consider any excess payable.
- Consider ancillary costs on the destruction of a major asset such as a building. There are usually demolition fees, local authority fees, architect and other professionals' fees and newer building codes requiring different construction. Cover for temporary accommodation might also be required.
- If the physical asset is subject to inflation then an automatic inflation-linked policy might be appropriate.
- If the asset is portable (e.g. a computer or mobile phone) will the cover extend off the business premises, in the UK or worldwide? Portable equipment is also often insured for accidental loss or damage. Assets such as stock or equipment may also be transported off the business premises and may need to be covered.

■ Ensure that assets (particularly contents) are sufficiently recorded so that in the event of destruction an undisputed claim may be lodged with the insurer. An assets register will usually provide an appropriate means to do this, but keep a copy of the register off the main premises. If an event occurs destroying property, the chances are that the assets register will be destroyed as well.

Business insurances

Fire and special perils cover

A fire policy is usually extended to cover a variety of additional risks known as special perils, such as explosion, riot, malicious damage, earthquake, storm, water damage, burst pipes and damage from impact with vehicles and aircraft.

It should be noted that the most common exclusion in such policies is in relation to flood and, accordingly, the non-profit organisation should consider the matter carefully if the property is situated in a flood prone area. Property that is undergoing alteration or addition is also often excluded.

Some plant, especially boilers, air conditioning, refrigeration and pieces of machinery may also be excluded, and special extensions necessary.

If the non-profit organisation has tenants on its property, then suitable arrangements will have to be made with the insurer.

One further matter that should be considered is the extent of cover provided by the policy in respect of goods that the non-profit organisation might not legally own, but has a legal responsibility to care for. Members may leave personal property (e.g. sporting equipment) in the care of the non-profit organisation and coverage should be considered.

Money

Cash and cheques are often excluded from fire and special perils policies, but money extensions are available. Money can also be covered when it is in transit or held overnight at a private residence. There are usually special conditions in relation to the amount of money a single person can carry, loss from an unattended vehicle, or loss from a safe where the key or combination has been left on the closed premises.

Theft and burglary insurance

A non-profit organisation's property (usually excluding money and vehicles) can be insured against theft and this ought to be considered where the non-profit organisation has premises. Insurance companies will often insist that security arrangements be in place before granting the policy. Depending on differing circumstances it may be necessary to install window bars, new locks, electronic security and security lighting. Covering property of members or other groups that is stored on the premises may also be considered.

Often such policies have a schedule of values for stock, and care should be taken where such stock may be subject to seasonal increases, for example at Christmas or at the beginning of the sporting season.

Note that 'walk in thefts' are not usually covered: there has to be forced entry. There is also an obligation on the non-profit organisation to ensure that the alarm systems are operative.

Fidelity guarantee insurance
A fidelity guarantee insurance provides an insured organisation with protection against defalcations of employees or officers of the organisation.

Glass
Glass insurance covers accidental damage other than that caused by fire or burglary. Temporary boarding and security arrangements are usually included in the policy. It may also be necessary to include damage to signs in this sort of extension.

Motor vehicle insurance
Vehicle and compulsory third-party insurance is fairly standard. The non-profit organisation should ensure that only those with appropriate qualifications drive any vehicles.

Lease agreements
Careful consideration should be given to insurance requirements when property is leased. When a formal lease is proposed for a building, sports field, car park, vehicle or piece of equipment there will often be written clauses defining responsibilities for insurance. Close attention should be paid to these requirements.

When the agreement is not in writing, careful consideration should be paid to exposure to liabilities.

Do not overlook the implications of:
- the holding of meetings or events in members' homes;
- service delivery in a client's home;
- free use or hire of a public hall or meeting place.

Business interruption

This relates to additional financial loss resulting from the destruction of business premises. The organisation, for example, may sell recycled clothing from a shop. The shop is destroyed and income is lost until it is replaced. The insurance may pay either actual loss of income or the additional cost of carrying on business, e.g. renting another shop.

Outdoor events – pluvious insurance

A non-profit organisation holding an outdoor event may be exposed to risks from bad weather restricting or cancelling events. The sum insured is usually related to the income anticipated from the event.

Pay close attention to how adverse weather is to be measured, as it may be from the nearest weather station, which may or may not experience that same rain as the venue.

Special events

Additional insurance may be necessary for conferences, exhibitions or sporting events. The risks to be covered will depend on the nature of the activity, but it may be necessary to:

- increase public liability for the duration;
- increase contents for displays or stock;
- increase financial loss cover in case the main attraction or venue fails;
- cover for carnival attractions and hired equipment.

Liability insurance

The insurance term 'public liability' is very loosely used. It is often called third-party insurance. It indemnifies an organisation in respect of claims that may be made against it for its legal liability for injury/loss or damages to persons or property.

One of the major issues is the amount of cover that is required. The cover needs to reflect realistically the assessment of damages by the courts, which appears to be ever increasing. Potential claims by injured children and highly paid professionals should not be overlooked.

✔ Consider whether coverage beyond the UK is required.

✔ Consider any excesses.

✔ Public liability policies need to be specific to the activities carried out by the non-profit organisation and so a sporting non-profit organisation's policy may be very different from those of a childcare centre, a trade association or a health care service. It is important to analyse the activity-specific risks of the non-profit organisation.

General public liability insurance

This type of policy usually provides the non-profit organisation and its members with an indemnity against its legal liability to pay damages for accidental injury and accidental damage to property. The standard policy covers the situation where the injury is caused by the action of the non-profit organisation or its members to a member of the public.

Accidents occurring on your property are commonly covered, but the situation in respect of (for example) a leased car park should not be overlooked.

Extensions to cover injuries to a member of the non-profit organisation or between members of the public attending an activity organised by the organisation may be necessary. An example of this may be a sporting fixture where neither team's players are members of the organisation.

Consideration should be given to liabilities incurred through goods sold by organisations, such as food, drink, clothing and equipment, toys and medical aids.

Professional indemnity insurance

Non-profit organisations that provide professional services to their members or the public ought to ensure that they have adequate professional indemnity insurance. The insurance is designed to cover the non-profit organisation from liability arising from its negligence or a breach of its duties to others.

Organisations that employ doctors, healthcare workers, lawyers, accountants, coaches, counsellors and the like to give advice or act for others are prime examples. For example, a sporting body should consider first aid treatment risks, coaches', referees', and umpires' liabilities.

The policy will be activated only when a claim is made on the policy. It will not necessarily cover events that happened in the policy period but were not notified to the insurer until a later date. Special extensions can be used to alter this situation.

Professional indemnity policies vary greatly depending on the professions involved, and the exclusions must be carefully understood. Extensions may be necessary for:

- defamation;
- fidelity guarantee;
- loss of documents;
- Trade Practices legislation.

Consideration may also be given as to whether the individual professional is covered as well as the organisation and, especially, whether volunteers are included.

Directors' and officers' insurance

Organisations might also consider whether they need or have adequate directors' and officers' insurance. Although there are several different types of policies currently on the market, the most common policy is the 'split' policy, which provides two types of cover:

1 Company reimbursement (which provides insurance to the organisation in respect of its liability pursuant to indemnities lawfully given to its directors or officers).
2 A Directors and Officers liability policy (which provides insurance to the director or officer for personal liability in respect of which he is not entitled to an indemnity from the company).

This form of insurance is particularly complicated and the terms of cover are highly technical. Accordingly, before taking out such a policy, an organisation and its directors or officers should consult with their insurance brokers or legal advisers in relation to these matters.

There will usually also be obligations imposed to make full disclosure of any circumstances which might give rise to a claim, and in relation to the financial and solvency position of the organisation. Steps should be taken to ensure that this obligation is complied with before entering into the policy.

It should be noted that the Directors and Officers policy will exclude claims arising from fraud or dishonesty on the part of a director or officer although, by special request, the 'innocent' or non-involved directors or officers may obtain cover where they are liable for the fraud or dishonesty of a co-director.

Overseas travel

This insurance can be obtained on a specific one-off basis for staff and volunteers travelling overseas. If there is an amount of travel overseas, then an annual policy can be arranged for automatic blanket cover.

Legal expense

This insurance may cover solicitors' and barristers' fees relating to specified disputes. Legal expenses have the ability to exceed the actual award of damages in some cases.

Consideration should be given as to whether this applies to tribunals as well as courts.

Some insurance companies offer free legal help lines to provide legal advice on the steps that should be taken when a potential claim arises. The premiums are usually quite expensive.

Accident cover

This type of insurance is not dependent on anyone being found to be legally negligent. It will be activated by injury as a result of participation in a non-profit organisation's activity. It is very common in sporting contexts, schools and childcare organisations. The payment under the policy is usually pre-determined, such as £50,000 for death, or £2,000 for household assistance during recovery. The premiums will vary according to the risks associated with the activity and the schedule of benefits. Premiums for professional athletes are considerably higher than for amateurs, for example.

Consideration should be given as to whether the schedule of benefits is realistic, given the premium.

Consideration should be given to the geographical cover – the UK or worldwide?

Consideration should also be given to the events upon which the benefits will be paid and the class of persons whom the policy covers.

Accident cover for voluntary workers

Volunteer workers are the backbone of many non-profit organisations and injuries caused to volunteers ought to be insured against. The organisation should ensure that the policy is at least sufficient to cover medical expenses and salary lost because of the accident.

Exclusions should be closely scrutinised in these policies. Some have age limits on volunteers, and some non-profit organisations have many volunteers well beyond these age limits.

Organisations that are offered volunteer labour from schools, tertiary institutions and governments should establish that such people are covered adequately under an insurance policy – either their own or that of the supplying body.

Risk identification

General risk identification checklist

- ✔ Chattel/contents loss
- ✔ Company records loss
- ✔ Compliance with Government grant conditions
- ✔ Compliance with own constitution
- ✔ Computer record loss or corruption
- ✔ Contractual liabilities
- ✔ Corporate law regulations
- ✔ Discrimination legislation
- ✔ Employment
- ✔ Fraud and theft
- ✔ Fundraising regulations
- ✔ Glass and signs
- ✔ Health regulations
- ✔ Interruption of business or services
- ✔ Lotteries
- ✔ Motor vehicles (own or use by volunteers)
- ✔ Negligence in delivery of services
- ✔ Nuisance, such as excessive noise and activity
- ✔ Pollution
- ✔ Product liability
- ✔ Professional negligence
- ✔ Property loss
- ✔ Special events/activities

✔ Staff travel
✔ Taxation
✔ Volunteers
✔ Workers' compensation
✔ Workplace health and safety

The diagram on the following page clusters the risks facing non-profit organisations under five broad headings:

- governance
- outcomes
- physical
- relationship
- financial.

Within each of these areas, specific examples of risks are identified. The diagram can be adapted and used as a prompt when auditing risk in your organisation.

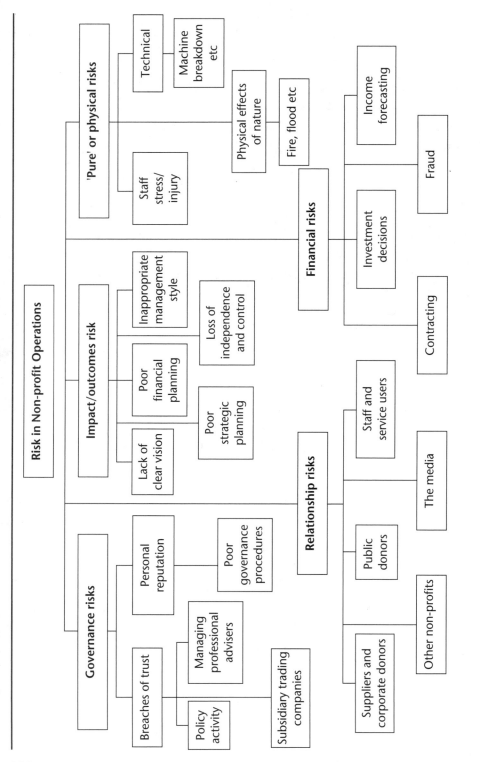

Resource **4** Volunteers

Ideas for motivating volunteers (and your staff too)

Recognition when a volunteer joins your organisation

- Send a letter of welcome (maybe a small welcome gift too).
- Provide a good role description; issue name tag, ID card, etc.
- Provide an induction (including an organisation tour).
- Assign a space to the volunteer (place to put coat, bag, on-going work, etc.), if appropriate.
- Publish names of new volunteers in employee/volunteer newsletter.
- Introduce the new volunteer to other staff.
- Introduce the volunteer to their team leader.
- Develop a talent inventory of the volunteers.

Recognition on a daily or weekly basis

- SMILE!
- Informal thank you from staff and the volunteer's supervisor.
- Document their time for future evaluation.
- On the job praise – with specific comments.
- Provide good supervision.
- Seek feedback from volunteers (suggestions/improvements).
- Show awareness/sensitivity to religious practices of volunteer (holidays, customs, prayer rituals).
- Have board members talk with the front line volunteers.
- Take time to talk.
- Say 'we missed you'.
- Recognise personal problems and needs.
- Use a volunteer suggestion box.

Recognition on a monthly basis

- Volunteer of the Month.
- Set aside time for supervision and evaluation.
- Articles in newsletters.
- Provide opportunities to attend volunteer conferences/workshops.
- Letters to the papers about your organisation's volunteers.

Recognition at the completion of a special event or project

- Say 'thank you'.
- Send letter of thanks to the volunteer, their boss, or their school
- Write an article about the project for the local newspapers or the organisation's publication.
- Take the volunteer(s) out for lunch or a coffee break.
- Promotion – give the volunteer more responsibility.
- Wall of fame – post up a picture of the volunteer with a summary of the project.
- Write a letter to prominent public figures.

Recognition at meetings with staff or groups

- Tell others about the volunteer projects and individual volunteer accomplishments.
- Show slides or videos of the volunteers at work.
- Invite volunteers to staff meetings.
- Provide volunteers with outside training resources.

Recognition on occasions, at events, etc.

- Send your volunteers a birthday card.
- Have an informal birthday party.
- Send a get well card.
- Remember special events in their lives (child's wedding, job promotions, anniversaries).

Recognition when a volunteer leaves the organisation

- Give a letter of thanks.
- Give a certificate/pin of appreciation.
- Write a letter of recommendation.

- Write a letter of appreciation/commendation to the volunteer's present employer.
- Have an exit interview.

Where to recognise your volunteers

- Volunteer Office or lounge.
- Hallway in building/cafeteria.
- In the community.
- At shopping centres – on display boards.
- In the media – newspaper articles, local TV shows, professional journals.
- In your organisation's newsletter or on your website.

Reproduced by kind permission of Volunteer Canada:
www.volunteer.ca/volunteer/celebrate_recognition_hints.htm

Volunteer rights

Unlike paid staff, volunteers are not covered by workplace agreements. Volunteers, however, do have rights, some of which are enshrined in legislation and some of which are the moral obligations of an organisation involving volunteers. The following list is the basis of your rights as a volunteer. As a volunteer you have the right:

- to work in a healthy and safe environment;
- to be interviewed and employed in accordance with equal opportunity and anti-discrimination legislation;
- to be adequately covered by insurance;
- to be given accurate and truthful information about the organisation for which you are working;
- to be reimbursed for out-of-pocket expenses incurred on behalf of the organisation for which you are working;
- to be given a copy of the organisation's volunteer policy and any other policy that affects your work;
- not to fill a position previously held by a paid worker;
- not to do the work of paid staff during industrial disputes;
- to have a job description and agreed working hours;
- to have access to a grievance procedure;
- to be provided with an induction to the organisation;
- to have your confidential and personal information dealt with in accordance with the principles of the Data Protection Act; and
- to be provided with sufficient training to do your job.

Resource 5 Draft board role descriptions

The following role descriptions for board officers are intended to provide a guide only, and may be adapted according to the particular emphasis that your organisation places on each role.

Position Title: Chairperson of the Board

Function:
- As Chairperson of the board, assure that the board fulfils its responsibilities for the governance of the Anywhere Community Association (ACA).
- Be a partner to the CEO, helping him/her to achieve the mission of the ACA.
- Optimise the relationship between the board and management.

Qualifications/Skills:
- Completed two years of board membership term and have an understanding of parliamentary procedures.

Term:
- The Chair serves for a two-year term.

Requirements:
- Commitment to the work of the ACA.
- Knowledge and skills in one or more areas of board governance: policy, finance, programmes and/or personnel.
- Willingness to serve on at least one committee.
- Attendance at monthly board meetings.
- A time commitment of between five and eight hours per month (includes board preparation, meeting, sub-committee and meeting time).
- Attendance at Annual General Meeting.
- Be informed of the services provided by the ACA and publicly support them.
- Prepare for and participate in the discussions and the deliberations of the board.

- To foster a positive working relationship with other board members and ACA staff.
- Be aware and abstain from any conflict of interest.

Responsibilities:
- Provide leadership and direction to the board.
- Chair meetings of the board. See that it functions effectively, interacts with management optimally, and fulfils all of its duties. With the CEO develop agendas.
- Serve as ex-officio member of other board committees.
- Call special meetings if necessary.
- Arrange for Vice to Chair meetings in the absence of the Chair.
- With the CEO, recommend composition of the board committees. Recommend committee chairpersons with an eye to future succession.
- Work with the nominating committee to recruit new board members.
- Assist the CEO in recruiting board and other talent for whatever volunteer assignments are needed.
- Periodically consult with board members on their roles and help them assess their performance.
- Establish overall long- and short-term goals, objectives and priorities for the ACA in meeting the needs of the community.
- Ensure board members receive agenda and minutes in a timely manner.
- Reflect any concerns management has in regard the role of the board or individual trustees. Reflect to the CEO the concerns of the board and other constituencies.
- Prepare a review of the CEO and recommend salary for consideration by the appropriate committee.
- Oversee searches for a new CEO.
- Annually focus the board's attention on matters of organisational governance that relate to its own structure, role and relationship to management.
- Work in partnership with the CEO to make sure board resolutions are carried out.
- Serve as an alternate spokesperson.
- Enhance relationships with other community groups and agencies.
- Fulfil such other assignments as the Chair and CEO agree are appropriate and desirable for the Chair to perform.
- Adhere to general duties outlined in the board member job description.

Based on material prepared by, and reproduced by kind permission of Minnesota Council of Non-profits, www.mncn.org/bdpos.htm

Position Title: Vice Chair

Qualifications/Skills:

- Completed one year of board membership term and have an understanding of meeting procedures.

Term:

- The Vice is selected by Executive Committee to serve for a one-year term.

Requirements:

- Commitment to the work of the ACA.
- Knowledge and skills in one or more areas of board governance: policy, finance, programmes and personnel.
- Willingness to serve on at least one committee.
- Attendance at board meetings.
- A time commitment of five hours per month (includes board preparation, committee and meeting time).
- Attendance at Annual General Meeting.
- Be informed of the services provided by the ACA and publicly support them.
- Prepare for and participate in the discussions and the deliberations of the board.
- To foster a positive working relationship with other board members, and ACA staff.
- Be aware and abstain from any conflict of interest.

Major Duties:

- Fulfil Chair position in the absence of the Chairperson, at monthly board meetings.
- Be an active member of the Executive Committee.
- A signing authority on behalf of the board for financial and legal purposes.
- Adhere to general duties outlined in the board member job description.

Position Title: Secretary

Qualifications/Skills:
- Good communication and written skills.

Term:
- The Secretary is appointed by Executive Committee for a two-year term.

Requirements:
- Commitment to the work of the ACA.
- Willingness to serve on at least one committee.
- Attendance at monthly board meetings.
- A time commitment of five hours per month (includes Board preparation, meeting, committee and meeting time).
- Attendance at Annual General Meeting.
- Be informed of the services provided by the ACA and publicly support them.
- Prepare for and participate in the discussions and the deliberations of the board.
- To foster a positive working relationship with other board members, and ACA staff.
- Be aware and abstain from any conflict of interest.

Major Duties:
- Keeping the minutes of the ACA, monitoring and verifying their accuracy, and circulating to all directors.
- Keeping the register of members and allowing members to inspect it.
- Ensuring the change of records for any land owned by the ACA on its incorporation afterwards.
- Ensuring that the rules are in a legible state.
- Lodging financial statements.
- Notifying the relevant authorities of a change of officers.
- Notifying the chief executive of the ACA's insurance.
- Providing notice for the convening of all general meetings and meetings to hear membership appeals.

Position Title: Treasurer

Qualifications/Skills:
- Completed one year of board membership and have the ability to read / understand / interpret financial statements.

Term:
- The Treasurer is appointed by the Executive Committee to serve a two-year term.

Requirements:
- Commitment to the work of the ACA.
- Willingness to serve on at least one committee.
- Attendance at monthly board meetings.
- A time commitment of five hours a month (includes Board preparation, meeting, committee and meeting time).
- Attendance at Annual General Meeting.
- Be informed of the services provided by the ACA and publicly support them.
- Prepare for and participate in the discussions and the deliberations of the board.
- To foster a positive working relationship with other board members, and the general staff.
- Be aware and abstain from any conflict of interest.

Major Duties:
- Ability to read / understand / interpret financial statements for board members.
- Chair the Finance Committee.
- A signing authority on behalf of the board for financial matters.
- Ensure audited financial statements are presented to the board on an annual basis.
- Calls the motion at Annual General Meeting to appoint the Auditor.
- Act as a resource to other committees.
- Adhere to general duties outlined in the board member job description.

Position Title: Board Member

Function:
- Provide governance to the ACA, represent it to the community, and accept the ultimate legal authority for it.

Qualifications/Skills:
- Knowledge and skills in one or more areas of board governance, e.g. policy, finance, programmes or personnel.

Term:
- Board members are elected by the membership at the Annual General Meeting. Board members serve for a two-year term. Board members may be re-elected for two additional terms.

Requirements:
- Commitment to the work of the ACA.
- Willingness to serve on at least one committee and to participate actively in the work of the board.
- Attendance at monthly board meetings.
- A time commitment of five hours per month (includes board preparation, meeting and committee meeting time).
- Attendance at Annual General Meeting.
- Be informed of the services provided by the ACA and publicly support them.
- Prepare for and participate in the discussions and the deliberations of the board.
- Be aware and abstain from any conflict of interest.

Major Duties:
- Govern the organisation by the broad policies developed by the board.
- Establish overall long- and short-term goals, objectives and priorities for the ACA in meeting the needs of the community.
- Recommend policy to the board.
- Promote the organisation membership through community networking, etc.
- Be accountable to the funders for the services provided and funds expended.
- Monitor and evaluate the effectiveness of the organisation through a regular review of programmes and services.
- Provide candid and constructive criticism, advice and comments.
- Approve major actions of the ACA, such as capital expenditure and major programme and service changes.

- Annually review the performance of the board and take steps to improve its performance.
- Seek nominations for election to the board when appropriate.
- Prepare for and participate in the discussions and the deliberations of the board.
- Foster a positive working relationship with other board members, and ACA staff.
- Be aware of and abstain from any conflict of interest.
- Be assured that management succession is properly being provided.
- Appoint independent auditors subject to approval by members.
- Review compliance with relevant material laws affecting the ACA.

Based on material prepared by and reproduced by kind permission of www.boarddevelopment.org.

Resource **6** Working with consultants

The use of consultants could be a major issue for your donors and supporters, who may positively dislike the idea that some of their donations will go to a paid consultant. You need to think very carefully before going down this particular road.

If you decide to go ahead, you must produce a clear brief against which you can compare quotes from different people (consultants expect to tender for business). Once you have identified your consultant, you must agree precise terms in a clearly written contract. The Institute of Fundraising has a useful set of guidelines for charities wishing to appoint a consultant.

If you are paying someone not directly employed by you to sign appeal letters on your behalf, to visit donors or to make phone calls to donors, the Charities Act 1992 requires them to declare their status as a professional fundraiser and how they are being paid. There must also be a written agreement in a prescribed form between the charity and the professional fundraiser. A standard agreement can be obtained from The Institute of Fundraising, or see *The Fundraisers Guide to the Law* published by the Directory of Social Change for a model.

Payment by results

You may be tempted to pay commission rather than a flat fee to link cost with performance. This is problematic:

- Under the Charities Act 1992, if the consultant asks for money they have to make a declaration that they will receive a part of the donation as a commission, which can affect the chances of getting support (although if they simply advise on strategy or write out the letter for you to sign, no declaration needs to be made).
- The Charities Commission is not keen on commission-based fundraising. They feel that the charity should employ someone based on their competence to do the job and the expectation that they will succeed, and pay the consultant on this basis. But payment could include a success fee if certain targets are achieved.

- If you have not made a financial commitment, you have less incentive to manage the consultant effectively.
- The consultant might cherry pick – get those donations you were expecting anyway, and do little more.

If you cannot afford a professional fundraiser, which is a common situation for small organisations, you could:

- look for sponsorship to cover the costs of the consultancy – show it as a cost-effective investment in the future of your organisation;
- seek a grant for an initial feasibility study – the Charities Aid Foundation makes grants for this;
- find someone to do the work for nothing – a long shot!
- do the work yourselves, but gather around you people with the required expertise to advise you.

How to select an adviser

Whoever you decide to choose, there are a number of steps to go through:

1 Be absolutely sure of the help you need. Is it just to devise the strategy, or do you need additional help with its implementation? Do you need someone to do a specific task done, or just advise?
2 Write a good brief and clear job description covering what needs to be done, the timetable and the specific objectives.
3 Have a selection of people or companies to choose from – ensuring that you choose the best.
4 Agree the basis of payment. Is this acceptable? What control over success and failure will you retain? How will expenses be charged? How much notice is required to terminate the arrangement if you are dissatisfied?
5 Obtain and follow up references. If you do not get good – or indeed any – references, proceed only with the greatest caution.

Nina Botting and Michael Norton, *The Complete Fundraising Handbook*, 4th edn, Directory of Social Change (London, 2001), pp32–3

Resource **7** Robert's rules of order

Where formal voting is required the parliamentary-minded will be aware that there are set procedures for considering a decision. The most widely adopted are *Robert's Rules of Order*, which provide for a structured and logical approach. To summarise:

- One of the board members will **move** that a decision be made (this is proposing that the board go on record in favour of a certain definite action).
- Another member of the group will **second** the motion, which means 'support' for the action proposed. (The second is necessary to be certain that the issue is of interest to more than one person.)
- Once the motion has been made and seconded there is **discussion**, **clarification**, and **debate**.
- When the subject has been covered fully, there is the **vote**.
- Prior to both discussion and vote, the person in the chair should restate the motion to be certain everyone knows what is being discussed and decided.

The next level involves a situation in which the group considers that it might want to make some changes in the motion as originally offered. In the course of the discussion it may become obvious that the motion doesn't quite say what the board now has in mind. This is the way that slightly more complicated scenarios would unfold:

- The motion.
- The second.
- The chairperson restates the motion.
- Discussion, clarification and debate.
- Someone suggests that the original motion be amended and another person seconds the idea. (At that point it will usually happen that the proposer and seconder of the original or main motion will agree to the amendment even though a vote on the amendment has not been taken. Technically, once a motion has been made and seconded it involves the whole assembly, but if no one offers objection to the amendment, no vote is usually taken.)

- If the persons who moved and seconded the original motion do not agree to the amendment, or if anyone else voices an objection, then there is discussion, clarification and debate on the amendment itself.
- After the group has adequately considered the amendment, the chairperson restates the motion to amend and the group votes *on the amendment.*
- Once the amendment has been accepted or rejected, the group returns its attention to the original motion.
- If the amendment had been passed, the main motion would now be known as 'the original motion as amended'. If the amendment had been defeated, it would simply be the original motion.
- Debate would proceed on the original motion. It could be amended again, in which case it would be the new amendment that gets the informal or formal consideration.
- When the amendments have been disposed of, the board votes on the original motion (as amended, if that's the case). Although that is slightly more complicated, it is simply the group's way of deciding whether the original motion needed some changes before it reflected the combined view of what should be done.
- If the main motion is defeated, the same basic proposal cannot be brought forward again at the same meeting. That's to keep the losers from filibustering by bringing the same motion up again and again. (There is an exception: if one person who was on the winning side of the vote realises that he or she may have made a mistake, such as misunderstanding what the motion called for, he or she can move for reconsideration, at which point the board decides whether to allow this reconsideration.)

Brian O'Connell, *The Board Member's Book: Making a Difference in Voluntary Organisations*, The Foundation Center (New York, 1985), pp106–7.

Resource **8**
CEO recruitment

Active searching

The board's proactive stance towards CEO recruitment would be demonstrated if the search and selection panel did not rely solely on the results of one or two advertisements. The panel, possibly with input from the incumbent CEO, should also consider drawing up a circulation list of organisations to contact with details of the post, in order to alert potential candidates (they may not be reading the recruitment pages of the national or trade press).

A decision also needs to be taken on whether members of the selection panel are going to network within relevant industry sectors to identify prospects, and encourage them to apply for the post; or whether the task of networking should be entrusted to an Executive Search agency (in which case, ensure the agency has a proven track record of searches in relevant fields of work).

If the board is embarking on its own search process it is essential that confidentiality and high standards of professionalism guide its approach. Conversations with prospects should be treated as strictly in-confidence. Names should not be bandied around the organisation – a prospect who may ultimately decide not to apply does not want word getting back to their current employer that they are on the job market (especially if they aren't!). Similar sensitivity applies to when and how references with current employers are taken up. In some cases, health checks and criminal record checks will be required. Adopt a minimalist approach, asking only for essential information, and keeping within the letter and spirit of the laws against discrimination. If in any doubt, clear the application form and line of questioning with a personnel professional or lawyer with relevant experience.

Other issues for the selection panel or the board as a whole to consider include:

- whether the outgoing CEO will have an involvement in the process;
- whether other staff will be consulted, and on what basis;
- whether key stakeholders (e.g. funding agencies) will be consulted, and how;
- contingency plans in the event that the recruitment process does not at first succeed.

The interview

The interview process itself should be planned, consistent and searching. In some cases it will be appropriate to have more than one interview round, or to split interviews between two panels covering different topics areas. In most cases it would be unwise to depend solely on the interview. It is a truism in the personnel field that interviews are a poor means of assessing job suitability. Hence the use of structured tests (in-tray exercises or similar), informal time with the candidates, use of Myers-Briggs or other personality profiling tools, and even a day-on-the-job assessment – all of which can be supplemented by taking up references in a way that focuses referees on the specific requirements of the job, probes the candidate's previous achievements in detail, and discourages generalised character witnessing. However, the reality is that most organisations will depend heavily on the results of the interview – so it's all the more important for the interview to be well planned.

The same board members who make up the selection panel should make up the interview panel. It is worth considering the addition of an appropriate and experienced outsider, to provide expertise and focus. Normally, the Chair of the board will be a member of the selection/interview panel, and will chair it.

The interview should be structured to secure the maximum information additional to that which has been provided in the written application. The greatest value the interview can add to the process is to probe the prospective CEO's previous achievements thoroughly, through a series of open questions requiring a full explanation (and which discourage yes/no answers). Of course, the candidates will be asked about their ideas and policy suggestions, their style of leadership, the relationship they expect to have with the board, and so on. But whilst candidate responses to these may be interesting, and will certainly reveal how quick-witted the candidates are and how well they communicate, the fact remains that all these responses may constitute a 'performance'. The hard data lies in their track record – investigate it thoroughly, then use referees to verify. Telephone references give the opportunity to probe, and explore specific questions relating to the candidate's ability and track record – but notes should be taken during a telephone reference and filed in the same way that a written reference would be.

An interview plan

Have a plan: It is best to have a structure to the interview, outline it to the candidate, and follow it yourself.

Develop rapport: Be natural and friendly with the candidates. Make them feel relaxed so that their behaviour is natural.

Take notes: Notes help you remember what was said. Keep them short to avoid lengthy breaks in eye contact.

Open and closed questions: Use open questions to obtain a general picture. Use closed questions to probe.

Leading questions: Make sure that the way questions are asked does not tell the candidate the reply to give.

Talking time: The purpose of the interview is to provide you with information on the candidate. Therefore he or she should talk 75 per cent of the time, you only 25 per cent.

Prejudice and bias: Your judgement of the candidate should depend on the facts, not on bias.

Relevance: The content of the interview should provide relevant information on whether the candidate is suitable for the job.

V. Shackleton, *How to Pick People for Jobs*, Fontana (London, 1989), pp100–1

In order to provide a consistent and rational basis for decision-making (which candidate are we going to recommend be appointed?) and, indeed, to provide a framework to resolve disagreements between interview panel members, it is important to confirm an evaluation system, probably including a scoring process against specific criteria. These criteria will relate to the candidate specification which was agreed at the time the job description was prepared, with weightings allocated to each criterion being discussed amongst the panel members (before the interviews have started).

Finally, when a new CEO is appointed, it is important for the board to provide support, guidance and regular communication during the early days. It is tempting for boards to be lulled into a false sense of security by a capable CEO who has been in post for many years. An assumption develops that this is the way relationships normally are between boards and CEOs – a high level of understanding, clear delineation of who does what, and reports as the board wants them. It may not be nearly so obvious to the incoming CEO. Time needs to be invested in their induction to ensure there is a common understanding of the parameters of their role, and that they have a grasp of the current issues facing the organisation. They may not fully share the aptitudes or attitudes of the previous CEO, which may call for some adjustment on the board's part, or at least open dialogue to avoid misperceptions.

Resource 9 CEO performance review

1   The Performance Review of the CEO is intended to be a constructive tool in the appraisal of key staff against the job descriptions that form part of their employment contracts. The reviews are designed to assist in the analysis of staff weaknesses and strengths in the performance of their duties. The criteria and measures against which the CEO will be assessed are intentionally broad and unweighted.

2   The Performance Reviews of the CEO remain strictly confidential to the board and CEO.

3   Copies of the reviews shall be retained ONLY by the Chair of the board, off premises, either in hard or soft copy.

4   These Terms of Reference for the CEO Review have been developed in consultation with the CEO and have received the approval of the full board.

5   These Terms of Reference are subject to the Company Disciplinary Procedures, including warning and dismissal procedures, which form part of all Employment Contracts with the company.

6   The CEO Reviews may be referred to and used by both the board and the CEO to support contract renegotiations, including conditions such as duration of contract and remuneration.

Frequency

7   The CEO Reviews will be conducted annually with half-yearly progress reviews, unless otherwise stated in Employment Contracts.

Process

Constitution of panel

8   The Performance Review Panel will consist of three board members including the Chair.

9   The board will seek input to the reviews only from the CEO unless cause may be shown to seek input from other internal and/or external sources.

10 The process for the CEO Reviews is subject to Company Review Policy as follows:

Part A – The CEO undertake a personal review against criteria and measures. This review will take the following shape:

- CEO to review his/her own work under appropriate range of headings, including key areas of responsibility and/or key elements of the Strategic Plan.
- Assessment of adequacy of supervision and direction, including suggestions for improvement.
- Assessment of concerns and difficulties being experienced that are constraining performance.
- Suggestions for training and/or changes that would enable the CEO to better perform in his/her position.

Part B – The board undertake a review against criteria and measures. This review will take the following shape:

- The Board to review the CEO's performance against same appropriate headings as the CEO's personal review.
- Assessment of how the CEO implements agreed plans and policy directions.
- Assessment of both external (government, public, community/industry, etc.) and internal (other company staff/employees, permanent, casual workers, volunteers) relations.

Part C – The CEO Performance Review Panel will then convene with the CEO for discussion about the reviews undertaken in Parts A and B. At this discussion the CEO and board will jointly develop appropriate objectives to address variances and performance measures.

(Note: Part C to form the basis of the subsequent review.)

Criteria and measures

1 Criteria have been kept to a minimum to encapsulate entire areas of performance and to ensure the scope of the review is sufficiently wide-ranging to allow all matters to be raised and accommodated within the review.

2 Measures have been kept to an absolute minimum for clarity and simplicity and will consist only of:

- Exceeds expectations
- Satisfactory
- Needs some improvement
- Highly unsatisfactory

Resource **10** Board self-assessment questionnaire

Under each section of the questionnaire the board member should be given an opportunity to add qualitative comment – amplifying on their assessment and indicating how board performance might be improved.

At the end of the questionnaire, the board member should be given the opportunity to make any broader comments on areas for improvement, and perhaps to focus on the improvements which he or she thinks should form the highest priorities.

Performance Element	Yes	Partly	No	Don't know
Mission, Policy and Planning				
I am familiar with the current mission statement				
The board has approved a mission statement which is appropriate for the organisation's current role				
The board focuses its attention on long-term significant policy issues rather than short-term administrative matters				
The board has articulated policies relating to our main areas of service delivery				
The board has articulated policies relating to our organisational processes (e.g. conflict of interest policies, risk management policies, financial authorities, staff selection and grievance procedures)				
The organisation has developed a strategic plan and monitors its implementation regularly				
Organisational and Industry Knowledge				
I am knowledgeable about the organisation's current activities and services The board periodically considers amendments to the range of programmes and services in the light of changed circumstances				

continued

Performance Element	Yes	Partly	No	Don't know
The board fully understands the external environment in which it is operating				
Relationship with the CEO				
A written job description clearly spells out the responsibilities of the CEO				
A climate of trust exists between board and CEO				
The board appraises the CEO systematically, and remunerates him/her appropriately				
Marketing and Fundraising				
The board has approved an effective marketing and communications strategy for the organisation				
I understand the fundraising strategy for the organisation				
The board assists the fundraising in practical ways – providing contacts or contributing directly				
Financial and Risk Management				
The organisation has developed good financial controls				
The board discusses thoroughly the annual budget of the organisation and its implications before approving it				
The board receives regular financial reports that are accurate, timely and clearly comprehensible				
The board has agreed key financial indicators and monitors these routinely				
The board has approved risk management strategies				
Board composition and processes				
The board currently contains a sufficient range of expertise to make it an effective governing body				
The board has effective recruitment and induction processes				
The board holds effective meetings				
The board's size and structure is adequate				

Resource **11** Looking ahead: a 7-point plan

1 *Schedule key board events and programmes*

2 *Develop your board*
- Develop a needs analysis for the board development programme.
- Review the board size and mix; if needed decide on a new governance structure.
- Develop a board profile.
- Identify board competencies.
- Identify and recruit new board members.
- Induct new board members.

3 *Think strategically*
- Develop a strategic plan.
- Develop a communications strategy.
- Develop a fundraising strategy.
- Develop risk management strategy.

4 *Clarify board expectations*
- Implement a code of conduct.
- Implement a conflict of interest policy.
- Develop board role descriptions.

5 *How well is the board doing?*
- Plan a board retreat – plan an away day for the Chief Executive, the senior management team and the board.
- Carry out a governance audit (a board self-evaluation exercise).
- What value does the board add to the organisation?
- Review board information and board meetings.

6 *How well is the Chief Executive performing?*
Assess the Chief Executive's performance.

7 *Plan for next year*
Send out the schedule for next year's board meetings.

NCVO Trustee Board Development Programme Factfile. Reproduced by kind permission of the National Council for Voluntary Organisations (NCVO).

Website: www.ncvo-vol.org.uk/main/about/does/trustee_governance/briefings.htm

E-mail: trustee.enquiries@ncvo-vol.org.uk

Tel: 020 7713 6161.

Resource **12** Further reading and resources

All books published by DSC are available from DSC's website www.dsc.org.uk or call 020 7209 515 for a free catalogue. All prices were correct at time of going to press.

Part 1: Introduction

Further reading for Chapter 2 (Why do we have a board?)

Carver, John, *Boards that Make a Difference*, Jossey-Bass Inc. (San Francisco, 1997).

Eastwood, Mike, *The Charity Trustee's Handbook*, Directory of Social Change (London, 2001).

Garratt, Bob, *The Fish Rots from the Head: The Crisis in our Boardrooms: Developing the Crucial Skills of the Competent Director*, HarperCollins Business (London, 1997).

Harvard Business Review on Non-profits, Harvard Business School Press (Boston, 1999).

Houle, Cyril O, *Governing Boards*, Jossey-Bass Inc. (San Francisco, 1997).

Hudson, Mike, *Managing Without Profit: The Art of Managing Third-sector Organisations*, 2nd edn, Directory of Social Change (London 1999).

Kevin Nunan *The Good Trustee Guide: A Resource Organiser for Members of Governing Bodies of Charitable Companies*, 3rd edn, NCVO Publications (London, 1999). (Available from the Directory of Social Change.)

Further reading for Chapter 3 (Recruitment: the new board member)

McFarlan, F Warren, 'Don't Assume the Shoe Fits', *Harvard Business Review*, Nov–Dec 1999, pp65–80.

Part 2: Responsibilities

Further reading for Chapter 4 (Letter of the law)

Adirondack, Sandy and Taylor, James Sinclair, *The Voluntary Sector Legal Handbook*, 2nd edn, Consulting Editors Sinclair Taylor & Martin Solicitors, Directory of Social Change (London, 2001).

Berry, Graham and Pia, Paul (eds), *Care, Diligence and Skill*, Scottish Arts Council (Edinburgh, 1995).

Phillips, Andrew, *Charitable Status: a practical handbook*, 5th edn, published in association with Bates, Wells & Braithwaite, Directory of Social Change (London, 2003).

Further reading for Chapter 5 (Keeping to the straight and narrow)

Baxt, Robert, 'Risk Management, a New Development in Legal Practice', *Company Director*, September 1994, p45.

Borowka, H, 'Understanding Risk Management', *Occupational Hazards*, November 1991, pp57–60.

Glendon, A Ian and McKenna, Eugene F, *Human Safety and Risk Management*, Chapman & Hall, (London, 1995).

Livermore, John, *Exemption Clauses and Implied Obligations in Contracts*, The Law Book Company Limited (Sydney, 1986).

McGregor-Lowndes, Myles, *Working Paper No. 11: Facing up to the Liabilities of Nonprofit Enterprise: A Strategy to Minimise and Finance Liabilities*, Program on Nonprofit Corporations Working Paper Series, Queensland University of Technology, November 1992.

Further reading for Chapter 6 (Cheques and balances)

Cornforth, Chris and Edwards, Charles, *Good Governance – Developing Effective Board-Management Relations in Public and Voluntary Organisations*, The Chartered Institute of Management Accountants (London, 1998).

Eastwood, Mike, *The Charity Trustee's Handbook*, Directory of Social Change (London, 2001).

Ernst & Young's Corporate Governance Series of publications is available at the website EY.com (http://www.ey.com/global/content.nsf/Australia/Library). Amongst other titles, the series includes:

- Best Practices in Board Reporting
- Directors' Duties
- What is Corporate Governance?
- Setting up an Audit Committee
- Understanding Audit Committees
- A Corporate Governance Statement
- A Guide to the Corporations Law
- Audit Committees and their Directors
- Benchmarking Audit Committee Performance
- Understanding Accounting Standards

Further reading for Chapter 7 (People matter)

Adair, John, *The Skills of Leadership*, Gower Publishing (Aldershot, 1984).

Adirondack, Sandy, *Just About Managing*, London Voluntary Services Council (London, 1998). (Available from Directory of Social Change.)

Burnell, John, *Managing People in Charities*, ICSA Publishing / Prentice Hall (Englewood Cliffs, NJ, 1997).

Forbes, Duncan, Hayes, Ruth and Reason, Jacki, *Voluntary But Not Amateur: A Guide to the Law for Voluntary Organisations*, 6th edn, London Council of Voluntary Services (London, 2000). (Available from Directory of Social Change.)

Peters, Tom and Austin, Nancy, *A Passion for Excellence: The Leadership Difference*, William Collins Sons & Co (Glasgow, 1985).

Stewart, Valerie, *The David Solution: How to liberate your organization through Empowerment*, Gower Publishing (Aldershot, 1990).

Taylor, Gill, *Managing Recruitment and Selection*, Directory of Social Change (London, 1996).

Further reading for Chapter 8 (Policy and planning toolkit)

Drucker, Peter F, *Managing the Non-Profit Organisation: Practices and Principles*, Butterworth Heinemann (Oxford, 1992).

Lawrie, Alan, *The Complete Guide to Business and Strategic Planning for Voluntary Organisations*, 2nd edn, Directory of Social Change (London, 2001).

Ohmae, Kenichi, *The Mind of the Strategist: Business Planning for Competitive Advantage*, Penguin (Harmondsworth, 1982).

Further reading for Chapter 9 (Marketing, advocacy and fundraising)

Botting, Nina and Norton, Michael, *The Complete Fundraising Handbook*, 4th edn, Directory of Social Change (London, 2001).

Forrester, Susan, *The Arts Funding Guide*, 6th edn, Directory of Social Change (London, 2002).

Gilchrist, Karen, *Promoting your Cause*, Directory of Social Change (London 2002).

Lattimer, Mark, *The Campaigning Handbook*, 2nd edn, Directory of Social Change (London 2000)

Rosso, Henry, *Achieving Excellence in Fundraising: A Comprehensive Guide to Principles, Strategies and Methods*, Jossey-Bass Inc. (San Francisco, 1991).

Taylor, Russell Willis, *Fundraising for Museums and the Arts*, Museums & Galleries Commission (London, 1995).

Part 3: Board processes

Further reading for Chapter 10 (Effective board meetings)

Bader, Barry S, *Planning Successful Board Retreats: A Guide for Board Members and Chief Executives*, National Center for Nonprofit Boards (Washington DC, 1993).

Beck, Ken and Beck, Kate, *Assertiveness at Work: A practical guide to handling awkward situations*, Guild Publishing (London, 1990). (First published by McGraw-Hill Book Company.)

Comer, Lee and Ticher, Paul, *The Minute Taker's Handbook*, Directory of Social Change (London 2002).

Masaoka, Jan, 'Board Meeting Packets', BOARD CAFÉ: *The Newsletter Exclusively for Members of Nonprofit Boards of Directors* (e-mail newsletter published monthly by CompassPoint Nonprofit Services), www.board-cafe.org, San Francisco, 28 January 2001.

'Robert's Rules', in Brian O'Connell, *The Board Member's Book: Making a Difference in Voluntary Organisations*, The Foundation Center (New York, 1985), pp106-7.

Further reading for Chapter 11 (Committee structures)

Eastwood, Mike, *The Charity Trustee's Handbook*, Directory of Social Change (London, 2001).

Further reading for case study (Evolution of boards: leadership and stewardship in a dynamic environment)

Dart, R, Bradshaw, Pat, Murray, Vic, and Wolpin, Jacob, 'Boards of Directors in Non-profit Organisations – Do they follow a life-cycle model?' *Non-profit Management and Leadership*, Vol. 6, No. 4 (Summer 1996), pp367–79.

Stewart-Weeks, Martin, Seminar 'Governance in Not-for-Profit Organisation', 26 March 2001, Queensland University of Technology.

Wood, Miriam, 'Is Governing Board Behaviour Cyclical?' *Non-profit Management and Leadership*, Vol. 3, No 2 (Winter 1992), pp143-50.

Further reading for Chapter 12 (The role of the chair)

Cook, Tim and Braithwaite, Guy, *A Management Companion for Voluntary Organisations*, Directory of Social Change (London 2000).

Leigh, Andrew, *Perfect Decisions: All you need to get it right the first time*, Arrow Books (London, 1993).

Further reading for Chapter 13 (The board and the chief executive)

ACEVO, Appraising the Chief Executive, 2nd edn, ACEVO (London 2002).

Carver, John, *Carver Guide: Board Assessment of the CEO*, Jossey-Bass Inc. (San Francisco, 1997).

Nason, John W, *Board Assessment of The Chief Executive: A Responsibility Essential to Good Governance*, National Center for Nonprofit Boards (Washington DC, 1990).

Further reading for Chapter 15 (Monitoring our progress)

Chait, Richard P, Holland, Thomas P and Taylor, Barbara E, *Improving the Performance of Governing Boards*, American Council on Education (Phoenix, AZ, 1996).

Letts, Christine W, Ryan, William P and Grossman, Allen, *High Performance Nonprofit Organizations: Managing Upstream for Greater Impact*, John Wiley & Sons Inc. (New York, 1999).

Szanton, Peter, *Board Assessment Of the Organization: How Are We Doing?* The National Center for Nonprofit Boards (Washington DC, 1993).

Further reading for Chapter 16 (Assessing and improving the board)

Carver, John, *Carver Guide – Board Self-Assessment*, Jossey-Bass Inc. (San Francisco, 1997).

Chait, Richard P, Holland, Thomas P and Taylor, Barbara E, *Improving the Performance of Governing Boards*, American Council on Education (Phoenix, AZ, 1996).

'Factfile 14: Board Self-Assessment', *Factfile on Governance*, NCVO website: www.ncvo-vol.org.uk/main/about/does/trustee_governance/briefings.htm.

O'Connell, Brian, *The Board Member's Book: Making a Difference in Voluntary Organisations*, The Foundation Center (New York, 1985).

Slesinger, Larry H, *Self-Assessment for Nonprofit Governing Boards*, National Center for Nonprofit Boards (Washington DC, 1993).

Other useful further reading

Allford, Marion, *Charity Appeals: The Complete Guide to Success*, JM Dent & Sons Ltd (London, 1993).

Axelrod, Nancy R, *The Chief Executive's Role in Developing The Nonprofit Board*, The National Center for Nonprofit Boards (Washington DC, 1988).

Black, G. David and Reiter, Robin, *Boards of Trustees and the Not-For-Profit Organisation* (Miami, 1988).

Botting, Nina and Norton, Michael, *The Complete Fundraising Handbook*, 4th edn, Directory of Social Change (London, 2001).

Carver, John, *The Chief Executive and the Renegade Board Member*, Jossey-Bass Inc. (San Francisco, 1991).

Carver, John and Mayhew Carver, Miriam, *Basic Principles of Policy Governance*, Jossey-Bass Inc. (San Francisco, 1996).

Carver, John and Mayhew Carver, Miriam, *Your Roles and Responsibilities as a Board Member*, Jossey-Bass Inc. (San Francisco, 1996).

Chait, Richard P, *How To Help Your Board Govern More and Manage Less*, National Center for Nonprofit Boards (Washington DC, 1993).

Charan, Ram, *Boards at Work: How Corporate Boards Create Competitive Advantage*, Jossey-Bass Inc. (San Francisco, 1998).

Cowe, Roger, 'Private money, public gain', *Guardian*, Wednesday 20 March 2002.

Crawford, Robert W, *In Art We Trust: The Board of Trustees in The Performing Arts*, Foundation for the Extension and Development of the American Professional Theatre (New York, 1981).

Dorsey, Eugene C, *The Role Of The Board Chairperson*, The National Center for Nonprofit Boards (Washington DC, 1993).

Duca, Diane *Nonprofit Boards, Roles, Responsibilities, and Performance*, John Wiley & Sons Inc. (New York, 1996).

Dwyer, David, *Program on Nonprofit Corporations: Market Orientation in the Nonprofit Sector (Working paper no. 23)*, Program on Nonprofit Organisations, Queensland University of Technology (Brisbane, 1993).

French, Erica, *Program on Nonprofit Corporations: Strategic Planning in a Non Profit Organisation – Valuing the Process (Working paper no. 66)*, Program on Nonprofit Organisations, Queensland University of Technology (Brisbane, 1996).

Genovese, Margaret with Vanderhoof, Dory, *How to Get the Board You Need: The Recruitment and Nominating Process*, Orchestra Ontario (Toronto, 1997).

Harvey-Jones, John, *Making It Happen: Reflections on Leadership*, Fontana (London, 1990).

Hilmer, Frederick G, *Strictly Boardroom: Improving Governance to Enhance Company Performance*, Information Australia (Melbourne, 1998).

Howe, Fisher, *Fund Raising and the Nonprofit Board Member*, National Center for Nonprofit Boards (Washington DC, 1990).

La Piana, David, *Beyond Collaboration: Strategic Restructuring of Nonprofit Organisations*, The James Irvine Foundation and the National Center for Nonprofit Boards (San Francisco, 1997).

Lindsay, Nicole, 'Philanthropy should be a force for change', *Financial Review*, Australia, 10 November 2000.

Lyons, Mark, *Third Sector: The contribution of non-profit enterprises in Australia*, Allen & Unwin (Sydney, 2001).

McCauley, Cynthia D and Hughes, Martha W, 'Leadership in Human Services: Key Challenges and Competencies', in D Young, R Hollister, V Hodgkinson and Associates (eds), *Governing, leading, and managing nonprofit organizations: New insights from research and practice*, Jossey-Bass Inc. (San Francisco, 1993).

McDonald, Catherine, *Program on Nonprofit Corporations: Board Members' Involvement In Nonprofit Governance (Working paper no. 16)*, Program on Nonprofit Organisations, Queensland University of Technology (Brisbane, 1993).

McDonald, Catherine, *Program on Nonprofit Corporation: The Meaning of Effectiveness (Working paper no. 32)*, Program on Nonprofit Organisations, Queensland University of Technology (Brisbane, 1993).

NCVO/Charity Commission Working Party on Trustee Training, *On Trust – increasing the effectiveness of charity trustees and management committees: report of a working party on trustee training set up by NCVO and the Charity Commission*, NCVO Publications (London, 1992).

Pascoe, Timothy, *Strengthening the Governance of Arts Organizations*, Arts Research Training and Support Ltd (Woolahra, Australia, 1979).

Robinson, Maureen K, *Nonprofit Boards that Work: The End of One-Size-Fits-All Governance*, John Wiley & Sons Inc. (New York, 2001).

Saidel, Judith R, 'The Board Role in Relation to Government: Alternative Models', in D Young, R Hollister, V Hodgkinson and Associates (eds), *Governing, leading, and managing nonprofit organizations: New insights from research and practice*, Jossey-Bass Inc. (San Francisco, 1993).

Scott, Katherine Tyler, *Creating Caring and Capable Boards*, Jossey-Bass Inc. (San Francisco, 2000).

Shackleton, Vivian, *How to Pick People for Jobs*. Fontana (London, 1989).

Smith, Damien J, Bowman, Steve and Millard, Sean C, *The Not for Profit Board and Management Guide*, Enterprise Care Consulting Group Pty Ltd (Melbourne, 1999).

Steane, Peter and Christie, Michael, *Nonprofit Boards in Australia: A Distinctive Goverance Approach (Working paper no. 84)*, Queensland University of Technology (Brisbane, 2000).

A Guide to Orchestra Governance, American Symphony Orchestra League (New York, 1991).

Responsibilities of Charity Trustees, Charity Commissioner for England and Wales (London, 1993).

VIDEO – Charity Trustees: 'the "crucial" guide to Trusteeship, Charity Commissioner for England and Wales (London, 1993).

'Third Sector Trustee – Don't sink, swim – Masterstrokes and the art of Trusteeship', *NCVO – voice of the voluntary sector*, September 1998. Quarterly supplement of *Third Sector* magazine.

The Art of Serving on a Performing Arts Board, Theatre Bay Area (San Francisco, 1998).

Useful non-profit websites

Organisation Address Description

Organisation	Address	Description
Minnesota Council of Nonprofits	www.mncn.org	Minnesota Council of Nonprofits site containing links to public policy reports, management, legal and fundraising resources, advice on starting a nonprofit organisation, and links to other nonprofit organisations in the USA.
BOARD CAFÉ: The Newsletter Exclusively for Members of Nonprofit Boards of Directors	www.compasspoint. org/index.html	Site for BOARD CAFÉ: The Newsletter Exclusively for Members of Nonprofit Boards of Directors, which also contains links to workshops, conferences, consultancy services and research on various topics such as human resources, IT, board governance, marketing and financial management.
The Charity Commission for England and Wales	www.charity-commission.gov.uk/ publications/ cc60.asp	The Charity Commission for England and Wales website, containing links to registered and supporting charities, investigation publications and reports on enhancing charities.
Volunteer Canada	www.volunteer.ca/ volunteer/celebrate_ recognition_hints. htm	Volunteer Canada's website, containing information on volunteering in Canada, Volunteer Centers, links to volunteer opportunities exchange, and celebrating volunteers which includes helpful hints on volunteer recognition.
National Centre for Volunteering	www.volunteer.org. uk/fromthetopdown. htm	Site for National Centre for Volunteering (UK) with information on working with volunteers, research, links to publications, campaigns and Volunteering Magazine, and the Volunteering Image Bank.
Board Development	www.boarddevelop ment.org	Site for board development training, accountability and governance in the Canadian Voluntary Sector, including checklists, sample job descriptions and links to training sites.
National Council for Voluntary Organisations (NCVO)	www.ncvo-vol. org.uk	NCVO's trustee and governance team is dedicated to improving the effectiveness of voluntary sector organisations by strengthening their governing boards and enhancing the skills of trustees who sit on them. Their services include good practice information, signposting, publications and events.
Directory of Social Change	www.dsc.org.uk	Site for the Directory of Social Change. Includes information on all DSC training and events, including the annual Charityfair, and an online bookshop where you can buy books from DSC and other publishers.

Index